Critical Essays on Norman Mailer

Critical Essays on Norman Mailer

J. Michael Lennon

G.K. Hall & Co. • Boston, Massachusetts

12/1986
Am. Lit. Cont.

Library of Congress Cataloging in Publication Data

Lennon, Michael.
    Critical essays on Norman Mailer.

    (Critical essays on American literature)
    Includes index.
    1. Mailer, Norman—Criticism and interpretation.
I. Title.   II. Series.
PS3525.A4152Z74 1986   813'.52   86-12144
ISBN 0-8161-8695-2

This publication is printed on permanent/durable acid-free paper
MANUFACTURED IN THE UNITED STATES OF AMERICA

CRITICAL ESSAYS ON AMERICAN LITERATURE

This series seeks to anthologize the most important criticism on a wide variety of topics and writers in American literature. Our readers will find in various volumes not only a generous selection of reprinted articles and reviews but original essays, bibliographies, manuscript sections, and other materials brought to public attention for the first time. Among the twenty selections in this volume on Norman Mailer are reprinted essays by Irving Howe, Tony Tanner, Alfred Kazin, John W. Aldridge, Joan Didion, and Diana Trilling. In addition to J. Michael Lennon's extensive introduction, which surveys both Mailer's career and the record of scholarly comment on his life and work, there are two essays written especially for publication in this book, one by Michael Cowan and another by Robert F. Lucid. We are confident that this volume will make a permanent and significant contribution to American literary study.

James Nagel, GENERAL EDITOR

Northeastern University

For Mary Mitchell Lennon

CONTENTS

INTRODUCTION

Henry James, Sr., once said of Ralph Waldo Emerson, "Oh you man without a handle!" The same cannot be said of Norman Mailer, although so many handles have been proposed for him that it could be argued he has none at all. Despite the large number of illuminating interpretations of Mailer's artistic evolution, ruling ideas, and place in American literature, no orthodox, encompassing view has yet emerged. The only book-length study considered indispensable, Richard Poirier's *Norman Mailer* (1972),[1] is necessarily limited in that twelve books by Mailer have appeared in the past thirteen years (see chronology of books), including two major works that are radically different from all his earlier ones, and from each other: *The Executioner's Song* (1979) and *Ancient Evenings* (1983).

The fact that Mailer's literary life is still happening—he now is in the same sort of major phase that Henry James, Jr., entered in his early sixties—only partly accounts for the lack of an accepted overview. Nor is the lack of fruitful consideration by first-rate critics a sufficient reason. More than a dozen critical books and several biographical studies of Mailer have been published, and this is the fifth critical collection to appear since 1971. Like its predecessors, it contains forceful and original analyses by long-time Mailerians: Poirier, Robert F. Lucid, Alfred Kazin, Diana Trilling, Tony Tanner, John W. Aldridge, and Michael Cowan, as well as the essays and reviews of other excellent commentators, appearing in such a collection for the first time. Because the earlier essays on Mailer by those named above, as well as those by other important Mailer critics—James Baldwin, Dwight Macdonald, Norman Podhoretz, and Richard Foster—have been reprinted and referred to so often, I decided early on to pass over the criticism of earlier collections, and to assemble a new but equally important selection of essays and reviews.

The reasons for the lack of an accepted overview of Mailer's work divide into two clusters, the first deriving from the protean nature of his work over the past forty-four years (he won *Story* magazine's college contest in 1941), and the second owing to the sharp disagreement about the merit of his ideas on sex, violence, and politics. As the letter from an irate reader of *The Naked and the Dead,* and Orville Prescott's response (both included

1

here) indicate,[2] this disagreement stretches back to 1948, when Mailer's first novel was published. It is safe to say that Mailer has elicited more vitriol than any other major American writer of this century, and probably as much as generated by Edgar Allan Poe in the nineteenth century. Except for Hunter Thompson, he is the only living American writer who is regularly caricatured by cartoonists. Yet he has been often called America's finest postwar writer.

Ambitious book reviewers from the early fifties on have tried to earn their spurs by savaging his latest book, often, as Joan Didion noted in her review of *The Executioner's Song*, by pointing to *The Naked and the Dead* as a "promise later broken and every book since as a quick turn for his creditors, a stalling action, a spangled substitute, tarted up to deceive, for the 'big book' he cannot write."[3] And the extravagant praise of his admirers, an equally large group, has only stoked the outrage of his detractors. For more than twenty-five years Mailer has occupied center stage of what he recently called "our godawful out-of-whack deranging spirit-leaching ongoing static-exhaling national gong show."[4] The hullabaloo about Mailer, properly analyzed, can tell us much about American aspirations and sensitivities, but it has often muddied perceptions of his work, especially when coupled with the tendency of English-speaking critics to give less attention to literary technique than their continental counterparts. Mailer's work, like Lord Byron's and Ernest Hemingway's, cannot be approached without crossing biographical territory, but not enough attention has been paid to Mailer as a connoisseur of narrative forms, styles, and perspectives. Several contributors to this collection, including Didion, Tanner, Brendan Gill, and Philip Bufithis, discuss with considerable subtlety Mailer's craftsmanship, while several others—Cowan, Kazin, Aldridge, Lucid, Martin Green, and Ihab Hassan—present provocative explanations of why critical and popular opinion on him is so polarized, why he is seen by some as the Charles Lindbergh, and by others as the Legs Diamond of American letters.

Other topics considered at length are Mailer's existential philosophy (Robert Solotaroff), his political views and activities (Green, Irving Howe, and Jack Newfield), his cosmology (George Steiner and myself), his views on women and feminism (Trilling, Ingrid Bengis, and Judith Fetterley), and his historical sense (Poirier).

Before considering the course of Mailer's career, which like a Stendhal novel is filled with sharp reversals, and the equally dramatic shifts in critical response to his work, it is worth noting that each of Mailer's major literary metamorphoses has been causally related to events and situations in his personal life—his six marriages, legal and money problems, political activities, literary and personal friendships and feuds and the like. In this regard, Mailer has compared himself—aptly—to Pablo Picasso.[5] But forging the innumerable links between Mailer's evolution and accomplishments as a writer and the rest of his life remains to be done, although Lucid's essay, an overview of his unfinished biography, is a brilliant beginning.

What can be said is that Mailer has pondered the same question when making all the crucial artistic decisions of his career. In each instance he has felt compelled to consider "in the most ghastly terms possible: how much of yourself should 'go public,' like a stock?" as he once put it.[6] The exigencies and opportunities of self-representation have preoccupied Mailer since the beginning of his career, and to a great extent are responsible for the variety of prose forms that he has used. His insistence on the preeminence of his novelistic mission is well known, and he has often compared it to those of Herman Melville, Theodore Dreiser, Thomas Wolfe, Ernest Hemingway, Henry Miller, John Dos Passos, James T. Farrell, John Steinbeck, and F. Scott Fitzgerald as well as the great European and South American novelists. But of Mailer's thirty-five books, only eight are certifiable novels, although, characteristically, he has argued that three or four more should be so classified.

His other prose forms are autobiography, biography, novella, short story, science fiction, sports and political reportage, interview (over a hundred), every sort of essay, newspaper and magazine columns, letter, literary criticism, debate, preface, introduction, memoir, book review, and philosophical dialogue (of the sort written by Poe). This apples-and-oranges list gives no hint of the ways he has combined and reconstituted these forms nor of the dazzling range of rhetorical approaches he has employed. In addition, he has written poems, plays, and screenplays.

In all of these endeavors, Mailer's constant self-admonition has not simply been, as often claimed, to find ways to advertise himself, but also to see himself "as a piece of material, as a piece of yard goods. I'd say, 'where am I going to cut myself?' It's a way of getting a psychoanalysis, I think," as he once noted in an interview.[7] Sometimes he reduces his presence to an Alfred Hitchcock walk-on; sometimes he comes on like a one-man zeitgeist juggling an array of metaphors; sometimes he is "nothing but a conveyor belt," which is how he described his narrative function in *The Executioner's Song*.[8] Roughly speaking, the above three quantities of presence—slight, tremendously expanded, and radically diminished—mark sequentially his development as a narrative artist: from his cameo as Private Roth in *Naked*, through Aquarius with his "bustling, manic, intrusive voice,"[9] to the disembodied narrator of *Song*.

I know it will be said that Mailer, more often than not, exposes more rather than less of himself. Agreed, but only if we look at the middle of his career, from *Advertisements for Myself* (1959) through *The Fight* (1975). It is usually forgotten that at the beginning of his career he felt strongly that his personal and artistic lives should be separate. He told an interviewer in 1948 that it was "much better when people who read your book don't know anything about you, even what you look like. I have refused to let *Life* photograph me."[10] This attitude is not surprising when his quiet, even sheltered life before the publication of *Naked* is recalled. He was born on 31 January 1923 in Long Branch, New Jersey, but grew up in a Jewish bastion of Brooklyn, Crown Heights, where his family moved in 1927. His father, Isaac Barnett "Barney" Mailer, was an accountant from South Africa who served as a supply officer in the British army in World War I and later emigrated to the United States. His mother, Fanny Schneider Mailer, a powerful figure in Mailer's life until her death in 1985 (his father died in 1972), came from a family who ran a hotel in Long Branch.

After graduation from Boys High School in Brooklyn in 1939, where he excelled, Mailer entered Harvard in the fall of that year as the German army marched into Poland. Enrolled as a student in aeronautical engineering, Mailer received his B.S., with honors, fours years later in this field, although most of his electives were in English. He was drafted in March 1944 and served with a combat unit in Leyte and Luzon in the Philippines. Discharged in May 1946, he returned to Brooklyn and wrote *Naked*. Its publication on 6 May 1948 launched one of the most celebrated and controversial careers in American literary history.

With a few exceptions, reviews of the 721-page novel, which traces the assault and capture of the fictional Pacific island of Anopopei, were extremely laudatory. The *Time* reviewer called it "perhaps the best novel yet about World War II," and compared Mailer's vivid battle scenes to Leo Tolstoy's in *War and Peace*.[11] John Lardner, writing in the *New Yorker*, also compared the novel with Tolstoy's masterpiece, not only for its "sharp colors," but also for its "orderly plotting."[12] The reviewer for *Newsweek*, in perhaps the most enthusiastic review, called Mailer "a writer of unmistakable importance" whose novel made the classics of World War I "look thin and pale by comparison."[13] Almost every reviewer paid tribute to the novel's ruthless and detailed realism, although there was a division of opinion on its obscene dialogue. Orville Prescott, writing in the *New York Times*, complained that the novel contained "more explicitly vile speech . . . than I have ever seen printed in a work of serious literature before."[14]

The strongest attack on the novel, which sold approximately 200,000 copies within eight months of publication, came from Harrison Smith in *Saturday Review*, who called it "a monument to destructiveness" that did not contain "a single meritorious character."[15] Yet in an earlier review in the same publication, Maxwell Geismar argued that the dialogues of General Cummings and Lieutenant Hearn, the novel's titular hero, permitted Mailer "to build up, often very eloquently, the historical and philosophical connotations of the war." In what was perhaps the most perceptive comment of *Naked*'s reviewers, Geismar said that the novel's virtue lay in its evaluation of "the American Army in war and peace, as a manifestation of contemporary society, as well as a weapon of conquest and destruction."[16] From this point on in his career, Mailer would be identified with themes of sex, violence, and political power in modern life, and be alternately praised and damned for these preoccupations.

The enormous success of *Naked* was in Mailer's words "a lobotomy to my past,"[17] and he recoiled from intrusions into his personal life, arguing in 1951 that the creative work of writers "has nothing to do with what they profess, which is usually silly."[18] He further elaborated this belief in 1954 saying that he was opposed to "using one's novels as direct expressions of one's latest ideas" (*Advertisements*, 226). Until the middle fifties Mailer subscribed to Flaubert's dictum that "the artist should be in his work, like God in creation, invisible and all-powerful; he should be felt everywhere and seen nowhere. And then art should be raised above personal affections and nervous susceptibilities."[19]

Despite Mailer's belief in the novelist as detached creator, and his preference for third-person omniscient narration, he turned to the first person in the two novels that followed *Naked: Barbary Shore* (1951) and *The Deer Park* (1955). He explained in a 1963 interview that he could not return to the third person until he had "developed a coherent view of life."[20] Believing, as did James (whose indirect influence on the young Mailer was enormous), that it is promiscuous to detail the consciousnesses of a great number of characters, as he had done in *Naked*, Mailer restricted his focus. The protagonists of the novels, Mickey Lovett and Sergius O'Shaugnessy, respectively, write as autobiographers. Yet Mailer later stated that "*The Deer Park* is not autobiographical. No one in it speaks directly for me" (*Advertisements*, 270). To avoid slipping into the slough of personal revelation, Mailer made his two heroes orphans, and one of them—Lovett—an amnesiac.

His distancing attempts were only partially successful, however. In his 1959 essay "The Mind of an Outlaw," he says that in the second draft of *The Deer Park* he changed O'Shaugnessy from an "overdelicate, oversensitive and painfully tender" character to one who had "some of the stubbornness and belligerence I also might have." But "the more my new style succeeded, the more was I writing an implicit portrait of myself as well. There is a shame about advertising yourself that way, a shame which became so strong that it was a psychological violation to go on" (*Advertisements*, 237–38). But Mailer did go on, and the O'Shaugnessy of the final version is endowed with some of Mailer's sensibility, even though the thematic focus is squarely on the moral struggles of other characters in the novel: Charles Eitel, Marion Faye, and Elena Esposito.

Despite its bold attempt to explore the politics of Cold War America, *Barbary Shore* was a critical and popular failure. Although almost every reviewer compared it to the novels of Franz Kafka, George Orwell, or Arthur Koestler, almost all the comparisons were unfavorable. Published at the height of the Cold War, the novel's espousal of socialism evoked harsh criticism. "Paceless, tasteless and graceless" was the verdict of *Time*'s reviewer, who labeled it "small-beer *Nineteen Eighty-Four*."[21] *Saturday Review*'s Maxwell Geismar, clearly disappointed, chided Mailer for writing a novel that seemed to say "that no normal sex life is possible until the neurosis of history has been resolved," a reversal of Freud's dictum.[22] Anthony West of the *New Yorker* said that it had "a monolithic, flawless badness, like Mussolini's play about Napoleon."[23] Even leftist critics like Irving Howe and Harvey Swados, while lauding his political commitment, were lukewarm in their praise. In a review in the *Nation*, Howe said that it lacked "dramatic tension" and interesting characters, and Swados, the *New Republic*'s reviewer, judged Mailer's political allegory guilty of "murkiness."[24]

The Deer Park, Mailer's Hollywood novel, was more successful, but like *Barbary Shore* it suffers from his inability at the time to develop a narrative consciousness flexible enough to handle both politics and sex, the worlds of Marx and Freud. None of the novel's reviewers was impressed by Mailer's narrator-novelist-hero. Several noted that he seemed to be modeled, unsuccessfully, on James Joyce's Stephen Dedalus. Brendan Gill, the *New Yorker* reviewer, said O'Shaugnessy was a "bumpkin," but nevertheless called Mailer "a passionate moralist" possessed of "the greatest and most reckless talent," and Malcolm Cowley, in his enthusiastic review in the *New York Herald Tribune Book Review*, said that " 'The Deer Park' is a serious and recklessly honest book about art," flawed only by the unreality of O'Shaugnessy.[25] The novel's sizable group of detractors, including Orville Prescott of the *New York Times*, all pointed to the decline of Mailer's art since *Naked*, a refrain that some critics have continued to sing up to the present.[26] The most common objection to the book was its sexual explicitness. "Not even good pornography," said Sidney Alexander in the *Reporter; Time* compared it to *Confidential* magazine.[27] Arthur Mizener, writing in *Partisan Review*, said that the book's central proposition is that happiness is "roughly proportional to the talent for sexual gymnastics."[28] Nevertheless, the novel left the impression, as Richard Chase put it in *Commentary*, that Mailer was "a novelist who is still very obviously going places."[29] Mailer responded to the book's unfavorable reviews by reprinting their most unflattering phrases in an ad in the *Village Voice*, the counterculture weekly he cofounded and named the same year that *Deer Park* was published, a gambit that may have helped the novel reach the number six spot on the best-seller list in the late fall of 1955.[30]

After *Barbary Shore* Mailer said, "I don't think of myself as a realist," and it is clear that he had no sympathy for the pieties of the conventional social novel.[31] But he had not yet found a way to lever his twin obsessions with revolution and psychosis into an illuminating juxtaposition. Mailer's dilemma was this: How could he create an authentic protagonist who was both free-standing *and* fictional while surmounting, on the one hand, the difficulties of revealing the consciousness of someone markedly different from himself, and on the other, avoiding the "psychological violation" of making his protagonist a doppelgänger? In his first three novels Mailer *could not* create a completely successful hero who was different from himself, and he *would not* create one who was the same.[32]

Mailer's belief in disinterested literary creation began to evaporate after *The Deer Park*. According to him, his battle with the publishing industry over the supposed obscenity of the novel punctured his "nineteenth century naïveté" and transformed him into "a psychic outlaw" (*Advertisements*, 233–34). He now raked through the "personal affections and nervous susceptibilities" that Flaubert and James believed the artist should transcend. His essays of the late fifties, "The White Negro," "The Mind of an Outlaw," and the "Quickly" columns for the *Village Voice* (collected in *Advertisements*) were expressions of his latest intellectual enthusiasms and personal experience. Yet he was unable to exercise his powerful autobiographical impulse in a novel until 1965, a decade after *The Deer Park*, when *An American Dream* was published. In the intervening years, he wrote and assembled three collections of assorted prose: *Advertisements* (1959), *The Presidential Papers* (1963), and *Cannibals and Christians* (published in 1966, but comprised mainly of pieces written before 1965).

The occasional pieces that make up these miscellanies are held together by italicized "Advertisements," "Notes," "Postscripts," and "Arguments" that are often more compelling than the pieces themselves, although each collection contains three or four pieces praised even by some of Mailer's detractors. "The White Negro," his 1957 prospectus for a hipster-hero questing for new energies in "the Wild West of American night life" (*Advertisements*, 339), is the most important of these. It marks the first full articulation of Mailer's "bizarre yet compelling attempt to reassert the sanctity of private life against the pressures of a mass technocracy," as George Steiner described it in his *Encounter* review of *Advertisements*.[33]

The majority of *Advertisements*' reviews were unfavorable, but the praise that was given was exceptionally strong. Harry T. Moore in the *New York Times Book Review* said Mailer was "the most versatile if not the most significant writer of his generation," and *Partisan Review*'s Irving Howe called him "enormously, even outrageously talented," although he noted Mailer's failure to create a major character in his books.[34] Gore Vidal, reviewing for the *Nation*, gave Mailer his "highest praise" for being "honorable," but contradicted this by criticizing him for being "too much a demagogue" seeking "crude celebrity."[35] The tone of those who did not like the book is typified by Charles Rolo in the *Atlantic* and Charles Poore in the *New York Times*. Rolo attacked Mailer's "ugly-tempered perversity" and Poore his "endlessly seething indignation."[36] The core of critical displeasure was summed up by John Chamberlain in *National Review*, who ended his review by saying, "our 'individualists' are hypnotized by phantoms which just aren't there."[37] But this was still pre-assassination America. Vietnam and Selma were still faraway places.

The pattern of remarkably angry condemnation peppered with high praise that marked *Advertisements*' publication occurred again with *Presidential Papers*. The assassination of President John F. Kennedy (to whom the collection is addressed) a few days after the book appeared undoubtedly shaped the response of some reviewers, but Mailer's disillusioned injunctions to Kennedy could not have endeared him to the eastern press establishment in any case. Garry Wills of *National Review* and John Kenneth Galbraith, reviewing for the *New York Times Book Review*, both argued that Mailer was piqued by the failure of his ideas to interest the Kennedys; Wills called these ideas "absurdities."[38] In a long review in the *New Republic*, Richard Gilman called Mailer's self-exposure "tactical humility," and berated him as an "anathematizer of research and contemplation" who "finds it intolerable that thought and action should remain separate."[39] Still, Midge Decter in *Commentary* had enthusiastic praise for the collection, saying, "I mean quite simply that he owns America. . . . the whole country gives itself up to him in a range of natural assumption and reference."[40] With a few exceptions, the rest of the reviews were negative.

The much warmer reception of *Cannibals* in 1966 is not attributable to its superiority to the earlier collections; indeed, it has less claim to structural coherence. It is, however, more unrelenting and incisive in its attacks on the technological society. Mailer's rebukes were applauded by reviewers for their accurate rendering of the angry and frustrated national temper. No longer alone in his indignation about Vietnam, the F.B.I., American materialism, and the situation of blacks, Mailer was now hailed for his cultural prescience. John Wain, for example, writing in the *New Republic*, said Mailer "is trying to position himself so as to stand face to face with the true identity of our time, our time in America."[41] A. Alvarez's review in the *Observer* and Malcolm Muggeridge's in *Equire* were almost as enthusiastic, and Tony Tanner, in *Partisan Review*, said, "I would be a lot less worried if Norman Mailer were a lot less worried."[42] Oscar Handlin, reviewing in *Atlantic*, was alone in his conclusion that "Mailer is at his worst as a social critic."[43] The title of Eliot Fremont-Smith's review in the *New York Times*—"A Nobel for Norman?"—indicates the sharp reversal of opinion toward him.[44]

Mailer's bitter struggles with the literary establishment and his existential conviction that sexual and political timidity were sapping western culture were not the only factors that drove him in on himself. His emerging belief in an embattled God whose destiny was linked to the actions of men was of equal importance. Mailer has written that "every other one of his notions had followed from that [conception]."[45] For all of these reasons, Mailer from the late fifties on was doing precisely what he had earlier abhorred, namely, using his personality and experience as the "armature" (*Advertisements*, 219) of his writing. "Let others profit by my unseemly self-absorption," he said in one of his *Village Voice* columns, "and so look to improve their own characters" (*Advertisements*, 313). This cocky attitude enraged the more conservative members of the literary community, and Mailer was regularly dismissed as a loud-mouthed lout with no future. He has been written off so many times that an innocent observer might wonder if the establishment was alarmed by the possibility that he did have one.

Finally, what Mailer later called the "imperative of self-interest"[46] became too pressing, and in late 1963 he contracted with *Esquire* to write a serialized novel. He had kept his fictional and private worlds locked apart since *Deer Park,* only to discover that connecting "the world of affairs, institutions, society, realism, Marx, Tolstoy" and the "world of mood, hallucination, projections, surrealism, Freud, Dostoyevsky"[47] could not be accomplished until he channeled his personal experience into his fiction. The first spans of this "radical bridge from Marx to Freud" (*Advertisements,* 365) as he called it, were completed in *An American Dream,* which came out in revised book form in 1965.[48] If Stephen Richards Rojack, the novel's narrator and moral fulcrum, is not the doppelgänger of Norman Kingsley Mailer, he is a fictional first cousin. Certainly there can be no doubt that Rojack's "not inconsiderable thesis that magic, dread, and the perception of death were the roots of motivation" is also Mailer's.[49] The fear of "psychological violation" had proven to be baseless.

The division of opinion on *Dream,* which was reviewed more widely than any of his previous books, was nearly absolute. There were few half-and-half reviews. Leading critics and literary figures such as Granville Hicks, Philip Rahv, Eliot Fremont-Smith, Stanley Edgar Hyman, Tom Wolfe, and Elizabeth Hardwick said that the novel was a failure.[50] On the other side of the chasm, Leo Bersani, Richard Poirier, Conrad Knickerbocker, Joan Didion, Paul Pickrel, and John W. Aldridge acclaimed it as a major achievement.[51]

It is only mildly reductive of the positions of those who attacked the novel, the neo-Elizabethan plot of which revolves around Rojack's murder of his wife, to say that they are fairly represented by those of Rahv and Fremont-Smith. The former found Mailer's "low-level mysticism " to be "a programmatic statement of his own desires, power-drives and daydreams," and the latter saw the book as "Norman Mailer's fantasy of Norman Mailer . . . a continuation of the public diary Mailer has been entertaining us with for years."[52]

The positions of those in the opposed camp were not far from those of Didion and Knickerbocker. She claimed the experience of *Dream* to be "the essence of New York," and "perhaps the only serious New York novel since *The Great Gatsby,*" while he said it "beats with the pulse of some huge night carnivore. It defines the American style by presenting the most extreme of our realities—murder, love and spirit strangulated, the corruption of power and the powerful."[53] The fact that Mailer had stabbed his second wife, Adele, with a penknife five years earlier (receiving a suspended sentence when she refused to press charges), was of course known to all of the reviewers, although only Wolfe and *Time's* anonymous critic mentioned it in their reviews.[54] It is clear that the novel's detractors were unwilling to disassociate Rojack's nightmarish experiences from Mailer's.

The book's defenders, with few exceptions, tended to see the novel as myth, fantasy, or allegory. Aldridge, one of the few who did not lean on this interpretation, saw it as "a religious book" that delineated "the various ways a man may sin in order to be saved, consort with Satan in order to attain God."[55] Mailer liked Aldridge's review well enough to pay for its reprinting in the same number of *Partisan Review* containing Hardwick's harshly negative review.

Mailer states in *Advertisements* that "to write about myself is to send my style through a circus of variations and postures, a fireworks of virtuosity designed to achieve . . . I know not what. Leave it that I become an actor, a quick-change artist, as if I believe I can trap the Prince of Truth in the act of switching a style" (18). The role he chose in his next novel, *Why Are We in Vietnam?* (1967) was that of D.J., "disc jockey to America," a teenage Texan who divides himself into narrating and participating selves in his account of a big game hunt in Alaska two years earlier. The novel alternates between third-person "Chaps," which tell the hunting story, and self-reflexive first-person "Intro Beeps," which tell the story of the story. The problem with this division is that Mailer made the D.J. of the "Intro Beeps" so frenetic and weird that it is hard to imagine him as the source of the marvelous nature writing of the narrative chapters. At the novel's close we learn that D.J. has enlisted in the Marines because he wants to go where the action is: "Vietnam, hot damn!" are the last words of the novel. D.J.'s blindness and bloodlust, his failure to grasp the significance of what he presents, make us wonder if he could ever have seen it so well. The descriptions of the armed confrontations and unarmed communings with the natural world of the Brooks Range in *Vietnam* were the first nature writing in his work after *Naked,* and they are superior because the natural world in *Vietnam* is the incarnation of a prodigious and divided anima. The forests and mountains vibrate with supersensory messages, much as the forests of Lebanon do in *Ancient Evenings*.

A number of critics, including Richard Poirier, have argued that *Vietnam* is the book closest to Mailer's natural gifts.[56] Without disputing this, I would merely say that D.J. (who might be described as Mailer's crazy nephew from Dallas) is tangential to the principal curve of his development, which through the sixties continued to spiral inward. Freud, in Mailer's program, would serve as a gloss for Marx. He vested more of himself in D.J. than in O'Shaugnessy or Lovett, but he seemed to be wary of making him as autobiographical as Rojack. Mailer admitted as much when he later said, "I was full of energy when I was done, but the work was by the same token impersonal."[57]

Once again the reviewers were sharply split. The issue for most of them was whether or not the novel's exceedingly obscene language is an objective correlative for the Vietnam War. So the *Village Voice's* reviewer, Eugene Glenn, called *Vietnam* "a triumph, powerful, original, brilliant in substance and in formal means," and Eliot Fremont-Smith, in the *New York Times,* called Mailer "this country's most intrepid polemical metaphorist, not its Hemingway but its Swift."[58] The other half was as strong in its disapproval. Charles T. Samuels, the *Nation's* reviewer, called the novel "a tissue of clichés out of Hemingway and Faulkner," while Christopher

Nichols, writing in *National Review*, said that it was heavy with "the Mailerian mephitis of scatologia and sodomy."[59] *Newsweek* and *Time*, as usual, were pro and con, respectively.[60]

In his discussion of *Deer Park* in *Advertisements*, Mailer says that "the most powerful leverage in fiction comes from point of view" (238). In the years following *Advertisements*, he became intensely interested in questions of aesthetic leverage, but was involved in so many public activities that these experiments with narrative forms and perspectives were and are almost unnoticed. Tired of the first person, he began using the indefinite pronoun "one" as a way of gaining a bit of distance on the antecedent "I" in the nonfiction of the early and middle sixties.[61] But he also referred to himself with almost every other personal and impersonal pronoun and swiveled his perspective, often in the same essay, through all three persons in what can only be called pronomial confusion. Mailer recognized the problems of unifying his fragmented self behind the single letter "I," and therefore sought ways to reveal opposed aspects of himself. One example is his 1961 self-interview, "The First Day's Interview," where he says that his "subject is *a* Norman Mailer, a weary, cynical, now philosophically turned hipster of middle years."[62]

It was in these minor pieces that he first described himself in the third person. This unusual point of view, used successfully by Henry Adams in his *Education* (which Mailer read at Harvard), gave him the perfect method of linking and revealing several of his chief avatars, public and private. He used it again in *The Armies of the Night* (1968), an account of the 1967 march on the Pentagon. Mailer went on with the method, the "third-person personal" it could be called, in all of his narratives of public events and cultural phenomena through 1975. Never before or since has he stayed in the same groove for so long, an unmistakable tribute to the method's splendid legitimacy. The wave of Mailer's comeback, which began with *Dream* in 1965, reached its high-water mark in 1968 with the publication of *Armies*, and his account of the tumultuous political conventions of 1968, *Miami and the Siege of Chicago*. The paradox is that he was able to join and hold together so many of his ideas, experiences, and fragments of self with a method that sundered his protagonist into teller and told, Mailer-now and Mailer-then. This division of self by fiat, the resolution of twenty years of point-of-view uncertainties, was a masterstroke and the most significant aesthetic decision of Mailer's career through the sixties.

Mailer disarmed the literary world with *Armies*. The combination of detached, ironic self-presentation, deft portraiture of literary figures (especially Robert Lowell, Dwight Macdonald, and Paul Goodman), a reportorially flawless account of the march itself, and a passionate argument addressed to a divided nation resulted in a sui generis narrative praised by even some of his most inveterate revilers. *Time*'s reviewer, for example, said that "his fervent and intense sense of legitimately caring" for the nation made it "an artful document, worthy to be judged as literature."[63]

Old supporters of Mailer felt vindicated. Macdonald, writing in *Esquire*, not only found Mailer's reconstruction of the events of the march to be a "prodigious" act of memory, he called the book "a journalistic masterpiece by any standard and, by contemporary ones, a literary triumph"; Malcolm Muggeridge, also in *Esquire*, said *Armies* was "the best piece of reporting these old eyes have rested on for many a year, if ever"; Alfred Kazin, reviewing for the *New York Times Book Review*, compared the self-absorption of Mailer with that of "the best American writers in the 19th century [who] talked about themselves all the time—but in the romantic American line, saw the self as the prime condition of democracy." Kazin concluded with this thought: "Mailer's intuition in this book is that the times demand a new form. He has found it."[64]

There was some debate concerning the relative merits of the book's two sections. Most reviewers favored the longer, first part, "History as a Novel," in which Mailer's baroque presence dominates the events, over part 2, "The Novel as History," an overview of the march from a conventional perspective. What few negative reviews there were appeared in right-wing publications—*National Review* and the *Chicago Tribune*, for example. Mario Puzo, writing in the latter, called *Armies* "the most excruciating exhibition of pomposity available in our literature."[65] Lawrence Raab's concluding comment in a review in the *American Scholar* sums up what the bulk of the reviewers said or implied: "As a document of our times it is of great and perhaps enduring importance."[66] Published twenty years to the day after *Naked*, *Armies* won both the Pulitzer Prize and the National Book Award.

Mailer's favorite epithet is "once a philosopher, twice a pervert." It may seem that he violated the logic of Voltaire's line by using the third-person personal in the nonfiction narratives that succeeded *Armies*, but this is not strictly true. If he still continued to refer many aspects of American culture to his own psyche for explanation, he did so less often and he steadily reduced his presence in these narratives. While he is abundantly present in *Armies* and *Miami*, in *Of a Fire on the Moon* (1970), his account of the Apollo moon flight, he is less so, saying he feels "detached this season from the imperial demands of his ego." In *St. George and the Godfather* (1972), his narrative of the 1972 conventions, he becomes "modest and half-invisible,"[67] and by 1975 when he published *The Fight*, his account of the Muhammad Ali–George Foreman contest in Zaïre, he admits that "he was no longer pleased with his presence," and "his mind, he noticed was beginning to spin its wheels."[68]

Mailer was indeed bogged down on this front, but he was moving, as always, on several others. In the same year as the Pentagon march, dramatic versions of *Deer Park* and *Why Are We in Vietnam?* were staged. From 1967 to 1970 he produced and starred in three experimental films, "Wild 90," "Beyond the Law," and "Maidstone." And in 1969, just before going off to cover the moon shot for *Life*, he ran (and lost) in the Democratic primary for mayor of New York. These activities cut into the energy he could expend explaining American politics for his readers. Even Watergate could not bring him back. He made a half-hearted attempt to follow the proceedings of the Ervin Committee but grew depressed at the "clouds of moral ambiguity" surrounding the scandal. "It felt," he said, "as if an old magic had disappeared."[69]

Generally speaking, critical and popular enthusiasm for the books that succeeded *Armies* declined as Mailer's involvement in the public events of the late sixties and early seventies slowly diminished. The process was gradual and each of his books of the period was hailed with superlatives by several reviewers, but by the time Saigon had fallen and Nixon had resigned, their praise seemed almost perfunctory.

Miami and the Siege of Chicago, also nominated for a National Book Award, was highly acclaimed. Peter Shaw, reviewing for *Commentary,* said that Mailer had found "a way to approximate the accomplishments of the classic American writers."[70] But most reviewers agreed with Eliot Fremont-Smith, the *New York Times'* reviewer, that it was "more conventional" than *Armies.*[71] Jack Richardson, for example, in a highly complimentary review in the *New York Review of Books,* noted that Mailer had allowed the Miami and Chicago conventions "to unfold for the most part unchallenged by his imagination."[72]

Of a Fire on the Moon received more favorable than unfavorable reviews, but the old pattern of contradictory response began to reestablish itself. Benjamin DeMott's review in *Saturday Review* straddled the extremes. He complained of Mailer's "unremitting self-involvement and self-regard" but also argued (somewhat paradoxically) that this self-involvement "blesses him as an enthusiast," one who writes "pages that physically breathe with the vitality of the writer's will to pack in the whole, nail the kit complete—all two million functioning parts, every sensation, every fear, every lucked-out crisis" of the Apollo 11 mission.[73] So it went in the rest of the reviews: excited encomiums for Mailer's ability to drill through NASA's layers of bureaucracy with his diamond-hard ego, and protest against the revelation of his personal beliefs and metaphysics, especially his "Manichean ox-team—his God and Devil in harness pulling on the universe in opposite directions," as Christopher Lehmann-Haupt described it in the *New York Times.*[74]

The stimulus for his next book, *The Prisoner of Sex* (1971) was the publication of Kate Millett's *Sexual Politics* the year before. Millett had called Mailer "a prisoner of the virility cult,"[75] among other things, and Mailer responded with a disputatious examination of the sexual assumptions of the growing women's liberation movement, which included original critiques of the writings of Henry Miller and D. H. Lawrence. His arguments were received with few cheers by feminists and since almost every female reviewer attacked the book, and half the males as well, the ratio of favorable to unfavorable reviews enjoyed by *Fire* was reversed with *Pris-*

oner. The range of counterpoint in the negative reviews is too broad to summarize here, as are the defenses of those like Anatole Broyard, who called it "Mailer's best book" in the *New York Times.*[76] Brigid Brophy's conclusion in the *New York Times Book Review* that "his essay is modeled on a dribble: long and barely continuous,"[77] while not typical, is closer to the tone of the majority of the book's reviewers than is Broyard's. With the publication of *Prisoner*, and his appearance the same year at Town Hall in New York to debate Germaine Greer, Jill Johnston, Diana Trilling, and other feminists, Mailer became the number one whipping boy of the women's liberation movement, a position he holds to this day.

Mailer's fourth collection, *Existential Errands*, containing his essays, reviews, letters, prefaces, etc., from 1966 to 1971, appeared in 1972. It was not reviewed widely, partly because it lacked, as Mailer notes in his preface, the personal emphasis of his earlier collections, but those who did review it liked it. Robert W. Haney's comment, in a *Christian Science Monitor* review, that the miscellany "should win him the title of America's Proteus of the pen," was representative.[78]

St. George and the Godfather appeared the same year as *Errands* and just in time for Mailer to have his say on George McGovern (yes) and Richard Nixon (no) before the presidential election. Reviewers were generally congratulatory, but most felt that *St. George* was inferior to *Armies* because, as Robert Solotaroff noted in the *Nation*, the former lacked the latter's "excitement generated by a sense of new stylistic possibility."[79]

In relinquishing his position as Aquarius-in-charge-of-construing-American-culture in 1976, Mailer wrote that "the history of the republic had gone down into the mines again, and the novelist was left with his fiction."[80] The fiction he was left with was a long novel about ancient Egypt, begun in 1971 and worked at in stretches between other books throughout the decade. He published more than a book a year from 1971 until 1983, when *Ancient Evenings* finally appeared, an enormous achievement considering the massive research and writing effort the Egyptian novel required. Apart from *Evenings*, perhaps the best way to describe his writing in the seventies is to say that after his interest in himself as a protagonist dwindled along with the revolutionary expectations of the sixties, Mailer devoted the following years to a series of works on famous/infamous Americans: Marilyn Monroe in *Marilyn* (1973); Muhammad Ali in *The Fight* (1975); Henry Miller in *Genius and Lust: A Journey through the Major Writings of Henry Miller* (1976); Gary Gilmore in *The Executioner's Song* (1979); and Monroe again in *Of Women and Their Elegance* (1980). If the sixties are Mailer's autobiographical decade, the seventies may fairly be called his biographical period—again, excepting his work on *Evenings*.

Perhaps too much should not be made of it, but the two most ambitious and successful of these books—*Marilyn* and *Song*—deal with people Mailer never met. In both cases Mailer compensated by interviewing a number of people (hundreds for *Song*) who had known Monroe and Gilmore. For *Marilyn*, he also studied earlier biographies and twenty-six of her thirty films; for *Song* he pored over thousands of pages of letters to and from Gilmore, not to mention the voluminous legal documents and press reports bearing on him. Lacking firsthand knowledge of his subjects, Mailer conceived the biographies as imaginative rather than documentary efforts. His intentions may be seen in the fact that he titled the first chapter of *Marilyn* "A Novel Biography," and gave *Song* the subtitle *A True Life Novel*.

Although none of the major reviewers of *Marilyn* (which includes 111 photographs of Monroe assembled by Lawrence Schiller), was unequivocal in his praise, only a few panned it completely. Most found merit in portions of the biography—Mailer's analysis of the traffic between Monroe's public and private selves, and her marriage with Arthur Miller, for example—but attacked Mailer's speculation that she was murdered and derided his ana-grammatic musings on the similarities of their names. Some reviewers agreed with *Commonweal*'s reviewer, Saul Maloff, that the biography was a "free-form fantasia" that scanted the facts of Monroe's life.[81] Others, like the *New York Times*' Christopher Lehmann-Haupt and the *New Republic*'s John Seelye, felt the book lacked "the personal, subjective engagement that we associate with Mailer's writing since the early 60's," as Seelye put it.[82] The majority of the reviewers gave more space to Monroe's life than to the book itself, yet many of them complained that Mailer included too many items of gossip. Pauline Kael, reviewing for the *New York Times Book Review*, described the book as "an offensive physical object, perhaps even a little sordid," but nevertheless called it "brilliant."[83] In what was probably the shrewdest evaluation, Ingrid Bengis, writing in *Ms.*, lauded Mailer's "passionate effort of mind and feeling" applied "to really knowing what it must feel like to be a woman," but pointed out that while "The Bitch goddess is, and always has been, the female equivalent of Mailer himself," there is one huge difference between them: "Mailer was in a posi-tion to choose his role; Marilyn was not. Sex was the only thing she knew she had."[84] The generally unfavorable reviews did not adversely affect sales. *Marilyn* was a best-seller and a Book-of-the-Month Club selection; its first printing of 285,000 copies sold out.

There was considerably less interest in the five books Mailer published in the six years between *Marilyn* and *Song*, although two of these, *The Fight* and *Genius and Lust*, were important additions to his canon, demon-strating as they did his flagging interest in self-examination and the recipro-cal absorption in the lives of other Americans. It could be argued that Mailer's literary fecundity in the late sixties and seventies irked the literary world, especially since he had not yet produced the "descendant of *Moby Dick*" promised in *Advertisements* (156). His lesser efforts, therefore, were often ignored or undervalued. *The Fight* was better received than *Genius and Lust*, although no reviewer went beyond the *Boston Globe*'s George V. Higgins, who said in his review of the former, "Nobody else could have done it."[85] Several of the reviewers of *Genius and Lust* balked at Mailer's claim that Miller was America's greatest living writer, and so questioned the need for a 569-page anthology of his work.[86] Eighty of these pages consist of Mailer's appreciation of Miller; this commentary drew opposed evaluations. Richard Gilman, in a *Village Voice* review, said that Mailer had commented on Miller's unique "autobiographically tilted books" with "a brilliance and originality I haven't seen in any other writing about Miller," and went on to note Mailer's debt to Miller in those sections of the commentary dealing with "man's sense of awe before woman."[87] One of the most negative critiques came from Frederick Crews (in the *New York Review of Books*) who called it an example of Mailer's "incidental, bill-paying, publicity-generating work."[88]

While Mailer uses his experience and private self, although somewhat sparingly, in writing about Monroe, he does not speak in propria persona in *Song*, except for some designedly perfunctory comments in a brief afterword. "Only someone who has been writing for 30 years," Mailer told an interviewer, "would be willing to relinquish his ego. I couldn't have done it 15 years ago."[89] But thirty years earlier Mailer did use the same point of view. *Song* and *Naked* are both told by unidentified, omniscient narrators who wheel their perspectives through a large cast of characters, range freely in time and space, and knit several plot strands into a tremendous social tapestry. The huge cast of characters in *Song* is, of course, one reason he returned to this point of view. But his choice was more complicated. Another reason is that he had all but recovered from the anomie he had experienced during the Ford and Carter years. Assertion began to give way to conjecture in Mailer's writing during the seventies and this trend continued through *Song*, which like its forebear, Dreiser's *An American Tragedy*, was written in the interrogative mood. Nevertheless, by 1979 Mailer was much more in possession of that "coherent view of life" which he found lacking in himself in the period of uncertainty after the publication of *Naked* and again in the mid-seventies. In *Song*, he did not have all the answers, but he knew which questions to ask.

Habituated to Mailer's refractive presence in his nonfiction narratives of the late sixties and early seventies, almost every one of the numerous reviewers of *Song* remarked on his conspicuous absence. So much had been made of his identification with Monroe in *Marilyn* that it was scarcely noticed that he had been quietly paring away his presence as early as *Fire*. In the nine years after it was published, Mailer tinkered with his image, dialing it up two intensities, then down three, searching, it seemed, for a new and more perspicacious focus on himself. And then he was gone. It is significant that the books for which Mailer has received almost universal praise—*Naked*, *Armies*, and *Song*—are narratives in which he is either absent or seen from a distance, a reflection not so much of their preeminence among his works (although they are, along with *Dream*, *Advertisements*, and *Evenings*, his best) as of Americans' stubborn suspicion of literary self-presentation.

Only a few reviewers of *Song* felt that Mailer's "absence is so pronounced that it dominates the book like an empty chair at a family dinner," as Richard Stern argued in his *Chicago* magazine review. He said that *Song* "is so unremittingly unmailerian, it is also antimailerian; an act of literary suicide analogous to the legal suicide that is the book's core."[90] Earl Rovit, while applauding the book in the *Nation*, agreed with Stern to the extent of concluding that *Song's* readers are "unguided by the author and unconfronted with a meaningful shape of experience."[91]

The overwhelming majority of *Song's* reviewers, however, either agreed or would sympathize with Frank McConnell's opinion, in a review in *New Republic*, that Mailer's decision to relate Gilmore's life and death from the perspectives of literally hundreds of people demonstrated "narrative technique of real genius."[92] There was disagreement over the relative merits of the book's halves, "Western Voices," which traces Gilmore's life up to his conviction, and "Eastern Voices," which recounts the three-way struggle among those who wished to see him executed, those who did not, and those who wanted to tell the story, in all its macabre sensationalism, of Gilmore's fight to have the court's capital sentence carried out. Lawrence Schiller, Mailer's past collaborator on *Marilyn*, and his future collaborator on *Song*, won the story rights and his and Mailer's interviews with just about everyone associated with Gilmore became the *Ur-Song* upon which Mailer built his 1,056-page best-seller and Pulitzer Prize–winner (for fiction). Partly because of Schiller's record of recording the final moments of other criminals and celebrities, partly because of the media's disinclination to read about their own activities, and partly because of the force of "Western Voices," which Joan Didion described in the *New York Times Book Review* as "a fatalistic drift, a tension, an overwhelming and passive rush toward the inevitable," the second half was not as admired as the first.[93] Lucid, in his *Philadelphia Inquirer* review, described "Western Voices" as the discovery of "the voices and, therefore, the existence of a lost world in our culture," one similar to that made by John Steinbeck in *The Grapes of Wrath*. With *Song*, Mailer gained the attention of a generation too young to have protested the Vietnam War. Didion, in the concluding sentence of her review, called it "an absolutely astonishing book."[95]

What was not known in the seventies, but which can now be surmised, is the effect that the decade-long immersion in the culture of ancient Egypt was having on Mailer's other work. As he created the new and initially alien consciousness of the protagonist of *Ancient Evenings*, Menenhetet I, he was, in a complex, decade-long compensation, slowly effacing himself in his nonfiction narratives. This self-effacement was not a matter of humility; rather, it was part of Mailer's program to clarify and balance those parts of his psyche which had become shopworn or ambiguous by delineating their equivalents in Monroe, Ali, Miller, and Gilmore. It would be simplistic to say that he identified with these four, or with Menenhetet (as Richard Poirier emphasizes in his *Times Literary Supplement* review of *Evenings*),[96] but certainly the cardinal virtues and vices of Mailer's four American egotists are manifested in the Egyptian, who has learned from a Jewish slave how to father himself and lives four lives in the course of the novel. The goal of all of them, and Mailer too, is to achieve what he once called "the energy of new success" (*Advertisements*, 241), and so gain the power, like Menenhetet, to create new selves.[97]

Of the roughly forty reviews of *Ancient Evenings* I have read, only six or seven are middling or indecisive. The rest are evenly divided between denunciations and hosannas. The tenor of the antitheses goes like this: "a new and permanent contibution to the possibilities of fiction and our communal efforts at self-discovery" (George Stade); "considerably less than a heroic venture botched in the execution. It is, bluntly speaking, a disaster" (Benjamin DeMott); "it may well appear as one of the great works of contemporary mythopoesis" (Anthony Burgess); "a ineradicable abyss of stone. Mailer has written his epitaph" (Sam Coale).[98]

The chief reason for the collective Manichaeanism of the reviewers is their diametrically opposed opinions on the merit of Mailer's conception of the violent, magical, and carnal religiosity of the ancient Egyptians. He wanted to re-create a society unaffected by Western culture's ruling beliefs—Judaic monotheism, Christian compassion, Faustian progress, romantic love, and Freudian guilt. Half of the reviewers, more or less, felt that he accomplished this. The other half felt that, far from imagining such a society, Mailer was "plowing away at his old tired obsessions," as James Wolcott stated in his review in *Harper's*.[99] Demott and the other detractors agreed. Leslie Fiedler argued in a *Psychology Today* review that "he is able to project once more his lifelong fantasy of becoming the 'Golden Goy'" through "his surrogate, Menenhetet."[100]

Several of the book's reviewers noted that Mailer erroneously attributed a belief in telepathy and reincarnation to the Egyptians, although few if any recognized that his interest in them was as much technical as substantive. The telepathic powers of his characters allow them to perform the narrative work of omniscience and the novelist becomes, ostensibly, the amaneunsis of what they receive or pluck from the minds of others. Reincarnation gave Mailer a simple pretext for extending the story over four lives instead of one, although it is Menenhetet's first life as Ramses II's charioteer-general and harem master that receives the most attention.

Apart from these unhistorical attributions, there is no evidence that Mailer departed much from the available evidence on the nature of Egyptian society. His ideas (explained in postpublication interviews) that the Egyptians were "a warring people of viciously sexual and brutally violent habits," a people for whom "The Establishment . . . *was* the gods, a tyrannical establishment of the gods" can perhaps be qualified but not contradicted.[101] The criticism that Mailer remade Egyptian society along the lines of his own interests, therefore, is unfair, although he certainly chose a culture amenable to them. "Why are we in Egypt?" asked Harold Bloom in his generally favorable review in the *New York Review of Books*. "Where else could we be? Mailer's dialectics of sex and death have found their inevitable context," he answered.[102]

Richard Poirier's review of *Evenings* in the *Times Literary Supplement* goes along with Bloom's line of thinking to some extent. Poirier said that Mailer has presented a culture that gives "sanction to what in his other works often seems eccentric or plaintively metaphysical." *Evenings*, therefore, is the "most self-revealing" of Mailer's books. In an exceptionally subtle manner, Poirier elaborated on this contention, arguing that "the cental condition of nearly all his writing depends not on . . . the famous Mailer ego, but rather on self-fragmentation and dispersal," and that the novel's complexity and length, its votive interest in magic, spirits, and incantatory language, permitted Mailer not so much to be "his own subject," as "to be found instead within a larger expressive structure of which his voice is only one part looking for other parts." The sex and violence that the novel's deprecators focused on, while clearly important, are not nearly as crucial to *Evenings'* significance and meaning as "the power of the word" (*Evenings*, 709), which it, like Joyce's novels, so exalts. "This is his most audacious book," Poirier said at the close of his review, "largely because behind it all is the desire, once and for all, to claim some ultimate cultural and spiritual status for the teller of stories, the Writer."[103]

Ancient Evenings, with its evocations of the marvels and horrors of the tomb, court, battlefield, harem, and tomb again, is many things but first of all it is a great epistemological adventure. Although the work of understanding it has only just begun, its spiraling narrative skeins and multiple inlaid perspectives, and their push-pull relationships with the biographical narratives of the seventies may be the most important matters in its future critical consideration.

In *Tough Guys Don't Dance* (1984), Mailer returned to America, or at least to its shore. The murder mystery, which may prove to be more than a holding action, is set in Provincetown, the resort at the edge of the country where the Puritans, founders of WASP culture, first landed. Like *Ancient Evenings*, *Tough Guys* was a best-seller and a Literary Guild selection, although the reviews, predictably, were evenly divided. Singled out for praise in even some of the unfavorable reviews was the father of Tim Madden, the novel's narrator-hero, another in the long line of mentor figures in Mailer's fiction stretching back to General Cummings in *Deer Park* and McLeod in *Barbary Shore*.[104]

The almost schizophrenic response of reviewers to Mailer's books, taken one by one, is not mirrored in the scholarly and critical studies of his work. For the most part, he has been treated respectfully and extensively from the fifties on by a large number of deliberative critics. The following summary characterizes and briefly comments on the major emphases of this work, although because of its volume, only the most important and representative contributions are discussed.

The first of these is John W. Aldridge's *After the Lost Generation* (1951). Aldridge had high praise for Mailer's "terrifyingly accurate picture of the conditions of actual warfare" in *Naked*, but judged it to be "half triumph, half failure," because the novel's ostensible heroes, Red Valsen and Lieutenant Hearn, lack the strength of purpose to do more than feebly oppose the fascism of Sergeant Croft and General Cummings. The novel is "a potent condemnation of the fascistic military system," Aldridge concludes; what it lacks is "a set of values, a hierarchy of law in terms of which evil and good, futility and hope, could be meaningfully opposed."[105]

The next important critical study did not appear until 1959 when Norman Podhoretz published a long, mostly celebratory article. Podhoretz, a close friend at the time, also pointed to the weakness of Hearn as a character and the forceful depiction of Croft and Cummings. He departs from Aldridge, however, in arguing that the latter figures are not only "more admirable" than intended, but are the novel's "natural heroes," a point later confirmed by Mailer[106] and repeated by admirers and detractors ever since as evidence of Mailer's fascination with the exercise of power, moral or amoral. Podhoretz also established the framework for later discussions of Mailer's politics by tracing his rejection first of liberalism and then of revolutionary socialism in favor of the existential philosophy ennunciated in "The White Negro," and by noting that Mailer "must always work everything out for himself and by himself, as though it were up to him to create the world anew."[107] Mailer thought enough of the essay to reprint a portion of it as the introduction to the 1963 Grosset & Dunlap paperback edition of *Barbary Shore*.

Mailer's frank and incisive criticisms of his contemporaries in *Advertisements* drew rejoinders from several of them (Myrick Land's account of this battle, including interviews with most of the principals, appeared in 1963).[108] The most important of these was James Baldwin's, published in 1961 in *Esquire*. Baldwin, while rating Mailer as "an absolutely first-rate talent," severely criticized "The White Negro." "Why," he asked, "malign the sorely menaced sexuality of Negroes in order to justify the white man's own sexual panic?" Yet his own comment in the essay that "to become a Negro man, let alone a Negro artist, one had to make oneself up as one went along" supports rather than contradicts the existential propositions of "The White Negro."[109]

Ihab Hassan, in his landmark study of the contemporary American novel, *Radical Innocence* (1961), follows Podhoretz in his discussion of Mailer's obsession with power, but in one of the most persuasive studies of *Naked* to date, takes issue with Podhoretz and Aldridge by positing Hearn as an ironist and scapegoat who both links and opposes the Faustian Cummings, with his demonic chess-board approach to war, and his "earthly double," Croft, whose power lust is "primitive, almost feral."[110] The length-iest attack on "The White Negro" came from George Alfred Schrader, who argued in a 1961 article that Mailer's hipster-hero, like "Kierkegaard's es-thetic hero, the 'sensuous-erotic genius,'" is marooned in a despairing present. He concludes that Mailer must either "go on to an ethical-reli-gious courage in which he affirms existence with all its infinite blemishes— or remain in pathos."[111] Schrader's somewhat abstract analysis was squarely countered by Diana Trilling in a 1962 *Encounter* essay. She was the first to present a sustained argument for his placement "in the forefront of modern writers," despite what she calls "his detachment from cultural tradition." Reprinted several times since then, Trilling's essay must be considered one of the half-dozen finest summary critiques of Mailer's artistic and intellec-tual character. The subtleties of her wide-ranging and enthusiastic assess-ment cannot be redeployed here, but the shape of her argument, based on the contention that "the sum of his contradictions . . . bears striking resem-blance to present-day America" is indicated in the following passage.

> . . . so much moral affirmation coupled with so much moral anarchism; so much innocence yet so much guile; so much defensive caution but such headlong recklessness; so much despair together with so imperious a demand for salvation; so strong a charismatic charge but also so much that offends or even repels; so much intellection but such a frequency of unsound thinking; such a grand and manly impulse to heroism but so inadequate a capacity for self-discipline; so much sensitiveness and so lit-tle sensibility; so much imagination and such insufficient art . . . . a tal-ent which necessarily lives on the sharp edge of uncertainty.[112]

The critic in largest disagreement with Trilling in the early sixties was Christopher Lasch, who devoted a section of his 1965 volume, *The New Radicalism in America (1889–1963)*, to Mailer. More sympathetic are the short studies of Harris Dienstfrey on Mailer's fiction, published in 1964; of Edmund L. Volpe, who compared Mailer and James Jones, also in 1964; of Kingsley Widmer, who compared Mailer and Paul Goodman in his 1965 volume *The Literary Rebel;* and Paul B. Newman's "Mailer: The Jew as Existentialist" (1965).[113] Lasch identifies Mailer as a descendant of earlier radicals Randolph Bourne and Lincoln Steffens but contends that Mailer's desire to shift the nation's consciousness is doomed because his undertak-ing is "flawed by the old confusion of politics and culture."[114] Lasch's belief that politics can exist in a culture-free quarantine was subscribed to by a number of Mailer critics after the publication of *Advertisements*. A corol-lary to this idea, also advanced by many Mailer critics, is that Mailer should eschew political journalism for fiction, as well as the obverse, that his most credible skills are reportorial and applying them to fiction is a waste of time. For the past twenty-five years Mailer's severest critics have lam-basted him for being either a factualist or a fictionalist, or for confusing the two,[115] while his admirers have delighted in his conflation of narrative realms.

John W. Aldridge's 1966 essay on Mailer, a brilliant enlargement of his 1965 review of *Dream*, presents a dialectical view of Mailer's artistic dilemma after *Naked:* for his continuing success he needed a large popular audience, but his "suicidally belligerent habits" in print and in public in the period before the 1957 publication of "The White Negro" had antagonized a large part of his already shrunken readership. Mailer was able to resolve this problem, Aldridge says, "by persuading the public to hate him [so] that he could give up the idea of trying to persuade the public to love him." In the late fifties, after giving up his desire for large, quick successes, he was able to develop "a prose idiom of higher sensitivity to the exact condition of contemporary consciousness than any we have had in fiction since the best work of Faulkner."

Three very different studies of Mailer—none of them as important as Aldridge's essay—were published in 1967. Because of the large influence of Podhoretz's pioneering essay on Mailer, his mid-life autobiography, *Making It,* is of special interest. Although he includes only a brief section on Mailer, he admits that he used his friend as an exemplary model in the "frank, Mailer-like bid for literary distinction, fame and money" which *Making It* constitutes.[117]

Also in 1967, Howard M. Harper, Jr., devoted a chapter of *Desperate Faith* to Mailer, generally following the interpretations of Podhoretz and Trilling in his competent summaries of Mailer's fiction through *Dream;*[118] and James Toback's more unconventional essay appeared in *Commentary.* Toback defines Mailer as a "latter-day hell-fire Puritan preacher" as motivated by dread and as concerned with afterlife as Jonathan Edwards.[119] In 1968 Toback published an account of the filming of "Maidstone" on Long Island. Chiefly of value as a rough chronicle of Mailer's interaction on the set with a variety of friends, opportunists, and cranks, Toback's article paints an ambiguous picture of Mailer and his final movie-making gamble (Mailer put up over $100,000), which Toback characterizes as Mailer's "Brook Farm, his community, created and creative."[120]

Responding to Mailer's comeback, a number of commentators published articles on him the same year that Toback's appeared in *Esquire.* Richard Foster was the author of two. The first, "Mailer and the Fitzgerald Tradition," explores the striking similarities between the fictional male characters of the two writers: "modern versions of Spenserian knights, their heroes move through mazes of sexual ambiguity inhabited by true and false goddesses."[121] In his monograph on Mailer the same year, Foster extended the parallel, but went far beyond it and produced the longest and one of the most penetrating critiques of Mailer to that time. Especially valuable is his delineation of the strengths and weaknesses of Mailer's style, which he sums up as "a *forcing* style: it exerts force upon reality; it seeks to *force* reality into the matrix of an idiosyncratic vision. This *urgency* is the key to Mailer's most prominent strengths."[122]

David Hesla's 1968 article argues that Mailer fails as a thinker. He mainly repeats more emphatically the criticisms of Podhoretz and Trilling, noting that he "thinks as if no one in the history of the world has ever thought before him." He is more successful in his second role of novelist, Hesla says, but all of his novels are flawed because Mailer's "craft fails him at that point in his work where invention must take over from experience."[123] Other important contributions that year came from Jack Newfield and Robert Langbaum. The former's colorful sketch traces Mailer's steps during one day in early 1968.[124] Langbaum's essay is distinguished by his closely reasoned argument that with *Dream* and *Vietnam* Mailer broke through a new style. The "hallucinated realism" of these books, he contends, allowed Mailer to link "conscious and unconscious levels of existence," the worlds of Marx and Freud.[125]

The four books on Mailer published in 1969 were the beginning of a critical torrent. Two of these were concerned with Mailer's candidacy for mayor of New York. Joe Flaherty's *Managing Mailer* details the campaign from his campaign manager's vantage point, and Peter Manso's *Running against the Machine* collects the campaign's position papers and various press reports. Together they comprise a fairly complete overview of Mailer's mayoralty bid.[126] The first two book-length studies of Mailer are serious but imperfect efforts. Donald L. Kaufmann's *The Countdown* is the weaker. Written in a pseudo-Mailer style, it works backward from chapter 10 to chapter one for obscure reasons. Because he ends his consideration of Mailer's work with *Cannibals*, he is able to announce that Mailer's interest in politics is past, an error that does not generate confidence in his other interpretations. He is, however, thoughtful on the beast/seer conflict in Mailer's work, and on the morality play–type choices faced by Rojack.[127] Barry H. Leeds' *The Structured Vision of Norman Mailer* is itself well-structured and clear in its conventional intentions, the largest of which is to trace the growing optimism in Mailer's novels through *Dream* (*Vietnam* is seen as a regression). His analysis of Mailer's point-of-view problems and their resolution in *Armies* is excellent, and unlike Kaufmann he examines all of the books through *Miami*, not excepting Mailer's poetry or the dramatic version of *Deer Park*.[128]

Four short studies published in 1970 opened a decade of confusing debate about the meaning and value of Mailer's work. William Hoffa's retrospective analysis of his writing in the fifties is premised on the claim that the "objectivity and detachment" of Mailer's first three novels is indebted to the realistic heritage of nineteenth-century American literature.[129] Ihab Hassan's essay on *Vietnam* recalls D. H. Lawrence's idiosyncratic criticism of American literature in its orphic assertions and direct adress to the author. Hassan was perhaps the first of a number of critics who felt compelled by Mailer's personal tone to reply in kind.[130] Helen A. Weinberg devoted a chapter of *The New Novel in America: The Kafkan Mode in Contemporary Fiction* to Mailer. Skipping *Naked* and *Vietnam*, she traces the emergence of his "activist hero" from *Barbary Shore* to *Dream*.[131] Finally, Jerry H. Bryant, in an able recapitulation, characterizes Mailer's moral posture: "self-discovery must precede the establishment of satisfactory societies."[132]

From 1966 to 1971 Mailer published thirteen books. His literary prodigality, not to mention his other ventures, drew a correspondingly turbulent outpouring from the critics. More was published on Mailer, and more of real merit, in 1971 and 1972 than in any two-year period before or since. A total of thirty-eight essays appeared in two critical collections, one edited by Robert F. Lucid (1971) and the other by Leo Braudy (1972), and in a special 1971 issue of *Modern Fiction Studies* devoted to Mailer. I have already commented on a majority of the essays in the two books, but the introductions of Lucid and Braudy should be endorsed for their original contributions to an understanding of Mailer. Lucid attempts to resolve the apparent conflict between Mailer's devotion to his public, image-making activities and his fealty to his artistic ones in a shrewd, unsummarizable analysis which, after reference to Emerson, Hemingway, and other public artists, arrives at the simple but, I think, irrefutable conclusion that Mailer became a public figure to enhance his imaginative resources as a private artist. All of Mailer's enterprises, even the embarrassing failures, are "exercises in imaginative-isometrics," efforts to keep in shape artistically. Braudy's introduction is less sharply focused, but his reading of *Miami* as "closer than any one of Mailer's works since *The Naked and the Dead* to a total vision of society" is useful for its insights into this work, usually overshadowed by *Armies*. The essays in the *MFS* issue deal with three of Mailer's novels (*Naked, Barbary Shore,* and *Vietnam*), the influence of Hemingway and Dos Passos, Mailer's cosmology, *Armies* and the portions of *Fire* published in *Life*. John M. Muste's careful argument that *Naked* may be more indebted to Dos Passos's *Three Soldiers* than to *U.S.A.*, and Robert Meridith's leftist critique of *Armies* are the most forceful and detailed of the essays; Richard D. Finholt's article also deserves recognition as the first extended treatment of Mailer's cosmology.[133]

Diana Trilling's speech at the notorious 1971 Town Hall symposium on feminism (published with a prefatory comment in 1977) gives a much clearer picture of the evening and the issues debated than does Germaine Greer's "My Mailer Problem," published in the September 1971 issue of *Esquire,* the cover of which depicts Greer in the clutches of a snarling King Kong Mailer. Where Greer is facetious and ambivalent, Trilling is clear and pointed. After repeating her belief that Mailer is "the most important writer of our time," she points out the disparity between Mailer's position as "so pre-eminent a spokesman for the unconditioned life" and the "dangerous poetic excess" of his stand against contraception.[134]

Several of the other notable contributions of this period are Richard

Schickel's ruminative essay on the filming of "Maidstone"; Allen Guttman's chapter on Mailer, "a non-Jewish Jew," in *The Jewish Writer in America;* Theodore L. Gross's chapter on Mailer the "quixotic hero" in *The Heroic Ideal in American Literature;* and Fredric Jameson's leftist exploration of ideology in *Vietnam*, in which he argues that "Mailer clings with incorrigible tenacity to everything he denounces," even though these things poison him, because "his sickness is his raw material." In an English Institute paper on *Armies* and *The Autobiography of Malcolm X*, Warner Berthoff analyzes *Armies* as an adaptation of "a classic American literary mode: the exploratory personal testament in which the writer describes how he has turned his own life into a practical moral experiment."[135]

Lucid's *The Long Patrol*, a 739-page anthology containing excerpts from thirteen of Mailer's books through *Fire*, and Aldridge's review of it and Lucid's critical collection, were also published in 1971. Lucid's introduction to the anthology and Aldridge's review masterfully illuminate Mailer's mediations between public affairs and private obsessions, "between his personal micro-hells and the major disasters of his age," in Aldridge's formulation.[136]

Three more important studies appeared during the years 1971–72, the golden moment of Mailer criticism. They constitute, along with the work of Aldridge and Lucid, the central achievements of this remarkable period. Each of the three critics (Martin Green, Richard Poirier, and Tony Tanner) offer provocative interpretations that can be only generally described here. Green's 1972 essay presents Mailer as the consummate expression of Faustian New York, opposed both to Erasmian liberalism (because of its rationalism), and Puritan radicalism (because of its selflessness). Describing Mailer's temperament as "outrageously indiscreet and personal" and "powerfully insightful and reflective," he calls him "the most important writer of his time." The fact that Green believed the time to be near-apocalyptic does not negate his vision, the quality of which is suggested by the double-page photograph it contains: Mailer leaning on a smog-draped New York City skyline.[137] Tanner's chapter on Mailer in *City of Words: American Fiction, 1950–70* (1971) is titled "On the Parapet." He also stresses Mailer's identification with New York, especially in *Dream*, which he argues brings together "the three different worlds of Mailer's first three novels—war *[Naked]*, politics *[Barbary Shore]* and sexual experience *[Deer Park]*." In a progression of stunning insights Tanner shows how *Dream* sharpens and then balances the dualisms of his earlier work (sex-politics, unconscious-conscious, etc.), most notably in the climactic scene where Rojack is able to "negotiate the edge where the worlds meet" in his walk around the terrace parapet of Barney Kelly's penthouse.

> . . . Mailer has no wish to exchange naturalism for supernaturalism and commit himself henceforth to a purely demonic mode of writing—for that too is only a version, a fixed reading. . . . Just as Rojack walks the edge of the parapet to signify his intention to remain unclaimed by both sides,

so Mailer walks a stylistic edge. He touches continually on two worlds—
the inner and the outer, the demonic and the political, the dreaming and
the waking, the structured and the flowing—and tries to be stylistically
adequate to all without being trapped by any one.[138]

No one who has written about Mailer has been consistently stimulating
over so many pages as Poirier. In *Norman Mailer* (1972), he is tremendously acute on Mailer's endlessly modulating rhetoric, "his dogged refusal
to put together a self at the cost of stifling any fragment of his personality."
Poirier challenges several received interpretations—for example, the view
that holds Mailer's characteristic tone to be hortatory—and support his arguments with tenacious examinations of Mailer's syntax and metaphor.
Poirier ranges freely among the works through *Prisoner* in his volume's
three chapters: on Mailer's career, his relation to history, and the enormous foundation of dualisms on which his vision of contemporary life is
based. He correctly calls Mailer "an anticapitalistic, anti-industrial, anti-
technological pastoralist," but it is clear that Mailer's vested opinions on
technology, magic, nature, violence, and sex (especially) are prized much
more for their literary than their referential or elucidatory value. So Poirier
terms Mailer's ditheistic cosmology "an *imagined* [emphasis mine] war between God and the Devil." However much or little one sympathizes with
Poirier's incredulity concerning Mailer's ideas on matters of faith and morals, his study must be seen as the most elaborate and developed critique of
Mailer to date.[139]

Three 1973 studies of Mailer demonstrated his standing as "the most
vivid image in American literary life today," as Nathan A. Scott, Jr., described him in one of these, a long essay, "Norman Mailer—Our Whitman." In detailed readings of all the works through the sixties, Scott makes
his case that Mailer is a "spokesman for the American conscience," a propo-
nent of what Whitman called "personalism."[140] Alfred Kazin covers most of
the same books in *The Bright Book of Life: American Novelists and Storytellers from Hemingway to Mailer*, but is less interested in a detailed examination of the oeuvre than in showing how Mailer has succeeded in imposing on us "his characteristic sense of imbalance, of different orders of reality
to be *willed* together." A New York Jew a few years older than Mailer,
Kazin is only slightly avuncular and ambivalent about Mailer's "cockiness."
Mainly, he is admiring, penetrating, deeply sensitive to the tradition of the
American writer as "a cultural force," and altogether convincing on how
Mailer has extended and modified this tradition.[141] John Henry Raleigh's
essay on "Mailer's historical *Weltanschauung*," the most systematic examination of this topic to date, provides deft analyses of Mailer's attitudes toward the nineteenth-century frontier and small town, the "dynamic, orgiastic, explosive, accelerating City" and postwar America generally.[142]

Two 1974 articles by Lucid on Mailer's hero-scapegoat status in the
American imagination reaffirmed his status as one of the most important

Mailer commentators. The linked essays explore the love/hate relationship of our public writers and their audiences, with special reference to Fitzgerald and Hemingway. Lucid argues that greater and greater demands have been placed on Mailer and that his response has been to disassemble himself into his various avatars—reporter, clown, cop, crook, etc.—in his books and movies, while simultaneously introducing the "radically new element" of detachment, most notably through the use of the third person in his nonfiction narratives.[143]

Gordon O. Taylor's extended discussion of the "tonal and strategic affinities" of Mailer and Henry Adams, especially in *Fire* and *The Education of Henry Adams*, was published in 1974, as was the first considered estimate of *Armies*'s powerful influence on the anti–Vietnam War movement, by Sandy Vogelgesang.[144] Laura Adams published two volumes on Mailer in 1974: *Norman Mailer: A Comprehensive Bibliography* and a collection of fifteen essays and reviews, *Will the Real Norman Mailer Please Stand Up*. The bibliography, still indispensable, contains listings of Mailer's unpublished manuscripts, theses, and dissertations, primary and secondary works (including interviews and reviews of secondary works), and a chronology of Mailer's life. The anthology includes discussions of Mailer's poetry and films, the dramatic version of *Deer Park*, his mayoral race, and useful overviews by Matthew Grace, Raymond A. Schroth, Richard M. Levine, and Adams herself in her introduction.[145]

Robert Solotaroff's book, *Down Mailer's Way* (1974), was the first major study to carefully examine Mailer's debts to and distance from the great European existential philosophers. His critique of "The White Negro" is the best published to date. In addition, his generally negative evaluation of *Dream* is valuable for its contrast with those of Tanner and Aldridge. Despite the fact that he overlooks the use of the third person in half the chapters of *Vietnam*, his argument that it is Mailer's most important novel because D.J.'s sensibilities differ more from Mailer's than do Rojack's reinforces Poirier's high estimate of the novel.[146]

The book-length studies by Jean Radford and Stanley T. Gutman published in 1975 resemble each other in their focus on Mailer's fiction and their emphasis of thematic matters. Radford's study (the first major British effort) is repetitive and marred by her belief that style is only of secondary interest to Mailer, but her analysis of the Eitel-Esposito affair in *Deer Park* captures all its nuances. Gutman's volume is better conceived and organized. Although he insulates some of Mailer's electricity in his thematic summaries, they are solid. His study is informed throughout by his awareness that Mailer's views and rhetoric are "firmly rooted in the Emersonian tradition."[147]

A year later Laura Adams published her third Mailer volume, a full-length study entitled *Existential Battles: The Growth of Norman Mailer*. Her dialectical approach divides his career into four stages centered on *Advertisements*, *Dream*, *Armies*, and the work from *Miami* to *The Fight*. Adams's analyses are not significantly different from those of earlier critics like Barry H. Leeds, but her discussions of Mailer's perspectival problems and his credentials as an American romantic are insightful.[148]

More than a dozen articles and chapters dealing with Mailer came out in 1977; only the briefest mention of some of these can be made here. Howard Silverstein's article in *American Imago* examined the "triangular relationship in which two or more men are interested in the same woman" in Mailer's novels; George Plimpton recounted Mailer's trip to Zaire to cover the Ali-Foreman fight in *Shadow Box*; George Stade made an elegant comparison of Mailer and Henry Miller in *Partisan Review*; one of the four chapters of Frank D. McConnell's *Four Postwar American Novelists* is devoted to tracing the shift in Mailer's novels from ideological to "visionary" politics; the first sustained effort to evaluate Mailer as a "new journalist" was made by John Hollowell; Morris Dickstein took Mailer as a touchstone figure in his history of the sixties, *Gates of Eden*; and my article on Mailer's attitude toward and involvement with the media was published in *Modern Fiction Studies*.[149]

Four of the six studies of Mailer published in 1978 and 1979 are valuable contributions. Jennifer Bailey's *Norman Mailer: Quick-Change Artist* consists largely of extended summaries of his work, and Mitchell S. Ross's chapter on Mailer in *The Literary Politicians* is a diatribe that has no merit as literary criticism but should be consulted by those interested in Mailer for its truly remarkable and sustained hostility.[150] The strength and weakness of Robert Ehrlich's *Norman Mailer: The Radical as Hipster* lie in his application of the philosophy enunciated in "The White Negro" to the rest of Mailer's works, although he also discusses the foreshadowing of later themes in *Naked*.[151] Robert Merrill's *Norman Mailer*, a volume in the Twayne series, is the work of a thoughtful critic. He is one of the few to recognize that Mailer did not intend *Dream* to be a romance or an exercise in fabulism. He holds that both *Dream* and *Vietnam* are "formal failures" because they are not "governed by a single synthesizing principle." His position on *Dream*, like Solotaroff's, stands in sharp opposition to those who rate the novel as one of Mailer's finest.[152] Philip H. Bufithis's *Norman Mailer* is distinguished by a clear style and a confident view of "the conflict between will and external power" in Mailer's work. His penultimate chapter on *The Fight* and *Genius and Lust*, "Awesome Men," is the most penetating evaluation of these books published to date.[153] Finally, Judith Fetterley's feminist critique of *Dream* was published in 1978. In one of the strongest Mailer essays of the seventies, she argues that "Mailer's fantasy of female power and male powerlessness" in *Dream* "serves to disguise and hence perpetuate the very reality it invents."[154]

Three studies published in the period 1980–81 are rooted in psychology. Andrew Gordon's Freudian study, *An American Dreamer*, is the most thorough examination of Mailer from this perspective; Robert J. Begiebing's *Acts of Regeneration* is Jungian; and my own article (coauthored with

Charles B. Strozier) compares the introspective-empathetic narratives of Mailer and Erik Erikson. Of the two full-length studies, Begiebing's is less doctrinaire. He makes a stong argument that Mailer is not a fabulist but can fairly be described as an "archetypal allegorist" in all of his major works except *Naked*.[155] Opposed to Begiebing on Mailer's fabulism is John Hellman, who devotes a chapter of his 1981 study of the New Journalism to Mailer.[156]

Two excellent reconsiderations of *Naked* were published in 1982. Bernard Horn's essay in *American Quarterly* holds that "the presence of *Moby-Dick* animates *The Naked and the Dead* in seven important ways," the most important of which is the derivation of the power lust of Cummings and Croft from Melville's protagonist ("the Ahab within"). Donald Pizer's chapter on *Naked* in his *Twentieth-Century American Literary Naturalism: An Interpretation* is a brief against two major opposed interpretations of the novel: (1) that it looks to "the proletarian attitudes and fictional forms of the 1930's"; and (2) that it is "an unsatisfactory anticipation of Mailer's later existentialism." Pizer finds some merit in both of these ideas, but maintains in a persuasive and thoroughly researched discussion that in *Naked* "Mailer has successfully created a symbolic form to express the naturalistic theme of the hidden recesses of value in man's nature despite his tragic fate in a closely conditioned and controlled world."[157] The same year John R. Cooley devoted a section of *Savages and Naturals: Black Portraits by White Writers in Modern American Literature* to Mailer, praising the characterization of Shago Martin in *Dream*, but agreeing with Baldwin that the image of blacks in "The White Negro" is stereotypical.[158] Alvin B. Kernan's essay on *Fire* as a portrayal of the "conflict of the two great myths, science and poetry, for the control of reality" was also published in 1982.[159]

The final work of importance published in 1982 was Hilary Mills's *Mailer: A Biography*.[160] As the first serious biographer, Mills was the first in the quarry of recollections. Her interviews with two of Mailer's wives, his early mentors (especially Jean Malaquais), associates and editors at the *Village Voice* and *Esquire*, and friends such as Vance Bourjaily, Norman Podhoretz, Mickey Knox, Buzz Farbar, John W. Aldridge, and José Torres are of incontestable value. But, for whatever reasons, she was unable to interview many others: his children, four of his wives, his former editor at Little, Brown, Roger Donald, his sister Barbara and cousin Cy Rembar, his secretaries Molly Cook and Judith McNally, and friends and collaborators such as Lucid, Peter Manso, Rip Torn, Eddie Bonetti, Lawrence Schiller, Milton Greene, Barbara Solomon, Eugene Kennedy, and many others. Mailer himself gave her only one interview, and this before the book was underway.[161] The biography has a number of other faults. First, it is poorly documented; citations for many items are missing and page numbers are usually left out. Second, she often relies on a single source for the reconstruction of an event. Third, her remarks on his books are exceedingly general. For example, she says that the murder of Deborah in *Dream* "would hook the sensationalists and carry them deeper into Rojack's mind, which brooded on the universal question of modern dread."[162] She gives little consideration to the mountain of serious criticism. Finally, she erects no interpretative framework, offers no clarifying hypotheses about his life to be tested. Mills's Mailer does not appear to have an inner life of any consequence.

The publication of *Song* in 1979 and *Evenings* in 1983 will likely lead to a flood of critical estimates such as occurred in the early seventies after Mailer published *Armies* and its successors. While many of the same matters will be debated—his interest in all varieties of sex, violence, and power, certainly—there will probably be a number of major reevaluations of Mailer's work. Anthony Burgess's selection in 1984 of *Naked* and *Evenings* as Mailer's two finest novels, and two of the ninety-nine best in English since 1939, is perhaps an indication of how sweeping this reevaluation will be.[163] The other three significant studies of Mailer published in 1984 did not consider *Evenings*. The question of whether Mailer can still be considered "the New Jeremiah," as Sam B. Girgus calls him in a 1984 study, is debatable given his great disappearing trick in *Song* and his removal to Egypt in *Evenings*. Girgus's chapter on Mailer in *The New Covenant: Jewish Writers and the American Idea* follows the earlier study of Nathan A. Scott, Jr., in linking Mailer with Whitman as the "moral consciousness of his culture," although he also includes a careful examination of Mailer's Jewish characters.[164] Martin Green's chapter on *Vietnam* in *The Great American Adventure* compares and contrasts Mailer's hunting narrative with those of Hemingway and Faulkner. Green maintains that "the expansion of the self in adventure is blocked" in the narratives of all three (unlike nineteenth-century adventure narratives), but for different reasons: in Mailer adventure is used didactically "as a blackboard diagram for imperialism," while in Hemingway it is "an antidote to the poisons of civilized life," and in Faulkner "as a ritual of spiritual renewal."[165] The remaining 1984 study is by Eric Homberger, whose chapter on the American novel of World War II includes an examination of Lieutenant Hearn as "the most fully-realized portrayal of a liberal in the American war novel."[166]

What Mailer will do next is unknown. He has toyed with the idea of writing a book on Russia since his 1984 visit there.[167] He was recently elected president of the American branch of the international writers organiztion, PEN, and his contacts with writers from around the world could lead to a variety of projects. But he also returned to America in 1984, published *Tough Guys* and an essay commemorating the hundredth anniversary of the publication of *Huckleberry Finn*.[168] His unpublished play about Marilyn Monroe, *Strawhead*, was staged in a closed production at the Actor's Studio in New York in 1985, and may appear on the off-Broadway stage. He is now at work on a new book, but it is unlikely that it will be a continuation of the projected trilogy begun with *Evenings*, and he is also considering writing some new screenplays. But predicting what Mailer will do next is a notoriously unsuccessful activity. The unlikely is invariably the thing he undertakes. The two original essays in this collection—Lucid's prolegomenon to his biography and Michael Cowan's essay[169] on Mailer's quest for roots—are excellent places to find clues to Mailer's future work. Both stress his Americanness. I doubt if either Lucid or Cowan would accept as a disavowal of interest in native themes Mailer's recent statement that "you can no longer write an all-encompassing novel about America."[170] Indeed, Mailer's saying so makes me wonder if he might just be raising the bar for himself, preparing for a still more imaginative leap. If this is the case, it will be good to have him home.

Several people helped me to complete this volume. For understanding and general support, I would like to thank my wife, Donna, and my sons, Steve, Joe, and Jim. Without the research and office assistance provided by Bill Furry, Marilyn Immel, my brother, Peter K. Lennon, and Gloria Taylor, I could not have completed this volume. The editorial advice of Bruce Holroyd, Robert F. Lucid, James Nagel, Larry Shiner, and Charles B. Strozier, greatly aided me. Finally, for getting me interested in books in the first place, I would like to thank my mother, Mary Mitchell Lennon, to whom this volume is dedicated.

J. MICHAEL LENNON

Sangamon State University

Notes

1. Richard Poirier, *Norman Mailer* (New York: Viking, 1972).

2. Orville Prescott, "Books of the Times," *New York Times* (20 December 1948), 23.

3. Joan Didion, "I Want to Go Ahead and Do It," *New York Times Book Review* (7 October 1979), 1, 26–27.

4. Norman Mailer, Foreword, *Dear Muffo: 35 Years in the Fast Lane*, by Harold Conrad (New York: Stein and Day, 1982), xxii.

5. See "An Author's Identity: An Interview with Michael Lennon," *Pieces and Pontifications*, by Norman Mailer (Boston: Little, Brown, 1982), 151.

6. Mailer, Interview with Digby Diehl, "Norman Mailer—Ego, Movies and the Moon," *Los Angeles Times* (21 February 1971), 12.

7. Mailer, Interview with Vincent Canby, "When Irish Eyes are Smiling, It's Norman Mailer," *New York Times* (27 October 1968), Sec. 2, 15.

8. Mailer, quoted by Ted Morgan in a review of *The Executioner's Song*, "Fine Lines," *Saturday Review* (10 November 1979), 57–58.

9. Lance Morrow, review of *The Executioner's Song*, "Doom as Theater," *Time* (22 October 1979), 102, 104.

10. Mailer, quoted in "Rugged Times," *New Yorker* (23 October 1948), 25.

11 Anon., "War and No Peace," *Time* (10 May 1948), 106–09.

12. John Lardner, "Pacific Battle, Good and Big," *New Yorker* (15 May 1948), 115–17.

13. Anon., "Men in War," *Newsweek* (10 May 1948), 86–87.

14. Orville Prescott, "Books of the Times," *New York Times* (7 May 1948), 21.

15. Harrison Smith, "Sizing Up the Comers," *Saturday Review* (12 February 1949), 9–11.

16. Maxwell Geismar, "Nightmare on Anopopei," *Saturday Review* (8 May 1948), 10–11.

17. Mailer, *Advertisements for Myself* (New York: Putnam's, 1959), 93. Subsequent quotations from *Advertisements* will be identified parenthetically in the text.

18. Mailer, Interview with Harvey Breit, *The Writer Observed* (New York: World, 1956), 201.

19. Gustave Flaubert, quoted in *Writers on Writing*, ed. Walter Allen (New York: Dutton, 1948), 137.

20. Mailer, Interview with Steven Marcus, *Writers at Work: The Paris Review Interviews* 3d ser., ed. George Plimpton (New York: Viking, 1967), 265.

21. Anon., "Last of the Leftists?" *Time* (28 May 1951), 110.

22. Maxwell Geismar, "Frustrations, Neuroses & History," *Saturday Review* (26 May 1951), 15–16.

23. Anthony West, "East Meets West, Author Meets Allegory," *New Yorker* (9 June 1951), 106–09.

24. Irving Howe, "Some Political Novels," *Nation* (16 June 1951), 568–69; Harvey Swados, "Fiction Parade," *New Republic* (18 June 1951), 20–21.

25. Brendan Gill, "Small Trumpet," *New Yorker* (22 October 1955), 173–75; Malcolm Cowley, "Mr. Mailer Tells a Tale of Love, Art, Corruption," *New York Herald Tribune Book Review* (23 October 1955), 5.

26. Orville Prescott, "Books of the Times," *New York Times* (14 October 1955), 25.

27. Sidney Alexander, "Not Even Good Pornography," *Reporter* (20 October 1955), 46–48; Anon., "Love Among the Love-Buckets," *Time* (17 October 1955), 122, 124.

28. Arthur Mizener, "Fiction Chronicle," *Partisan Review* 23 (Winter 1956):102–03.

29. Richard Chase, "Novelist Going Places," *Commentary* 20 (December 1955):581–83.

30. The ad appeared in the *Village Voice* sometime in November 1955. It is reproduced in *Advertisements*, 249.

31. Mailer, *The Writer Observed*, 199.

32. The material in this and the next two paragraphs is adapted from my article, "Mailer's Radical Bridge," *Journal of Narrative Technique* 7 (Fall 1977):170–88.

33. George Steiner, "Naked but not Dead," *Encounter* 17 (December 1961):67–70.

34. Harry T. Moore, "The Targets Are Square," *New York Times Book Review* (1 November 1959), 4; Irving Howe, "A Quest For Peril," *Partisan Review* 27 (Winter 1960):143–48.

35. Gore Vidal, "The Norman Mailer Syndrome," *Nation* (2 January 1960), 13–16. Reprinted in *Norman Mailer: The Man and His Work*, ed. Robert F. Lucid (Boston: Little, Brown, 1971), and in Vidal's *Homage to Daniel Shays: Collected Essays, 1952–72* (New York: Random House, 1972).

36. Charles Rolo, "Reader's Choice," *Atlantic* 204 (December 1959):166–68; Charles Poore, "Books of the Times," *New York Times* (3 November 1959), 29.

37. John Chamberlain, "About Us Squares," *National Review* (21 November 1959), 494–95.

38. Garry Wills, "The Art of Not Writing Novels," *National Review* (14 January 1964),

31–33; John Kenneth Galbraith, "The Kennedys Didn't Reply," *New York Times Book Review* (17 November 1963), 6.

39. Richard Gilman, "Why Mailer Wants to be President," *New Republic* (8 February 1964), 17–20, 22–24.

40. Midge Decter, "Mailer's Campaign," *Commentary* 37 (February 1964):83–85. Reprinted in Lucid collection.

41. John Wain, "Mailer's America," *New Republic* (1 October 1966), 19–20.

42. A. Alvarez, "Dr Mailer, I Presume," *Observer* (15 October 1967), 27; Malcolm Muggeridge, "Books," *Esquire* 66 (December 1966):104, 106.

43. Oscar Handlin, "The Artist and Society," *Atlantic* 218 (October 1966):144.

44. Eliot Fremont-Smith, "A Nobel for Norman?" *New York Times* (22 August 1966), 31.

45. Mailer, *Of a Fire on the Moon* (Boston: Little, Brown, 1970), 468.

46. Mailer, *Existential Errands* (Boston: Little, Brown, 1972), 110.

47. Robert F. Lucid, Introduction, *The Long Patrol: 25 Years of Writing from the Work of Norman Mailer* (New York: World, 1971), xvi.

48. The serialized version of *Dream* appeared in *Esquire* from January to August 1964. For a comparison of the *Esquire* and book versions, see Hershel Parker, "Norman Mailer's Revision of the *Esquire* Version of *An American Dream* and the Aesthetic Problem of 'Built-In Intentionality,' " *Bulletin of Research in the Humanities* 84 (Winter 1981):405–30.

49. Mailer, *An American Dream* (New York: Dial, 1965), 8.

50. Granville Hicks, "A Literary Hoax?" *Saturday Review* (20 March 1965), 23–24; Philip Rahv, "Crime Without Punishment," *New York Review of Books* (25 March 1965), 1, 3, 4; Stanley Edgar Hyman, "Norman Mailer's Yummy Rump." *New Leader* (15 March 1965), 16–17; Tom Wolfe, "Son of Crime and Punishment, Or: How to go eight fast rounds with the heavyweight champ and lose," *Book Week—Washington Post* (14 March 1965), 1, 10, 12–13; Elizabeth Hardwick, "Bad Boy," *Partisan Review* 32 (Spring 1965):291–94. The reviews of Hardwick and Wolfe are reprinted in the Lucid collection; Hyman's is reprinted in *Norman Mailer: A Collection of Critical Essays*, ed. Leo Braudy (Englewood Cliffs, New Jersey: Prentice-Hall, 1972).

51. Leo Bersani, "The Interpretation of Dreams," *Partisan Review* 32 (Fall 1965):603–08; Richard Poirier, "Morbid-Mindedness," *Commentary* 39 (June 1965):91–94; Conrad Knickerbocker, "A Man Desperate For a New Life," *New York Times Book Review* (14 March 1965), 1, 36, 38–39; Joan Didion, "A Social Eye," *National Review* (20 April 1965), 329–30; Paul Pickrel, "Thing of Darkness," *Harper's* 230 (April 1965):116–17; John W. Aldridge, "The Big Comeback of Norman Mailer," *Life* (19 March 1965), 12. The reviews of Bersani and Poirier are reprinted in the Lucid collection; Bersani's is also reprinted in Braudy's collection, and a longer version of Aldridge's is reprinted in Braudy's and Aldridge's *Time to Murder and Create: The Contemporary Novel in Crisis* (New York: McKay, 1966).

52. Rahv, 1; Fremont-Smith, 47.

53. Didion, 329; Knickerbocker, 38.

54. Anon., "The Public Act," *Time* (19 March 1965), 112; Wolfe, 1.

55. Aldridge, 12.

56. Poirier, *Norman Mailer*, 129–44 passim.

57. Mailer, *Errands*, 221.

58. Eugene Glenn, Review of *Why Are We in Vietnam?*, *Village Voice* (28 September 1967), 6–7, 41; Eliot Fremont-Smith, "Norman Mailer's Cherry Pie," *New York Times* (8 September 1967), 37.

59. Charles T. Samuels, "The Novel, USA: Mailerrhea," *Nation* (23 October 1967),

405–06; Christopher Nichols, "Psychedelic Freakout," *National Review* (31 October 1967), 1216–17.

60. Jack Kroll, "The Scrambler," *Newsweek* (18 September 1967) 103–05; Anon., "Hot Damn," *Time* (8 September 1967), D12–D13.

61. Most of these essays and prefaces are collected in *Errands*.

62. Mailer, "The First Day's Interview," *Paris Review* 26 (Summer-Fall 1961):140.

63. Anon., "The Weekend Revolution," *Time* (10 May 1968), 120, 124.

64. Dwight Macdonald, "Politics," *Esquire* 69 (May 1968):41–42, 44, 194, 196. Malcolm Muggeridge, review of *The Armies of the Night*, *Esquire* 70 (July 1968):20, 22; Alfred Kazin, "The Trouble He's Seen," *New York Times Book Review* (5 May 1968), 1–2, 26. Macdonald's review is reprinted in his *Discriminations: Essays and Afterthoughts, 1938–1974* (New York: Grossman, 1974). His witty account of Mailer's run-in with the Provincetown police, "Massachusetts vs. Mailer," is also included in this collection.

65. Jeffrey Hart, "Anti-Matter as Jet-Set Journalism," *National Review* (30 July 1968), 754–55; Mario Puzo, "Generalissimo Mailer: Hero of His Own Dispatches," *Chicago Tribune Book World* (28 April 1968), 1, 3.

66. Lawrence Raab, review of *The Armies of the Night*, *American Scholar* 37 (Summer 1968):540.

67. Mailer, *St. George and the Godfather* (New York: New American Library, 1972), 3.

68. Mailer, *The Fight* (Boston: Little, Brown, 1975), 31.

69. Mailer, *Some Honorable Men: Political Conventions, 1960–1972* (Boston: Little, Brown, 1976), xi, xii.

70. Peter Shaw, "The Conventions, 1968," *Commentary* 46 (December 1968):93–96.

71. Eliot Fremont-Smith, "Family Report," *New York Times* (28 October 1968), 45.

72. Jack Richardson, "The Aesthetics of Norman Mailer," *New York Review of Books* 8 May 1969), 3–4. Reprinted in Lucid Collection.

73. Benjamin Demott, "Inside Apollo 11 with Aquarius Mailer," *Saturday Review* (16 January 1971), 25–27, 57–58.

74. Christopher Lehman-Haupt, "Mailer's Dream of the Moon—I," *New York Times* (7 January 1971), 33.

75. Kate Millett, *Sexual Politics* (New York: Doubleday, 1970), 314.

76. Anatole Broyard, "Norman Writes a Dithyramb," *New York Times* (27 May 1971), 41.

77. Brigid Brophy, "Meditations on Norman Mailer, by Norman Mailer, against the Day a Norman Mailest Comes Along," *New York Times Book Review* (23 May 1971), 1, 14, 16.

78. Robert W. Haney, "Slapdash, Bang, and a Boom," *Christian Science Monitor* (26 July 1972), 9.

79. Robert Solotaroff, "The Glop of the Wad," *Nation* (15 January 1973), 87–89.

80. Mailer, *Some Honorable Men*, xii.

81. Saul Maloff, "Mailer's Marilyn," *Commonweal* (21 September 1973), 503–05.

82. Christopher Lehmann-Haupt, "Aquarius on Gemini—II," *New York Times* (17 July 1973), 37; John Seelye, "The Naked and the Dead," *New Republic* (1 September 1973), 25–27.

83. Pauline Kael, "A Rip-off with Genius," *New York Times Book Review* (22 July 1973), 1–3.

84. Ingrid Bengis, "Monroe According to Mailer: One Legend Feeds on Another," *Ms.* 2 (October 1973): 44–47.

85. George V. Higgins, "Another View of Foreman-Ali," *Boston Globe* (3 August 1975), A15.

86. See, for example, Peter S. Prescott, "In the Torrid Zone," *Newsweek* (15 November 1976), 109.

87. Richard Gilman, "Norman Mailer Searches the Tropics—'Mr. Miller, I Presume,' " *Village Voice* (4 October 1976), 43–44.

88. Frederick Crews, "Stuttering Giant," *New York Review of Books* (3 March 1977), 7–9.

89. Mailer, quoted by Ted Morgan in "Fine Lines," *Saturday Review* (10 November 1979), 57.

90. Richard Stern, "Where is that Self-mocking Literary Imp?" *Chicago* 29 (January 1980):108.

91. Earl Rovit, "True Life Story," *Nation* (20 October 1979), 376–78.

92. Frank McConnell, review of *The Executioner's Song*, *New Republic* (27 October 1979), 28–30.

93. Joan Didion, "I Want to Go Ahead and Do It," *New York Times Book Review* (7 October 1979), 1, 26–27.

94. Robert F. Lucid, "A Man Sought Death and, Too Late, Found Love," *Philadelphia Inquirer* (21 October 1979), 14M.

95. Didion, "I Want to Go Ahead and Do It," 26.

96. Richard Poirier, "In Pyramid and Palace," *Times Literary Supplement* (10 June 1983), 591–92.

97. Mailer discusses these four figures and his writing of the seventies in several of the interviews collected in *Pontifications*, ed. Michael Lennon, the second half of *Pieces and Pontifications* (Boston: Little, Brown, 1982), his fifth collection of assorted prose, written mainly in the seventies.

98. George Stade, "A Chthonic Novel," *New Republic* (2 May 1983), 32–35; Benjamin Demott, "Norman Mailer's Egyptian Novel," *New York Times Book Review* (10 April 1983), 1, 34–36; Anthony Burgess, "Magical Droppings," *Observer* (5 June 1983), 30; Sam Coale, "Mailer's *Ancient Evenings* Passes Painfully," *Providence Sunday Journal Arts and Travel* (1 May 1983), H18.

99. James Wolcott, "Enter the Mummy," *Harper's* 266 (May 1983):81–83.

100. Leslie Fiedler, "Going for the Long Ball," *Psychology Today* 17 (June 1983):16–17.

101. Mailer, quoted by Bruce Weber in "Mailer's Flight to Ancient Egypt," *Harper's Bazaar,* May 1983:104; and by Eugene Kennedy, "Mailer: 'It's Easier to Talk of Sex Than Death,' " *Bookworld—Chicago Tribune* (10 April 1983), 7.

102. Harold Bloom, "Norman in Egypt," *New York Review of Books* (28 April 1983), 3–4, 6.

103. Richard Poirier, "In Pyramid and Palace," 591–92.

104. See, for example, Denis Donoghue, "Death on the Windy Dunes," *New York Times Book Review* (29 July 1984), 1, 32–33.

105. John W. Aldridge, *After the Lost Generation: A Critical Study of the Writers of Two Wars* (New York: McGraw-Hill, 1951), 133–40.

106. Mailer, *The Presidential Papers* (New York: Putnam's, 1963), 136.

107. Norman Podhoretz, "Norman Mailer: The Embattled Vision," *Partisan Review* 26 (Summer 1959):371–91. Reprinted in *Doings and Undoings: The Fifties and After in American Writing* (New York: Farrar, Straus, 1964), and the Lucid collection.

108. Myrick Land, "Mr. Norman Mailer Challenges All the Talent in the Room," *The Fine Art of Literary Mayhem* (New York: Holt, Rinehart and Winston, 1963), 216–38. Land later revised the book (San Francisco: Lexikos, 1983).

109. James Baldwin, "The Black Boy Looks at the White Boy," *Esquire* 55 (May 1961):102–06. Reprinted in *Nobody Knows My Name* (New York: Dell, 1961), and in the collections of Braudy and Lucid. For an extended, overextended, account of Mailer's relationship with Baldwin, see W. J. Weatherby's *Squaring Off: Mailer vs. Baldwin* (New York: Mason / Charter, 1977).

110. Ihab Hassan, *Radical Innocence: Studies in the Contemporary American Novel* (Princeton: Princeton Univ. Press, 1961), 140–51.

111. George Alfred Schrader, "Norman Mailer and the Despair of Defiance," *Yale Review* 51 (December 1961):267–80. Reprinted in Braudy collection.

112. Diana Trilling, "Norman Mailer," *Encounter* (November 1962), 45–56. Reprinted in her *Claremont Essays* (New York: Harcourt, Brace & World, 1962) and the collections of Braudy and Lucid.

113. Harris Dienstfrey, "The Fiction of Norman Mailer," *On Contemporary Literature,* ed. Richard Kostelanetz (New York: Avon, 1964), 422–36; Edmund C. Volpe, "James Jones—Norman Mailer," *Contemporary American Novelists,* ed. Harry T. Moore (Carbondale: Southern Illinois Univ. Press, 1964), 106–19; Kingsley Widmer, "Several American Perplexes," *The Literary Rebel* (Carbondale: Southern Illinois Univ. Press, 1965), 175–98; Paul B. Newman, "Mailer: The Jew as Existentialist," *North American Review* 2 (July 1965):48–55.

114. Christopher Lasch, *The New Radicalism in America (1889–1963): The Intellectual as a Social Type* (New York: Knopf, 1965), 334–49.

115. The most vehement criticism of Mailer on this score is Richard Gilman's "Norman Mailer: Art as Life, Life as Art," *The Confusion of Realms* (New York: Random House, 1969), 81–153.

116. John W. Aldridge, "Norman Mailer: The Energy of New Success," *Time to Murder and Create: The Contemporary Novel In Crisis* (New York: David McKay, 1966), 149–63. Reprinted in Braudy collection.

117. Norman Podhoretz, *Making It* (New York: Random House, 1967), 352–56. See Podhoretz's *Breaking Ranks: A Political Memoir* (New York: Harper & Row, 1979), 263–67 for further comment on his relationship with Mailer.

118. Howard M. Harper, Jr., *Desperate Faith: A Study of Bellow, Salinger, Mailer, Baldwin and Updike* (Chapel Hill: Univ. of North Carolina Press, 1967), 96–136.

119. James Toback, "Norman Mailer Today," *Commentary* 44 (October 1967):68–76.

120. James Toback, "At Play in the Fields of the Bored," *Esquire* 70 (December 1968):150–55, 22, 24, 26, 28, 30, 32, 34, 36.

121. Richard Foster, "Mailer and the Fitzgerald Tradition," *Novel* 1 (Spring 1968):219–30. Reprinted in Braudy collection.

122. Richard Foster, *Norman Mailer,* University of Minnesota Pamphlets on American Writers, no. 73 (Minneapolis: Univ. of Minnesota Press, 1968). Reprinted in Lucid collection.

123. David Hesla, "The Two Roles of Norman Mailer," *Adversity and Grace: Studies in Recent American Literature,* ed. Nathan A. Scott, Jr. (Chicago: Univ. of Chicago Press, 1968), 211–38.

124. Jack Newfield, "On the Steps of a Zeitgeist," *Bread and Roses Too: Reporting About America* (New York: Dutton, 1971), 385–90.

125. Robert Langbaum, "Mailer's New Style," *Novel* 2 (Fall 1968):69–78. Reprinted in his *The Modern Spirit: Essays on the Continuity of Nineteenth- and Twentieth-Century Literature* (New York: Oxford Univ. Press, 1970).

126. Joe Flaherty, *Managing Mailer* (New York: Coward-McCann, 1969); Peter Manso, ed., *Running Against the Machine: The Mailer-Breslin Campaign* (New York: Doubleday, 1969).

127. Donald L. Kaufmann, *Norman Mailer: The Countdown (The First Twenty Years)* Carbondale: Southern Illinois Univ. Press, 1969).

128. Barry H. Leeds, *The Structured Vision of Norman Mailer* (New York: New York Univ. Press, 1969).

129. William Hoffa, "Norman Mailer: Advertisements for Myself, or a Portrait of the Artist as a Disgruntled Counter-Puncher," *The Fifties: Fiction, Poetry, Drama*, ed. Warren G. French (Leland, Florida: Everett/Edwards, 1970), 73–82.

130. Ihab Hassan, "Focus on Norman Mailer's *Why Are We In Vietnam?*," *American Dreams, American Nightmares*, ed. David Madden (Carbondale: Southern Illinois Univ. Press, 1970), 197–203.

131. Helen A. Weinberg, "The Heroes of Norman Mailer's Novels," *The New Novel in America: The Kafkan Mode in Contemporary Fiction* (Ithaca: Cornell Univ. Press, 1970), 108–40.

132. Jerry H. Bryant, *The Open Decision: the Contemporary American Novel And Its Intellectual Background* (New York: Free Press, 1970), 369–94.

133. Robert F. Lucid, ed., *Norman Mailer: The Man and His Work* (Boston: Little, Brown, 1971); Leo Braudy, ed. *Norman Mailer: A Collection of Critical Essays* (Englewood Cliffs, New Jersey: Prentice-Hall, 1972); "Studies of Norman Mailer," *Modern Fiction Studies* 17 (Autumn 1971):347–463.

134. Diana Trilling, "The Prisoner of Sex," *We Must March My Darlings: A Critical Decade* (New York: Harcourt, Brace Jovanovich, 1977), 199–210; Germaine Greer, "My Mailer Problem," *Esquire* 76 (September 1971):90–93, 214, 216.

135. Richard Schickel, "Stars and Celebrities," *Commentary* 52 (August 1971), 61–65; Allen Guttmann, "The Apocalyptic Vision of Norman Mailer," *The Jewish Writer in America: Assimilation and the Crisis of Identity* (New York: Oxford Univ. Press, 1971), 153–72; Theodore L. Gross, "Norman Mailer: The Quest for Heroism," *The Heroic Ideal in American Literature* (New York: Free Press, 1971), 272–95; Fredric Jameson, "The Great American Hunter, or Ideological Content in the Novel," *College English* 34 (November 1972):180–99; Warner Berthoff, "Witness and Testament: Two Contemporary Classics," *Aspects of Narrative: Selected Papers from the English Institute*, ed. J. Hillis Miller (New York: Columbia Univ. Press, 1971), 173–98. Reprinted in Berthoff's *Fictions and Events* (New York: Dutton, 1971).

136. Mailer, *The Long Patrol: 25 Years of Writing from the Work of Norman Mailer*, ed. Robert F. Lucid (New York: World, 1971); John W. Aldridge, "The Perfect Absurd Figure of a Mighty, Absurd Crusade," *Saturday Review* (13 November 1971), 45–46, 48–49, 72. Aldridge's review is reprinted in his study, *The American Novel and the Way We Live Now* (New York: Oxford Univ. Press, 1983).

137. Martin Green, "Norman Mailer and the City of New York: Faustian Radicalism," *Cities of Light and Sons of the Morning; A Cultural Psychology for an Age of Revolution* (Boston: Little, Brown, 1972), 58–89.

138. Tony Tanner, "On the Parapet," *City of Words: American Fiction, 1950–1970* (New York: Harper & Row, 1971), 344–71. Reprinted in *Will the Real Norman Mailer Please Stand Up*, ed. Laura Adams (Port Washington, New York: Kennikat, 1974).

139. Richard Poirier, *Norman Mailer* (New York: Viking, 1972).

140. Nathan A. Scott, Jr., "Norman Mailer—Our Whitman," *Three American Moralists: Mailer, Bellow, Trilling* (Notre Dame, Indiana: Univ. of Notre Dame Press, 1973), 15–97.

141. Alfred Kazin, *Bright Book of Life: American Novelists and Storytellers from Hemingway to Mailer* (Boston: Little, Brown, 1973), 71–77, 149–57, 236–41, 255–57 and passim.

142. John Henry Raleigh, "History and Its Burdens: The Example of Norman Mailer," *Uses of Literature*, ed. Monroe Engel (Cambridge: Harvard Univ. Press, 1973), 163–86.

143. Robert F. Lucid, "Three Public Performances: Fitzgerald, Hemingway, Mailer," *American Scholar* 43 (Summer 1974):447–66; "Norman Mailer: The Artist as Fantasy Figure," *Massachusetts Review* 15 (Autumn 1974):581–95.

144. Gordon O. Taylor, "Of Adams and Aquarius," *American Literature* 46 (March 1974):68–82; Sandy Vogelgesang, *The Long Dark Night of the Soul: The American Intellectual Left and the Vietnam War* (New York: Harper & Row, 1974), 9–10, 131–33, 149–51, 178–79.

145. Laura Adams, *Norman Mailer: A Comprehensive Bibliography* (Metuchen, New Jersey: Scarecrow Press, 1974); *Will the Real Norman Mailer Please Stand Up*, ed. Laura Adams (Port Washington, New York: Kennikat, 1974).

146. Robert Solotaroff, *Down Mailer's Way* (Urbana: Univ. of Illinois Press, 1974).

147. Jean Radford, *Norman Mailer: A Critical Study* (New York, Harper & Row, 1975); Stanley T. Gutman, *Mankind in Barbary: The Individual and Society in the Novels of Norman Mailer* (Hanover, New Hampshire: Univ. Press of New England, 1975). Jonathan Middlebrook also makes reference to Mailer's affinities with the American romantics in his impressionistic study, *Mailer and the Times of his Time* (San Francisco: Bay Books, 1976).

148. Laura Adams, *Existential Battles: The Growth of Norman Mailer* (Athens: Ohio Univ. Press, 1976).

149. Howard Silverstein, "Norman Mailer: The Family Romance and the Oedipal Family," *American Imago* 34 (Fall 1977):277–86; George Plimpton, *Shadow Box* (New York: Putnam's, 1977), 258–62 and passim; George Stade, "Mailer and Miller," *Partisan Review* 44 (Fall 1977):616–24; Frank D. McConnell, "Norman Mailer and the Cutting Edge of Style," *Four Postwar American Novelists: Bellow, Mailer, Barth and Pynchon* (Chicago: Univ. of Chicago Press, 1977), 58–107; John Hollowell, "Mailer's Vision: History As A Novel, The Novel As History," *Fact & Fiction: The New Journalism and the Nonfiction Novel* (Chapel Hill: Univ. of North Carolina Press, 1977), 87–125; Morris Dickstein, *Gates of Eden: American Culture in the Sixties* (New York: Basic Books, 1977), 51–54, 142–52 and passim; J. Michael Lennon, "Mailer's Sarcophagus: The Artist, the Media and the 'Wad,' " *Modern Fiction Studies* 23 (Summer 1977):179–87.

150. Jennifer Bailey, *Norman Mailer: Quick-Change Artist* (New York: Harper & Row, 1979); Mitchell S. Ross, "Norman Mailer," *The Literary Politicians* (Garden City, New York: Doubleday, 1978), 166–211.

151. Robert Ehrlich, *Norman Mailer: The Radical as Hipster* (Metuchen, New Jersey: Scarecrow Press, 1978).

152. Robert Merrill, *Norman Mailer* (Boston: Twayne, 1978).

153. Philip H. Bufithis, *Norman Mailer* (New York: Frederick Ungar, 1978).

154. Judith Fetterley, "*An American Dream:* 'Hula, Hula,' Said the Witches," *The Resisting Reader: A Feminist Approach to American Fiction* (Bloomington: Indiana Univ. Press, 1978), 154–89.

155. Andrew Gordon, *An American Dreamer: A Psychoanalytic Study of the Fiction of Norman Mailer* (Cranbury, New Jersey: Associated Univ. Presses, 1980); Robert J. Begiebing, *Acts of Regeneration: Allegory and Archetype in the Works of Norman Mailer* (Columbia: Univ. of Missouri Press, 1980); J. Michael Lennon and Charles B. Strozier, "Empathy and Detachment in the Narratives of Erikson and Mailer," *The Psychohistory Review* 10 (Fall 1981):18–32.

156. John Hellman, "Journalism as Nonfiction: Norman Mailer's Strategy for Mimesis and Interpretation in a Postmodern World," *Fables of Fact: The New Journalism as New Fiction* (Urbana: Univ. of Illinois Press, 1981), 35–65. For another perspective on Mailer's non-

fiction, see Ronald Weber's *The Literature of Fact* (Athens: Ohio Univ. Press, 1980), 81–87, 166–71 and passim.

157. Bernard Horn, "Ahab and Ishmael At War: The presence of *Moby-Dick* in *The Naked and the Dead*," *American Quarterly* 34 (Fall 1982):379–95; Donald Pizer, "Norman Mailer: *The Naked and the Dead*," in *Twentieth-Century American Literary Naturalism: An Interpretation* (Carbondale: Southern Illinois Univ. Press, 1982), 90–114.

158. John R. Cooley, *Savages and Naturals: Black Portraits by White Writers in Modern American Literature* (Newark: Univ. of Delaware Press, 1982), 137–60.

159. Alvin B. Kernan, "The Taking of the Moon: The Struggle of the Poetic and Scientific Myths in Norman Mailer's *Of A Fire On the Moon*," in *The Imaginary Library: An Essay on Literature and Society* (Princeton: Princeton Univ. Press, 1982), 130–61.

160. Hilary Mills, *Mailer: A Biography* (New York: Empire Books, 1982). Perhaps the best review of Mills's book is by Tom Carson, "The Time of His Prime Time," *Village Voice Literary Supplement*, no. 14 (February 1983):1, 10–12. It includes a good overview of Mailer's career.

161. Hilary Mills, "Creators on Creating: Norman Mailer," *Saturday Review* 8 (January 1981):46–49, 52–53. Reprinted in an abridged form in *Pieces and Pontifications*.

162. *Mailer: A Biography*, 277.

163. Anthony Burgess, *Ninety-nine Novels: The Best in English Since 1939* (New York: Simon & Schuster, 1984), 42–43, 132–33.

164. Sam B. Girgus, "Song of Him-Self: Norman Mailer," *The New Covenant: Jewish Writers and the American Idea* (Chapel Hill: Univ. of North Carolina Press, 1984), 135–59.

165. Martin Green, "Mailer's *Why Are We In Vietnam?*," *The Great American Adventure* (Boston: Beacon Press, 1984), 199–215.

166. Eric Homberger, "United States," *The Second World War in Fiction*, ed. Holger Klein (London: MacMillan, 1984), 173–205.

167. Mailer's essay on his Russian trip, "A Country, Not a Scenario," appeared in *Parade* (19 August 1984), 4–9.

168. Mailer, "Huckleberry Finn, Alive at 100," *New York Times Book Review* (9 December 1984), 1, 36–37.

169. Cowan's essay is a revised and greatly expanded version of "The Americanness of Norman Mailer" which was first published in the Braudy collection, and was reprinted in the Adams collection.

170. Mailer, "Modern Evenings: An Interview with Norman Mailer," by Michael Schumacher, *Writers' Digest* (October 1983), 34.

Chronology of Books
by Norman Mailer

1948	*The Naked and the Dead.*
1951	*Barbary Shore.*
1955	*The Deer Park.*
1957	*The White Negro.*
1959	*Advertisements for Myself.*
1962	*Deaths for the Ladies (And Other Disasters).*
1963	*The Presidential Papers.*
1965	*An American Dream.*
1966	*Cannibals and Christians.*
1967	*The Bullfight: A Photographic Narrative with Text by Norman Mailer.*
1967	*The Deer Park—A Play.*
1967	*The Short Fiction of Norman Mailer.*
1967	*Why Are We in Vietnam?*
1968	*The Idol and the Octopus: Political Writings on the Kennedy and Johnson Administrations.*
1968	*The Armies of the Night: History as a Novel, The Novel as History.*
1968	*Miami and the Siege of Chicago: An Informal History of the Republican and Democratic Conventions of 1968.*
1970	*Of a Fire on the Moon.*
1971	*King of the Hill.*
1971	*Maidstone: A Mystery.*
1971	*The Prisoner of Sex.*
1971	*The Long Patrol: Twenty-Five Years of Writing from the Work of Norman Mailer* (ed. Robert F. Lucid).
1972	*Existential Errands.*

1972   *St. George and the Godfather.*

1973   *Marilyn: A Biography.*

1974   *The Faith of Graffiti.*

1975   *The Fight.*

1976   *Genius and Lust: A Journey Through the Major Writings of Henry Miller.*

1976   *Some Honorable Men: Political Conventions, 1960–1972.*

1978   *A Transit to Narcissus.*

1979   *The Executioner's Song: A True Life Novel.*

1980   *Of a Small and Modest Malignancy, Wicked and Bristling with Dots.*

1980   *Of Women and Their Elegance.*

1982   *Pieces and Pontifications* (*Pontifications*, ed. Michael Lennon).

1983   *Ancient Evenings.*

1984   *Tough Guys Don't Dance.*

REVIEWS

Books of the Times *[The Naked and the Dead]*

Orville Prescott*

Dear Mr. Prescott:

I have just observed your name among the list of persons recommending *The Naked and The Dead* by Norman Mailer. I have read most of the book.

My purpose in writing this letter is a latent curiosity to learn, if possible, why a man of your standing and connections would recommend a book containing such filth. Of what earthly benefit could it be to society, or to an individual reading it? How could one read this book without a feeling of revulsion?

For instance, if you had a daughter in her teens, would you like to have her read it? Would you feel proud if she said: "Daddy, did you recommend this book?" Could you defend your actions?

Sincerely,
Grant Mason

Dear Mr. Mason:

Your letter seems to me to be based upon several misunderstandings of the function of literature. But, since you speak for a point of view still widely held in spite of many victories won against it during the last hundred years, I will try to answer you.

First, then, I recommend *The Naked and the Dead* because I believe it to be a remarkable work, dramatic, powerful, honest and moving: a successful transformation of war experience into creative fiction. I know of no other novel about the recent war of comparable importance.

It is true that it would have been much improved by drastic editing, by condensation and greater selectivity. Mr. Mailer lacks taste, judgment

*Reprinted from the *New York Times*, 20 December 1948, 23. Copyright 1948 by the New York Times Company. Reprinted by permission.

and maturity. But he is young and he is greatly gifted. It is true that his characters are not a fair cross section of American life. They are frighteningly primitive and generally deplorable. But it is the artist's privilege to choose his subject matter, the novelist's to write about what he pleases. It is lamentably true that in his effort to report faithfully the obscenity of soldier speech that Mr. Mailer did so to unfortunate excess.

But all this can not change the fact that Mr. Mailer wrote an exceptional book which deserves to be recommended to all serious readers of serious fiction, to everyone interested in knowing about America's participation in the Pacific war and to all who watch for the emergence of promising literary talent.

You ask how *The Naked and the Dead* could benefit society or the individual? There are two logical answers. The first is that a social or individual benefit is a hard thing to judge and depends on where you are standing in relation to what fence. Many people feel that greater knowledge about the true nature of our less privileged, less cultivated fellow citizens is a step toward substantial benefit. Doubtless Mr. Mailer is one of them.

The second answer is that there can be no such criterion applied to fiction. Did "Mr. Pickwick" benefit anyone except by amusing him? Did *The Red Badge of Courage* benefit anyone save by increasing his vicarious experience and so his knowledge of life? Fiction written to uplift is rarely good fiction. The primary purpose of fiction is to tell a story, to create people and to interpret life according to the author's vision of it.

How could one read *The Naked and the Dead* without a feeling of revulsion? I don't know. I was revolted, too. But much human behavior, as our tragic century so plainly shows, is revolting. To be revolted may be a healthy thing.

Your question about a teen-age daughter seems to me to be based upon a particularly erroneous premise. A girl of seventeen (shall we say?) presumably knows the facts of human biology and that many men behave badly and use vile speech. I think that she would react to *The Naked and the Dead* in one of two ways. Either she would dislike it intensely and read only a little; or she would become absorbed in its terrible picture of war and read it all. In either case I don't think that the obscenities, after their first shock, would matter much. They are not attractive. They could never make anyone wish to use a similar vocabulary.

Since Flaubert wrote *Madame Bovary*, and probably for long before that, efforts have been made to suppress books because they describe behavior which everyone knows to be commonplace. Would-be censors forget that no one can be demoralized by knowledge or by mere words. You do not have to read any book. Unless you are tied down while someone reads out loud, you read from choice.

Our daughters have to live in this world. As much as their share of free will allows they have to decide what kind of women they are going to be. They might well begin by deciding not to be the kind of women Mr. Mailer's soldiers talked about with such enthusiasm.

It would be artistic death to reduce all fiction to the insipid level of *Little Women* just because there are innocent young people in the world. There are adults too. Innocence based upon ignorance is a poor thing compared with decency based upon deliberate decisions in favor of honorable behavior.

Let those who are interested, as you yourself were, read *The Naked and the Dead*. Those who are not can ignore it, or stop reading it on page two.

Sincerely yours,
Orville Prescott

P.S. I have substituted another name for yours in case you do not wish your own to appear in print.

Some Political Novels *[Barbary Shore]*   Irving Howe*

At the drop of memory, literary people will tell you that the critics of the thirties sinned in judging novels by political rather than aesthetic standards. Some of these very people are now attacking Norman Mailer's new novel on grounds that are almost entirely political, and in a few reviews attacking with invective and bad faith; only Maxwell Geismar in *The Saturday Review* has discussed the book with some considerateness. *Barbary Shore*, as it happens, is a bad novel, but not because Mailer has chosen to defend an unpopular political point of view.

Apparently Mailer has taken to heart the dubious notion that naturalism is "exhausted" and Kafkaesque symbolism the only recourse for a serious novelist. *Barbary Shore* is crammed with symbols and can be read as a political allegory, but it does not do the first things a novel should: create dramatic tension and arouse interest in its characters. Since one cannot become involved with the weird collection of disembodied voices Mailer has brought together in a Brooklyn rooming-house, one does not care what they "stand for." The meaning of symbols in a work of art matters only when they enchant, disturb, or otherwise arouse us in their own right.

Another trouble is that Mailer writes badly. His lumpy and graceless prose is strewn with quasi-intellectual chatter and stiff with echoes of radical jargon, "progressive" journalism, and WPA living-newspaper skits.

*Excerpted from "Some Political Novels," *Nation*, 16 June 1951, 568–69. Reprinted by permission of the journal.

Once a writer has been exposed to such influences it is hard for him to develop a style, but there is no evidence in *Barbary Shore* that Mailer is even aware of the problem.

Because its action is merely a lifeless posturing and its prose is savorless, the political message of *Barbary Shore* does not seem to me very impressive. And for another reason: if the critic has no business judging a work of art in terms of political opinion, he has every right to judge the *quality* of its thought. Though I roughly agree with Mailer's position of intransigent socialism, I find myself embarrassed by his crude formulations and the tone of pious, apocalyptic certainty with which he delivers them. It is one thing to say that capitalism and Stalinism are both reactionary societies and that a political identification with the first may lead to a political victory of the second; but it is sheer cant to suggest that the absolute dictatorship of Russia and the limited but real democracy of the United States are, or are soon likely to be, "two virtually identical forms of exploitation."

I cavil at Mailer's tone not because doubt is necessarily good "in itself" or because the sort of "open mind" some liberals affect is particularly admirable. It is simply that if one is to try to remain a radical these days and not surrender to cynicism or weariness or atomic hysteria, one *must* be torn by doubts, one must reexamine every scrap of doctrine and every step of action to see where and why things went wrong, one must engage in the "soul searching" that is scorned equally by the kind of dogmatic Marxist who is content to have predicted catastrophes he did not avert and by the kind of complacent liberal who now boasts, after years of guilt over his timidity, that he was never "taken in." (The kind of liberal, I mean, who has discovered that the end does not justify the means but is reconciled to the probability of an atom war.)

The trouble is that Mailer has come to his radicalism a little late; he does not really know in his flesh and bones what has happened to the socialist hope in the era of Hitler and Stalin, and that is why he can refer so cavalierly to democracy and carry on like a stale pamphleteer. He is sincere and he is serious; I admire his courage in writing a book he must have known would bring him grief and attack. But I can only say that his relation to his material, like his presentation of it, is not authentic. Otherwise he would not seem so sure.

Small Trumpet [*The Deer Park*]   Brendan Gill*

The Hero of Norman Mailer's new novel, *The Deer Park* (Putnam), is a young man who decides to buckle down and become a novelist. Moreover, the book he is at such pains to write is the very book we hold in our

*Reprinted from the *New Yorker*, 22 October 1955, 173–75. © 1955, 1983, The New Yorker Magazine, Inc. Reprinted by permission.

hands. It is both his life and the work of art for which everything in his life has been a preparation. He is thus a cousin-german of Proust's great "I," of Joyce's Dedalus, and of all those other fictional heroes who have struggled to forgive the past by imposing meanings on it. It must be said, however, that next to Marcel and Stephen, Mr. Mailer's young man is a bumpkin. Tall, blond, and good-looking, he is perfectly finished off outside; inside, the firmament of his mind is still cooling. The young man has a preposterous name—Sergius O'Shaughnessy—and a scarcely less presposterous history, which he hurls at us in anguished gobbets. The sum of these gobbets is a big, vigorous, rowdy, ill-shaped, and repellent book, so strong and so weak, so adroit and so fumbling, that only a writer of the greatest and most reckless talent could have flung it between covers.

The story of *The Deer Park* is told in the first person, in a style curiously at war with itself. Sometimes Mailer-O'Shaugnessy is sloppy fancy: "He had had women who gave him their first honest pleasure [to whom he had given their first honest pleasure] and he had taken all the bows for his vanity, but he had never met so royal a flow of taste. It was remarkable how they knew each other's nicety between love-making and extravagance." More often, he is merely sloppy: "It may sound weird, but I was so excited with enthusiasm that I had to share it." Weird indeed, though not as weird as an ocasional mincing neatness: "I tried to write my novel about bullfighting, but it was not very good. It was inevitably imitative of that excellently exiguous mathematician, Mr. Ernest Hemingway, and I was learning that it is not creatively satisfying to repeat the work of a good writer." At first we assume that these contrary dictions have some purpose; surely they are intended to reveal the authentic mind and voice of the immature and perplexed narrator. In the end, our teeth on edge and our ears aching, we are roused to the perhaps ungenerous reflection that it is the author who is perplexed and that this one-man babel springs not from too much art but from too little.

The opening paragraphs of the novel offer a fair sample of the Mailer-O'Shaugnesy method:

> In the cactus wild of Southern California, a distance of two hundred miles from the capital of cinema, as I choose to call it, is the town of Desert D'Or. There I went from the Air Force to look for a good time. Some time ago.
>
> Almost everybody I knew in Desert D'Or had had an unusual career, and it was the same for me. I grew up in a home for orphans. Still intact at the age of twenty-three, wearing my flying wings and a First Lieutenant's uniform, I arrived at the resort with fourteen thousand dollars, a sum I picked up via a poker game in a Tokyo hotel room while waiting with other fliers for our plane home. The curiosity is that I was never a gambler. I did not even like the game, but I had nothing to lose that night, and maybe for such a reason I accepted the luck of the cards. Let me leave it at that. I came out of the Air Force with no place to go, no family to visit, and I wandered down to Desert D'Or.

This is an admirable method for sketching backgrounds quickly and for stating facts. When it must convey feelings, or when it slows down to hover over a thought and help tease it into life, the method is no longer workable. Mr. Mailer appears to have been aware of this hazard, and he drives us up and down *The Deer Park* at breakneck speed. It is a trip through unfamiliar country, for a time funny and then unnerving. We are appalled by nearly everything we see (though never so appalled that we actually shut our eyes), and when the trip is over, we catch our breath and measure not only the distance we have travelled but the hardships we have undergone. We have been battered and bruised into knowledge, and the bruises hurt.

If the capital of cinema must be Hollywood, then Desert D'Or must be Palm Springs. Mr. Mailer is a passionate moralist, and his rendering of the resort is a hideous and compelling one, in full color. The set that welcomes young O'Shaugnessy to Desert D'Or consists almost entirely of shrewd, gross, hard-drinking and sexually exacerbated swine. When he wishes to, Mr. Mailer can tick them off in a single sentence—" 'Treat me like a human being,' Munshin roared, and added in a tiny voice, 'I'm bleeding.' " Like most moralists, however, Mr. Mailer is relentless; having thrust his swine out into the scorching desert sun, he makes them caper for us till they drop. The only man in *The Deer Park* worthy of even limited admiration concludes, passing judgement on himself, "In the end that's the only kind of self-respect you have. To be able to say to yourself that you're disgusting." These producers, directors, actors, actresses, agents, pimps and call girls are the *Who's Who* of Desert D'Or— a *Who's Who* that is largely a matter of who sleeps with whom, for the power that is fought for and won in the studios can be made real only in bed. How is the victor to recognize himself without his spoils? These fat, loud, bald men and pretty, frantic girls are all haunted by the need for sexual conquest and the fear of sexual defeat, not because sex is important to them but because success is. Male and / or female, off they go in pairs, trios, and quartets, and for what? Why, like so many Horatio Alger heroes, in order to make good.

Young O'Shaugnesy tells us that he went to Desert D'Or in search of pleasure, but we know better; as all young men in novels do, he went in search of his soul. In the course of finding it, he also finds a girl with whom he is able to make love (for O'Shaugnessy has been having his troubles in that department); a brilliant, bitter man, who consents to serve him in the office of father and mentor and then mercifully consents to be outgrown; and a vocation. As the novel draws to a close, the young man imagines his old demi-father spurring him on—"So, do try, Sergius. . . . Try for that other world, the real world, where orphans burn orphans and nothing is more difficult to discover than a simple fact. And with the pride of an artist, you must blow against the walls of every power that exists the small trumpet of your defiance." But from this gauche echo of Dedalus the eager O'Shaughnessy turns to undertake a conversation with God ("If there is a God, and sometimes I believe there is one"). Though we readers have been unaware of it, he has been saving up a pippin of a question to put to the Diety. "Would you agree," he asks Him, "that sex is where philosophy begins?" This must be one of the crudest questions that God has had to deal with in eons, but He is equal to it. Who knows better than He, after all, that O'Shaugnessy has been staying at Desert D'Or and that he is trying to become a novelist? Marking His place in the copy of "Popular Science Monthly" that He has just been leafing through, God says, "Rather think of Sex as Time, and Time as the connection of new circuits." The young man is pleased with the reply.

Naked but Not Dead
[Advertisements for Myself]   George Steiner*

At Matthausen they tied together the legs of women in childbirth. In the Warsaw ghetto they gave each family one less residence permit than it had children, compelling each mother to select one of her own children for immediate shipment to the ovens. We all now live under the imminent possibility of a mass death so complete that it will go unrecorded, that there will be none left to mourn or remember.

Either literature is about these things, or it is about nothing. That does not mean it must deal explicitly with the bestiality and menace which surround us (the finest novel to come of the war, Cozzens' *Guard of Honour*, does not even touch on actual combat). It means that literature, to be taken seriously, must recognise in man more terror and bruising than there has ever been, that it must see him in the light of what he has of late inflicted and endured. If literature is to be more than trivial entertainment, the artist must recognise the hideous enlargement in the range of possible experience. Floor and ceiling have collapsed in the house of the classic imagination. The cellar, as Dostoevsky foretold, gapes large. We torture in it and we take shelter.

Very few writers have had the nerve or insight to look at the new manner of man. They have acted as if all the ravenings and unknowns shadowing our time were exterior, as if the wounds and recoveries were merely of the flesh. To read most current fiction is to be given the illusion that nothing very drastic has happened, that the soul has passed no time in Dachau or under the sheen of the bomb. Admittedly, the artist courts a grave risk in being honest; he may fall silent. Like Moses, in the final, dread cry of Schoenberg's *Moses Und Aron*, he may find that the word is no longer adequate. But if humane letters are to remain either humane or literate, the risk must be taken.

*Reprinted from *Encounter*, December 1961, 67–70. Reprinted by permission of the journal.

If we except William Golding, American fiction has shown more honesty in this regard than the current English novel. Salinger is a minor artist, often facile or mannered in his craft; but there is not a sentence in the inward rhetoric of his haunted personages that does not show the new, inhuman stress of the times. *Lolita* is, among many other things, a parable on the collapse of the classic conditions of feeling; Humbert Humbert is a displaced person, soul and body reft from their traditional moorings.

Norman Mailer is among the honest men. He strives to know, at the peril of moral chaos, what it is that has been loosed upon the world and whether art can cope with it:

> Probably, we will never be able to determine the psychic havoc of the concentration camps and the atom bomb upon the unconscious mind of almost everyone alive in these years. For the first time in civilised history, perhaps for the first time in all of history, we have been forced to live with the suppressed knowledge that the smallest facets of our personality or the most minor projection of our ideas, or indeed the absence of ideas and the absence of personality, could mean equally well that we might still be doomed to die as a cipher in some vast statistical operation in which our teeth would be counted, and our hair would be saved, but our death itself would be unknown, unhonoured, and unremarked . . . a death by *deus ex machina* in a gas chamber or a radio-active city. . . .
> The Second World War presented a mirror to the human condition which blinded anyone who looked into it.

Mailer approaches his obsessive theme [in *Advertisements For Myself*] with a complicated set of masks, with a doctrine and language drawn from four principal values. He is by origin a Jew, and by vocation a Socialist, Hipster, and Writer.

To the Jewish tenor of mind fiction does not come easily. The Judaic tradition is narrowed and ennobled by the predominance of argument and verity. For obvious historical reasons, Jews came late to *belles lettres;* but their approach to the novel—to its art of truthful lying—has retained a particular wariness—Kafka treated his art as if it was a vaguely embarrassing malady. Hermann Broch tended to think of fiction as something lacking ultimate seriousness; he moved away from his own novels towards epistemology and a psychology of politics. In fact, he wrestled continuously with the belief that in the face of man's present condition silence might be a better response than art.

Mailer's inheritance runs far below the surface. It scarcely appears in his conscious interests. Yet it helps account for two of his dominant traits. From the outset, Mailer has wanted to write "the big one," the novel or tract which would change men's social and moral existence. He is out "to trap the Prince of Truth" in order to direct the times towards a re-birth of the psyche. The other trait that speaks of Mailer's background is his frenzy for justice. It beats strong in *The Naked and the Dead;* it is the main theme in *Barbary Shore,* the sloppiest but most original of Mailer's novels. It has led him recently to a theodicy close to Kafka's and to some of the bleaker parables of the Talmud:

> God is in danger of dying. In my very limited knowledge of theology, this never really has been expressed before. . . . God is no longer all-powerful. The moral consequences of this are not only staggering, but they're thrilling, because moral experience is intensified rather than diminished. . . . It's the only thing that explains to me the problem of evil. You see, the answer may well be—how to put it?—that God Himself is engaged in a destiny so extraordinary, so demanding, that He too can suffer from a moral corruption, that He can make demands upon us which are unfair, that He can abuse our beings in order to achieve His means, even as we abuse the very cells of our own body.

In short: *Dieu a besoin des hommes*.

Mailer's Socialism is a queer brew. It sprang originally from the kind of personal, lyric infatuation with Marx which affected a whole generation of the American intelligentsia. The great bearded one (in a lineage of charismatic beards stretching from Moses to Hemingway) seemed to have foretold all that was nasty, brutish, and chaotic in American life. An angry generation drank avidly of his parched dogmatism. In Mailer something of the thirst and of the gratitude remains: "I happen to have got more from Marx than from anyone else I've ever read. I wouldn't want to jettison Grandfather." But, as he says himself, Mailer has drifted away from orthodoxy.

He is now a kind of pastoral Socialist. I mean by that that his socialism is founded primarily on a lyric image of private, domestic fulfillment, on a golden vision of a sensuous, liberated order of human relations in which economic, sexual and political energies would gather to unison rather than tension. There is a touch of Thoreau in Mailer's Utopia, and more than a dash of D. H. Lawrence: "Deeper than the love of property is the fear of the past, the fear of the vitality of the lower classes, the fear that if all men were to walk the earth equal, the upper classes would not long survive." There is that characteristically American notion that the machinations of evil, psychically infirm men—men of power, men of money—have marred the promised land: "I believe it was destined, by history if you will, to be the greatest country that ever existed. I don't think it's come near it." The bastards have done us in. Often, in his garrulous scorn, Mailer comes very near often to echoing Pound and Mencken:

> if I am to go on saying what my anger tells me is true to say, I must get better at overriding the indifference which comes from the snobs, arbiters, managers, and conforming maniacs who manipulate most of the world of letters. . . . There may have been too many fights for me, too much sex, liquor, marijuana, benzedrine and seconal, much too much ridiculous and brain-blasting rage at the miniscule frustrations of a most loathsome literary world, necrophilic to the core—they murder their writers, and then decorate their graves.

At the heart of Mailer's politics there is neither theory nor pro-gramme, but stark revulsion: "Just as people there's something godawful about the upper classes in America—they really are horrible people."

Opposed to them in a masked but decisive struggle for the salvation of the American soul is the Hipster. Mailer did not invent the type; it has roots in jazz and pacifism, in the *demi-monde* of the hobo and the drug ad-dict. But he gave it definition in his famous essay "The White Negro." The Hipster is the man who knows that the quick of life is threatened continully with destruction by war or totalitarian rule or by the slow death of confor-mity. To survive, to "live with death," he must exist without roots and set out "on the uncharted journey into the rebellious imperatives of the self." One is Hip or one is Square; there is no middle road. One is a pioneer on the Wild West trail of drugs, sexual liberty, and racial intermingling, or a mere *petit bourgeois* "trapped in the totalitarian tissues of American so-ciety."

The Negro is the matchmaker of Hip; marijuana the wedding ring. Banded together in a conspiracy of dissent, scorning the facile values of es-tablished morals and culture, Hipsters live "in the enormous present." They seek to realise a communion of soul and sex outside the barren ground of modern life and find in orgasm a counterpart to the Holy Grail (Mailer's own image). Being "philosophical psychopaths," men dedicated to the fulfilment of the self in an ecstasy of action, they lash out at the habits and safeguards of traditional society. They are drifters, addicts, pimps, thieves, sometimes murderers; they murder out of the mystic necessity to purge their own violence, for if he cannot empty his hatred, the Hipster cannot love. And love, "as the search for an orgasm more apocalyptic than the one which preceded it," is his sacred quest.

If we cut away the verbiage and adolescent posturing in all this, there remains a doctrine of vehement candour and a bizarre yet compelling at-tempt to reassert the sanctity of private life against the pressures of a mass technocracy. In a queer but real sense, the Hipster is the monk of the pres-ent dark ages. His style of life alternates between austere repose and vio-lent psychological stress. He has rejected the ambitions and comforts of the mundane world. Clad in his dark sweater, jeans and sandals, the Hipster is a living indictment of the American dream—of the belief in material suc-cess and "well-adjustments." Moreover, he cannot easily be bought off. In England the anger of the young is an accepted prelude to the complacency of the old. After spending a decade hurling red bricks at the Establishment, Lucky Jim ends up at the most elegant of Cambridge high tables. Even if he should want to, the Hipster cannot climb back into the citadel. Drug-addiction or inter-racial marriage create a context of needs and attitudes from which there is hardly any possibility of return.

Mailer himself has gone very near the edge. He could have moved on from *The Naked and the Dead* to further peaks of commercial success. He chose instead a tortuous, idiosyncratic road calculated to rouse against him the powers that be. It has brought him close to professional and personal disaster. Nothing rings truer amid the sprawling sentimentality of *Advertisements for Myself* than Mailer's reckoning of the cost: "I am everything but my proper age of thirty-six, and anger has brought me to the edge of the brutal. . . . I started as a generous but very spoiled boy, and I seem to have turned into a slightly punch-drunk and ugly club fighter. . . . I've burned away too much of my creative energy."

That, surely, is the key point. What of the Writer? What have the self-destructive candours of Mailer's life and doctrine produced? At the start there was a raw talent and a control of mood which make *The Language of Men* a small masterpiece, a story Chekhov would have delighted in. What now?

After the unshaped energies and acuities of *Barbary Shore* came *The Deer Park*. It is a small, sour book with flashes of macabre wit. But the stimulants Mailer was taking at the time seem to have shifted the whole thing out of focus; it ends up whining. It falls far short of Nathanael West's goring of Hollywood. Since *The Deer Park*, there has been little except the screeds of polemic and confession now gathered in *Advertisements*.

There are fine moments in this acrid chronicle. Mailer conveys beautifully the nightmares of diminished power. But the sense of the self as a bruised, clamorous *persona* grows all-embracing. Like a diver trapped in weeds, Mailer seems unable to break surface. He seems incapable of believing in, or making credible, any identity outside his own. All voices have dwindled to echo. It is here that drugs and Hipster ecstasies take their toll; even the "ultimate orgasm" is a private Nirvana, incommunicable to others except by metaphors of music or common trance.

This solipsism of desire, the dilemma of final privacy in the act of sexual communion, has provoked Mailer to the best piece of writing he has ever done. *The Time of Her Time* is a marvel of ribaldry and compassion. It is a story of sexual encounter and near-conquest set in Greenwich Village, in the neutral zone where the Hipster meets the college girl to seduce and argue, to pit Reich against Freud and Trotsky against Stalin. In an alley of cool cats, the hero opens a school for bull-fighters. What follows is a battle more humorous and decisive than any *faena*. All of Mailer's obsessions are concentrated and disciplined in this wry tale: the flailings and incompletions of lust, the poses struck by the uprooted heart, the need for words and gestures truer to the naked, anarchic beat of the time than any we possess. This wild, sad fable goes far towards justifying Mailer's sense of his own stature.

But the British reader will not find it in this book. It is "the considered opinion of some of the best legal and literary minds of the Realm," says Mailer, that "this piece cannot be printed in Britain." They are probably right (and the distinction points up neatly how much there is in *Lady Chatterley* of "safe" sentimental romance). *The Time of Her Time*, and other bits missing from the British edition of *Advertisements* are available in paperback at nearly any American drugstore. The story suggests that Mailer is not through yet, that he will stop being a case and start being a writer again.

In The Lion's Den *[Cannibals and Christians]*

Tony Tanner*

"In the meanwhile, 'these are thy works, thou parent of all good!' Man eating man, eaten by man, in every variety of degree and method! why does not some enthusiastic political economist write an epic on 'The Consecration of Canniblism.' " Norman Mailer on America in 1966? No, Charles Kingsley on England in 1850. And what about this? "The disgrace and grief resulting from the mere trampling pressure and electric friction of town life, become to the sufferers peculiarly mysterious in their undeservedness, and frightful in their inevitableness. The power of all surrounding them for evil; the incapacity of their own minds to refuse the pollution, and of their own wills to oppose the weight, of the staggering mass that chokes and crushes them into perdition, brings every law of healthy existence into question with them, and every alleged method of help and hope into doubt. Indignation, without any calming faith in justice, and self-contempt, without any curative self-reproach, dull the intelligence, and degrade the conscience, into sullen incredulity of all sunshine outside the dunghill, or breeze beyond the wafting of its impurity. . . . And thus an elaborate and ingenious scholasticism, in what may be called the Divinity of Decomposition, has established itself in connection with the more recent forms of romance. . . ." The sentiments could be Mailer's, but the prose is Ruskin's, from a brilliant lecture in which he shows how the conditions of modern urban living conspire to produce a fiction which is preoccupied with violence, madness, disease and death. One can almost see Mailer taking up this point when he suggests, in an interview, that the modern condition may be "psychically so bleak, so over-extended, so artificial, so plastic . . . that studies of loneliness, silence, corruption, scatology, abortion, monstrosity, decadence, orgy, and death can give life, can give a sentiment of beauty." Where Ruskin speaks of "Decomposition" Mailer talks about the "endless expanding realities of deterioration." I am not, of course, suggesting any direct links. But to appreciate Mailer's particular rhetoric it is worth recalling that from the start the modern city provoked sensitive men to seek out new uses of words, new metaphors, in an attempt to convey their apprehensions of the new horrors around them and to project their intimations of doom and apocalypse. Ruskin made the point clearly: "the peculiar forces of devastation induced by modern city life have only en-

*Reprinted from *Partisan Review* 34 (Summer 1967):465–71, by permission of the author.

tered the world lately; and no existing terms of language known to me are enough to describe the forms of filth, and modes of ruin" which are endemic to that life. When the young Kingsley explored the slums of London he could only transmit his response by describing it as hell, and its occupants as cannibals and victims. Dickens (in *Bleak House*) saw that same London as a foggy darkness permeated with a fatal pestilence which the city itself had nourished. In our time Norman Mailer seems to have made it a practice to expose himself to everything the modern city offers, or imposes, and he is echoing an older tradition when he selects as his key metaphors for modern American life cancer (or plague) and cannibalism. Mailer himself is very conscious of the importance of his quest for metaphors. Near the end of his latest book he says: "the argument would demand that there be metaphors to fit the vaults of modern experience." Modern man is being systematically dulled to the possible meanings of his environment and Mailer's contention is that "a future to life depends on creating forms of an intensity which will capture the complexity of modern experience and dignify it, illumine—if you will—its danger."

"Forms" is a word we might pick on to suggest one of the problems that Mailer has encountered. His insights are as idiosyncratic and intermittently brilliant as ever; his uncompromising willingness to expose and anatomize his own inner life (from cerebration to bowel movement) is still compelling; and his ability to feel his way into the mood of occasions of power (boxing matches, political conventions), and to empathize with the men who meet in the arenas of American life, remains remarkable. He offers endless diagnosis ("the country was in disease"); warnings of doom ("Apocalypse or debauch is upon us"); appeals to the latent panic in all sensitive men ("the legitimate fear we feel is vast"). It is vivid stuff, even if some of it is familiar stuff. But where are the new forms? Mailer has tried to provide a form for this collection by dividing it into four stages—Lambs, Lions, Respite and Arena—but it is a pretty arbitrary arrangement brought to a somewhat theatrical conclusion with a story about the end of the world. Essays, book reviews, poems, speeches, occasional stories, interviews—these are what make up the book and it would take more than an introductory assertion to metamorphose them into a new form. Instead, certain obsessions, worries and images provide a sort of febrile continuity, and Mailer offers one kind of justification when he says "if what you write is a reflection of your own consciousness, then even journalism can become interesting."

One drawback is that each piece was originally written for a specific occasion and was meant to have its own self-contained climax and impact. Brought together and read consecutively they provide perhaps one or two climaxes too many. Mailer at times gives the impression of crying wolf about once a page: so much high-pitched warning occasionally has the unintended effect of somewhat inuring us to the dangers that Mailer perceives. This is a pity because many of the dangers are very real, and there is a good deal of biting truth in these pages. An example at random: "an unjust war, an unnatural war, an obscene war brutalizes what is best in a nation and encourages every horror to rise from its sewer." Exaggerated, perhaps; but true enough to worry over. Such insights, or opinions—and they range over modern architecture, the Vietnam War, sex, politics, art, religion, psychology, etc.—are spasmodic; they are ejected from the prose which is kept simmering at a high degree of excitability just short of hysteria. Mailer's observations are passionate rather than considered, emerging from the heat of the moment; inevitably, for every one that seems penetratingly right, there is at least one that seems wildly wrong. The book, then, is one of those endlessly interrupted, endlessly renewed monologues from the extreme psychological edges of modern experience which Norman Mailer has offered us before and will, I hope, again. For all that it is not a new form. In its fragmentary spasmodic structure the book really exemplifies an aspect of modern life which Mailer catches vividly in a few pages on the cult of the absurd. "The absurd is an art which is built not only on interruptions but annoyance. . . . It assumes that annoyance, not love or passion or dedication or climax or interest or mood or mind or even matter, but annoyance is the foundation of modern existence, and the progressively most common condition for everyone alive is interruption and annoyance. . . . One plans to eat—one has to wait for the food to unfreeze; one calls a friend on quick impulse—the line is busy; start to contemplate—the refrigerator will begin to speak; look to pour a friend a drink—the telephone will ring; begin to watch a show—a commercial comes in!" (etc., etc.): "we are talking of modern man's ability to swallow nausea . . . his consciousness is formed on collisions and interruptions. . . . The children who came after the Second World War grew up . . . on interruption—so the arts of the mid-century are the arts of the absurd and deal with categories and hierarchies of discontinuity and the style of their breaks. Art is here on earth to uplift us, to encourage the religious and the nonreligious to feel a heavenly glow—so declared the caretakers of art for two thousand years. But now art is a heart pill—nitroglycerine—it binds shattered nerves together by shattering them all over again with style, with wit, each explosion a guide to building a new nervous system. . . . We live, remember, in a time which interrupts the mood of everything alive. . . . A people deadened by interruption go mad." What are the chances of creating new forms in such times, under such pressures and with such distractions as these? Mailer himself gives the impression of not being able to get beyond the interruptions long enough to develop those new forms he thinks are so necessary. He is constantly engaging in rhetorical clashes with the chaos of modern life which as constantly besets and interrupts him. In his sustained passion, tinged with madness, there is, oddly, a touch of Carlyle about him. He is a prophet of the Age of Interruption.

Like many prophets he is not too good on short-term predictions (Goldwater did not become a great power; Lindsay did get elected) and he can be irritatingly irresponsible. For instance, he continually utters his loathing of contraception as a sign of our modern sickness, but he has no comment to make on the more terrible problem of overpopulation; and for a man who sets so much store by the seed well planted, Mailer is unusually silent on the subject of children. Still, looking back at his previous collections, one readily concedes him the gift of being able to catch and articulate the general inner mood of certain key moments in postwar America: wrong about surface facts, he is often right about subterranean feelings. It is thus disturbing to note that although all his books have been frenetic, this one is more deeply pessimistic than any previous one. "If one's country lives like a woman in some part of the unconscious dream life of each of us, if beneath all our criticisms and detestations of America's vulgarity, misuse of power, and sheer pompous stupidity there has been still some optimistic love affair with the secret potentialities of this nation, some buried unvoiced faith that the nature of America was finally good, and not evil, well, that faith has taken a pistol-whipping in the last months. The romance seems not even tragic or doomed, but dirty and misplaced." It would be quite out of place for someone writing from England to pronounce on the current state of America; but judging from the depressing symposium on the subject in the last issue of *PR*, Mailer's antennae are picking up many bad vibrations which are indeed in the air. One knows that Mailer is fairly committed to a rather comminatory tone, and it would probably be quite possible to find a foolishness or an exaggeration on every other page of this book. The fact remains that I would be a lot less worried if Norman Mailer were a lot less worried.

To dispatch a summary of Mailer's topics and opinions from England to America would be to send rockets to Cape Kennedy. But seen from a distance his recent work does reveal a pattern which may be worth mentioning. Let me start with a tiny symptom, from this current book. Asserting, improbably enough, that he has learned more of his fictional technique from E. M. Forster than from any other writer, he quotes a sentence he particularly admires from *The Longest Journey*, thus—"Gerald was killed that day. He was beaten to death in a football game." Now, the sentence actually reads: "Gerald died that afternoon. He was broken up in a football match." Anybody can get a quotation wrong, but the transformation which Forster's sentence has undergone in Mailer's memory is revealing. What was originally seen as an unexpected accident has become a thuggish and murderous assault. Beaten to death, indeed! (Even allowing that Mailer is probably thinking of American football and Forster most certainly was not.) Mailer's imagination inhabits a world of extreme violence in which hostile forces threaten the annihilation of the individual at every turn. In this connection it is significant that Mailer feels a good deal of sympathy with the work of William Burroughs and his vision of a possible world to come. (One of his telling asides is: "If World War II was like *Catch-22*, this war will be like *Naked Lunch*.") Take this statement, for instance: "Life may now be intolerable to some other conception of Being—I would not know what else to call it but a plague—which is different from ourselves, more powerful perhaps, some conception so antagonistic to the Vision by which we try to discover our life that its presence has invaded our world, perhaps even our universe. The intent of such a plague is to deaden the soul of all of us, invite it to surrender." That could stand on the jacket of *Nova Express* summarizing the main dread in Burroughs' apocalyptic vision. I offered some comments on the demonism in Burroughs' work in a recent issue of *PR* and it is interesting to note that Mailer, in his own way, is also undoubtedly a demonist in as much as he sees existence as a battleground between superhuman forces. The paranoia and sense of proliferating invisible threats which seems endemic to life in the modern city ("the power of all surrounding them for evil," in Ruskin's words), rises to a crescendo in Mailer's writing. "New York is ill beyond relief. There are forces in the city, Left, Right, and Center, which are out of control . . . their only logic is to grow by themselves." And the forces which are seen as gradually bringing death to the modern world with malevolent purposefulness are ultimately "mysterious" (again, as Ruskin said they would strike the city-dweller). Underneath Mailer's specific political concerns there is a feeling that "the war between being and nothingness is the underlying illness of the twentieth century." The ultimate fear is not that Johnson may trigger off the war that ends us all—though that is there—but the fear that God "may have lost His way" and may now lose to the Devil. "It is the heart of existential logic that God's ultimate victory over the Devil is no more certain than the Devil's victory over God—either may conquer man and so give Being a characteristic Good or Evil, or indeed each may exhaust the other, until Being ceases to exist or sinks through seas of entropy into a Being less various, less articulated, less organic, more like plastic than the Nature we know." Again, that could come from Burroughs (note, in passing, the increasing popularity of the metaphor of "entropy"). Mailer thinks it is disastrous that modern man lives in an "antisupernatural" society, and he finds a greater psychic health in "medieval man . . . [who was] able to live with gods, devils, angels and demons, with witches, warlocks and spirits." It is one of Mailer's avowed intents to attempt to restore to modern man some of the more primitive dreads in the interest of renewed psychic vitality. This was clear in *An American Dream* where Rojack asserts: "Yes, I had come to believe in grace and the lack of it, in the long finger of God and the swish of the Devil. . . . I had come to believe in spirits and demons, in devils, warlocks, omens, wizards and fiends, in incubi and succubi. . . ." Interestingly, Rojack maintains that civilization is an "invasion of the supernatural . . . and the price we have paid is to accelerate our sense of some enormous if not quite definable disaster which awaits us." Mailer's demonism, then, is perhaps an attempt to provide identities for unidentified threats and forces, a way of transforming an enfeebling paranoia into a vitalizing dread. "Today the enemy is vague," he revealingly said in an earlier essay, and one can see how throughout his more recent work he has tried to dissipate that vagueness by postulating pairs of opposed extremes. Mailer once said he was excited by the "tendency to reduce all of life to its ultimate alternatives" and we can see various moves in that direction in some of his own pairings: "assassins and victims"; conformists and outlaws; the cancerous forces of control resisted by the brave healthy energy of the hero or the hipster; magician and artist (as in the classic account of the Liston-Patterson fight, which Mailer transformed into a cosmic victory of black magic over the weakened forces of light); "being and nothingness"; *Cannibals and Christians;* finally, "God and the Devil." As I said in relation to Burroughs, I think this simplifying schematization runs the risk of melodramatizing reality. That is not necessarily a totally bad thing, of course. A certain amount of timely melodrama may serve to awaken us to nightmare aspects of our common life to which we have become too easily acclimatized; it may revive feelings of nausea in too complacent stomachs. On the other hand, I still maintain that there is a real danger of complete loss of hope and passive despair lying in wait for the man who refers all the threats that he feels and the aids he needs to external non-human forces. For what can man himself do if he is caught in some vast conflict between angels and demons, a victim of voodoo, a suppliant of grace?

Still, Mailer's metaphors, even at their most extravagant, do serve to give rudimentary outlines to the sensed threats of modern city life. "Society is a sea," said Wallace Stevens; the image is apt since the sea is precisely that element of power which is least amenable to shaping and defining. Its shape is simply itself and all that swarms within it. Mailer, then, is trying to find metaphors for the sea of urban life in modern America—and for the beasts of that sea. His way of coping with the oceanic threats of society is not Stevens' way, and the difference is instructive. Stevens said: "Resistance to the pressure of ominous and destructive circumstance consists of its conversion, so far as possible, into a different, an explicable, an amenable circumstance." Mailer may want to make the destructive pressures explicable, but he is far from converting them into amenable circumstances as far as art is concerned. Stevens, intent on creating works of art despite all external interruptions, spoke of the artist's need for "a violence from within that protects us from a violence without. It is the imagination pressing back against the pressure of reality." Mailer's way—part bravery, part limitation—is not to press back with the imagination, but to let the violent pressures goad him to immediate outcry. For this he has an audience in mind, "that audience which has no tradition by which to measure their experience but the intensity and clarity of their inner lives" and his contention is that "I have a consciousness now which I think is of use to them." Take his most recent book, not as a new work of art, nor as a series of conclusions and prescriptions, but as the record of an unusually sensitive modern urban consciousness, and it has a great deal to tell us about the way we live now. Or, perhaps Mailer would say, the way we die now.

The Trouble He's Seen [The Armies of the Night]

Alfred Kazin*

Twenty years ago this week, when Norman Mailer published *The Naked and the Dead,* became famous and rich and pleased everybody, even old novelists on their way out, it looked as if a safe type were off to a traditional career. The novel was "the best of the American World War II novels"; it was on the side of Lieutenant Hearn, the young American progressive, and made a villain of epicene, Fascist-minded General Cummings; its characters made a comprehensible, "cross-section of American society," from Goldstein to Gallagher: the text was clearly indebted to many models—Dos Passos for narrative rhythm, Farrell for tough city background, Hemingway for nuance.

The Naked and the Dead is as intensely readable as it was in 1948, and still the only one of Mailer's novels that continually reads like a novel that is stable in conception, that doesn't become an exhibition or a Quest. There is a particular visual concentration behind its best scenes that was to reappear in everything he wrote later, a force of mind that had enabled this literary draftee out of Brooklyn and Harvard, in the Army often a clerk, to absorb other people's hardships and battles into himself. But what is most striking about it now is its intellectual discipleship. It could have been called *Main Currents in American Thought—A Novel.* "The best of American World War II novels" is no great praise, for that war didn't produce any new forms. The novelists were competing with the reporters on their own ground, and amidst the mountains of gritty documentaries, Mailer's novel in fact pleased because it was more intelligent and better written, and so was more recognizable.

Barbary Shore (1951) was not just a "disappointment": it showed that Mailer was not interested in being an "acceptable" novelist, that in his moody indignation with the moral failure of Socialism in Russia and the growth of authoritarian state power in the U.S.A., he was willing to throw a novel away in order to express political agony. He portrayed a struggle to the death between an ex-Bolshevik not yet ready to betray his dream of Socialism and an F.B.I. agent ready to betray anything. This dark, sad testament of a book, only distractedly a novel, was riddled with the intimations of a tie-up between the ex-Left and the Government's intelligence service. This (then) fantasy, one of many in Mailer's busy mind, nevertheless frightened him, demanded a solution, a reaffirmation of Socialism in Trotsky's terms. The author was stridently a moralist, disturbed by the lack of expected sequences. Faith seemed more important than fiction.

The author of *Barbary Shore* was still the nice Jewish boy from Harvard and very much a disciple—this time of the French radical, Jean Mala-

*Reprinted from the *New York Times Book Review,* 5 May 1968, 1–2, 26. © 1968 by The New York Times Company. Reprinted by permission.

quais. But around the time Mailer had such trouble completing *The Deer Park* (1955) to his satisfaction, there had appeared the toughie who hated the nice Jewish boy—and began talking about himself in public, with a bravado plainly designed to throw off anything that might soften him up in his opposition to America's cancer-breeding repressions. There was a new wife, a new Mailer and a new ideology—sexual courage, truth to the buried instincts. It looked as if Sade had displaced Marx, Wilhelm Reich had displaced Jean Malaquais. But the immediate crisis in this search for the politics and religion of sex, for solutions that would connect sex back to revelation, sex with the hidden message circuits of the mind that lead to God, was that Mailer never did like what he had finally made of *The Deer Park*. Several publishers turned it down, he became obsessed with the book, and has been writing about it or dramatizing it ever since.

Mailer was now living "the crisis of the novel." He thought constantly about writing novels, saw everyone as a possible character, made grandiose announcements of a whole series of novels. But he was so sensitive to politics, power and society in America, so engrossed in the search for solutions and revelations, that the moralist and the "celebrity" left little time to the novelist. He now made a feat of writing books quickly, as if hurling *An American Dream* month by month into *Esquire* and turning all his powers of mimicry into the *Why Are We in Vietnam?* would finally earn him self-approval as a novelist. Both are certainly brilliant *performances;* but in the first you are always aware of Mailer's favorite fantasies, in the second of his pride in a linguistic tour de force.

Still, a significant reason for Mailer's impatience has also been his acute sense of the national crisis, his particular gift for detecting political deterioration—and his professional feeling that the American scene at this time may be too thorny a subject to be left to journalists. It is the coalescence of American disorder (always an obsession of Mailer's) with all the self-confidence he feels as a novelist doing reportage that has produced *Armies of the Night*, his extraordinary personal tract on the unprecedented demonstration of Oct. 21–22, 1967, when thousands of the New Left attempted to "march on the Pentagon," fell into some brief but bloody skirmishes with armed guards, and a thousand people were arrested—among them, Norman Mailer.

Of course Mailer presents this book as *his* nonfiction novel—he simply cannot stop dreaming about himself as a novelist. But it is a fact that only a born novelist *could* have written a piece of history so intelligent, mischievous, penetrating and alive, so vivid with crowds, the great stage that is American democracy, the Washington streets and bridges, the Lincoln Memorial, the women, students, hippies, Negroes and assorted intellectuals for peace, the M.P.'s and United States marshals, the American Nazis chanting "We want dead Reds."

The book cracks open the hard nut of American authority at the center, the uncertainty of our power—and, above all, the bad conscience that now afflicts so many Americans. *Armies of the Night* is a peculiarly appropriate and timely contribution to this moment of the national drama and, among other things, it shows Mailer relieved of his vexing dualities, able to bring all his interests, concerns and actually quite traditional loyalties to equal focus. The form of this diary-essay-tract-sermon grew out of the many simultaneous happenings in Washington that weekend, out of the self-confidence which for writers is *style*, out of his fascination with power in America and his fear of it, out of his American self-dramatizing and his honest fear for his country.

Armies of the Night is a poorer title than the one Mailer gave to the portion of the book that appeared in the March issue of *Harper's*—"The Steps of the Pentagon"; but it does light up his main subject—the intellectuals, the students, the Negroes, the academic liberals and the marching women who personify the American opposition. From first to last, this book is about that opposition, its political and human awkwardness; that is why the book that seems too full of Mailer himself is really about Mailer's deepest political anxieties. Things are coming to a crisis, but the forces of protest symbolically assembled before the Pentagon seem to him limited in everything except courage. (It was the women particularly who, as the weekend drew to a close, were beaten by the guards.)

What makes the tract exciting is the interpretation by Mailer's favorite persona, the novelist-in-charge-of-practically-everything, of the Left as well as of the Authority it would like to challenge. Mailer's gnawing sense of possibility makes the book, and it plainly grows out of his frustrations as a novelist, his wild imaginative resources, his constant brooding over all *he* might do with what he sees. So the American opposition has been frustrated by the way in which the Vietnam war particularly, but also Negro-white relations and even the old primacy of business in this country, have shown every day how little the forces of protest and "resistance" have to do with American *institutions*.

A century ago the Transcendentalists—the purest of Puritans—were already maddened by the power exercised by bankers, politicians, slaveholders. The feeling of the American opposition today, publicly if not actually led by such pillars of the Protestant establishment as the Rev. William Sloane Coffin Jr. and Dr. Benjamin Spock, is not merely that the American war in Vietnam is hideously brutal and wrong, that we have no right to be devastating this country in the name of our theological anti-Communism, but that the political and moral sages who founded our culture have been succeeded by generals, politicians, executives, hucksters and "experts."

Nothing is more likely to drive a brilliant scholar at M.I.T. into a rage than the picture of ex-professor Walt Whitman Rostow of M.I.T. conferring with his boss on just where to bomb the North Vietnamese. "They" have all the power, and "we" have just imagination! This has been Mailer's grievance for many years. Given a novelist's belief that a novelist is the smartest of men anyway ("The novel is the one bright book of life," said

D. H. Lawrence. ("Only in the novel are *all* things given full play.") and *this* novelist's impatience to get into everything all the time and right away, one can see why Mailer in this book shows so much *brio,* so much wrath at the powerful, so much despair at those on the American Left who have been losing all their lives and perhaps like to lose.

For all his self-dramatization, Mailer is the right chronicler of the March on the Pentagon. For there is no other writer of his ability who, feeling so deeply about this "obscene war . . . the worst war the nation has ever been in," can yet be so aware of everything else around him—not least the intellectual staleness of his own side.

See him, for example, on the Friday night before the Saturday afternoon march, sipping bourbon from a coffee cup as he staggers up and down the stage of a Washington movie house, heckling his own audience and not forgetting to patronize Dwight Macdonald and Paul Goodman. All this was terrible, terrible, as that moral journal *Time* has told us. Mailer likes to be terrible, to clean all timidity, subservience and false respect out of his system. He is afraid of losers; they may be contagious.

But because these *Armies of the Night* are in reality his army, if not exactly an army after his own kind, it is a fact that Mailer does not trust his troops, or even his fellow writers on the Left, to be outrageous, strong and imginative enough—to have *style* enough with the Kennedy panache. Can the American opposition really take on the corporations, the police, the mass media? America Mailer variously calls "corporation land," "technology land." Just as the stones of Egypt were formed from the "excremental" ooze of the Nile, so the walls of the Pentagon seem to him primeval, ancient, blind.

But that Saturday afternoon, as the incongruous crowd made its *symbolic* challenge, Mailer felt "as if he stepped through some crossing in the reaches between this moment, the French Revolution, and the Civil War, as if the ghosts of the Union Dead accompanied them now to the Bastille," Not drinking or eating a thing all day, he knew ". . . they were going to face the symbol, the embodiment, no, call it the true and high church of the military-industrial complex, the Pentagon, blind five-sided eye of a subtle oppression which had come to America out of the very air of the century . . . yes, Mailer felt a confrontation of the contests of his own life on this March to the eye of the oppressor, greedy stingy dumb valve of the worst of the Wasp heart . . . smug, enclosed, morally blind Pentagon, destroying the future of its own nation with each day it augmented its strength."

Overwritten? Overwrought? It doesn't read so in the context. And think of how many nice young students from the best families at the best colleges are mentally confronting the Pentagon today, how many of America's best young men in the graduate schools are in fact preparing *their* contest with authority—how many of America's children, if only in the privacy of their minds, now find themselves in one form of opposition or another. Yet Mailer is by no means happy about the young opposition. "These mad middle class children with their lobotomies from sin" are too facile in their thinking, spoiled by American affluence, indifferent to waste, too quick to obliterate the complexities of our situation by drugs and pills. Mailer calls himself a "Left Conservative" and at a marvelous moment, watching the young men turning in their draft cards, confesses that this mass ceremony shocks him.

Mailer's put-down of other writers (among the demonstrators only Robert Lowell is recognized as a "peer," but Lowell doesn't write fiction) is, of couse, funny, because Mailer is always in character. If Ralph Ellison or Saul Bellow had passed by (hardly likely) Mailer would have been looking for Susan Sontag. But while he is careful to describe writers he can put down—or brilliant scholars like Noam Chomsky whose specialities he of course has ideas about—his judgments are infernally shrewd.

His portraits of the leaders are both impressive and funny—of Mailer's four wives, three used Dr. Spock's baby book, so Dr. Spock reminds him of all the trouble he has seen. For the first time one sees a leading American peacenik and resister addressing urgent questions to his "army"—Are *we* good enough? How can we overcome the "mediocrity of the middle-class middle-aged masses of the Left?" The general shoddiness of American standards just now? The marked tendency of authorities to lie? The general greediness of the middle classes? "The overpsychologized loins of the liberal academic intelligentsia" and the general tendency of "liberal academics to become servants of the social machine of the future?"

Salinger once counseled us to recognize Jesus Christ in the fat old lady. But Mailer asks—what about "grandma with orange hair," madly playing the slot machines in Las Vegas and ignoring the burned children in Vietnam? The conformism, inertia, gluttony and moral indifference—to say nothing of the power now stored in piled banks of coded knowledge—may in fact be too much for the rhetoricians of the New Left. Mailer feels that there is a dead nerveless area in the American Left, "comprised of the old sense of paralysis before the horrors of the gas chambers." And since he grew up with the failure and failures on the Old Left, he is tired of the lack of style, wit and intellectual grace. J.F.K. is his model, and he is proud that he finally got himself arrested—by trying to run a line of U.S. marshals like a football player. Then, having got himself arrested, he found himself in the paddy wagon with an arrested American Nazi shrieking hate at him. Waiting in the detention center to pay his $25 and so get back to New York in time for a party, he unexpectedly spent the weekend in jail because the United States Commissioner in charge thought that a man with *his* literary reputation and all should not get off as easily as the others.

"I am the man," said Walt Whitman. "I suffer'd, I was there." When a writer gets old enough, like Whitman, one forgets that he was just as outrageous an egotist and actor as Norman Mailer is. Yet Whitman staked his work on finding the personal connection between salvation as an artist and the salvation of his country. The best American writers in the 19th century talked about themselves all the time—but in the romantic American line, saw the self as the prime condition of democracy. I believe that *Armies of the Night* is just as brilliant a personal testimony as Whitman's diary of the Civil War, *Specimen Days*, and Whitman's great essay on the crisis of the Republic during the Gilded Age, *Democratic Vistas*. I believe that it is a work of personal and political reportage that brings to the inner and developing crisis of the United States at this moment admirable sensibilities, candid intelligence, the most moving concern for America itself. Mailer's intuition in this book is that the times demand a new form. He has found it.

The Perfect Absurd Figure of a Mighty, Absurd Crusade   John W. Aldridge*

The appearance of these two volumes, a retrospective collection of Norman Mailer's writings and a book of critical essays about him, is one of several recent indications that Mailer has at last begun to suffer the fate he has hoped for years would overtake him. There now seems to be widespread agreement—not only among his literary contemporaries but large segments of the reading public—that he is the most exciting and important writer in America. The interesting question is why the presumably self-evident fact of Mailer's genius has taken so long to be acknowledged, why even sophisticated people have had to *learn* to live with it as if it were a loathesome disease, after overcoming extremely powerful feelings of distaste, while legions of the semi-literate, the sort who never read books but know exactly which writers they detest, appear to harbor the most astonishing hostility to Mailer's face, physique, voice, manners, and morals and seem unable to understand why he was not put away long ago. This is rather odd when one considers that we have never expected our best writers to be particularly saintly, and there is a fine tradition among them of behavior ranging from the merely perverse through the boorish, sottish, deceitful, spiteful, disloyal, and infantile to the maddest reaches of paranoia and monomania. The examples of Poe, Whitman, Twain, Frost, Hart Crane, Hemingway, Faulkner, and Fitzgerald all testify in varying degrees to the fact that sometimes the only respectable thing about a writer is his writing. Yet these men have been accepted—in some cases, to be sure, only after they were decorously dead—because the quality of their work finally seemed to justify their peculiarities of character.

*Reprinted from *Saturday Review*, 13 November 1971, 45–46, 48–49, 72, by permission of the journal. Review of *The Long Patrol: Twenty-Five Years of Writing from the Work of Norman Mailer*, ed. Robert F. Lucid (New York: World, 1971), and *Norman Mailer: The Man and His Work*, ed. Robert F. Lucid (Boston: Little, Brown, 1971).

The trouble with Mailer is that not only has he been very much alive among us—unforgivably alive—but he seemed for too long a dubious quantity as a writer while his character grew steadily more outrageous. There was a period in the Fifties when he appeared to imagine that the way to achieve large literary success was to engage in brawls and try to get arrested, or to insult his readers by disparaging their intelligence—as he did to such good effect in the columns he wrote at the time for *The Village Voice*. His strategy then may well have been to create such an offensive public image that people would be moved to read him if only out of hate. But the practical result was that too many people decided that nobody who acted that foolish could possibly be worth reading. Significantly, it was not until the appearance in 1959 of *Advertisements For Myself*, a collection offered quite nakedly, even abjectly, as an appeal for serious recognition, that the tide of opinion began to turn in Mailer's favor, and it did so not because that book contained old material hitherto unappreciated or prompted a reconsideration of his novels, but because in writing about his frustrations and mistakes, the wreck of his literary hopes, the corrosions of failure that drove him to behave badly, he produced a prose so remarkably much better than anything he had done before that a large number of readers saw for the first time how very good a writer he was—because then, for the first time, he was that good.

Mailer also discovered in *Advertisements* what has since become his most complex and vital subject—himself as combined victim, adversary, hero, and fool being simultaneously humiliated and aggrandized as he engages the ogres and windmills of contemporary history. He had learned a great deal about the dramatic possibilities inherent in the multifoliate subject of Norman Mailer, and he was destined as time passed to learn a great deal more. But by 1959 his remarkable sensitivity to the intricate telegraphies of status had already taught him this much: that to be taken seriously as a man and writer you do not *demand* the approval of the public, for this puts you in the position of appearing to feel arrogantly superior to them and insisting on what is rightfully your due. The far better way is to make the public feel superior to you by demonstrating how pathetic you have become in trying to win their approval and just how much their approval means to you. Furthermore, you could always count on good Americans to believe that recognition should come to those who have worked for it hard enough, and Mailer in *Advertisements* had explained with fine eloquence how terribly hard he had worked for it. If, as Leslie Fiedler once remarked, nothing succeeds for Americans like failure, it is equally true that confession of failure is not only cleansing to the soul but absolutely wonderful for one's public image.

Having apparently learned all this by 1959, Mailer went on to learn something even more essential to his future prosperity: how to make himself into the kind of writer who would finally neutralize through his work some of the mistrust and hostility he had generated through his public behavior. He achieved this in two ways. First, he began making much more direct use in his fiction of his own well-publicized obsessions and aberrations—his interest in the mystical properties of the orgasm in *The Time of Her Time*, the spiritually regenerative effects of wife-murder in *An American Dream*, the cathartic possibilities of the scatological in *Why Are We in Vietnam?*. This had the effect of dissociating these ideas from his public self and the essays and interviews in which he had first presented them as shockingly offensive personal interests, and giving them the safely general and objective quality of fictional themes. As such, they might still seem offensive, but at least they would be identified with his imaginary characters and no longer be taken as quite such literal evidence of his own moral corruption.

At the same time he was also discovering how to project in his work— primarily in the meta-journalism he began to write in the late Sixties—a self-image which became steadily more attractive, not so much because the things he described himself as saying and doing had suddenly ceased to seem outrageous, but because a new note of humor had come to characterize the description and to give it an air of ironic detachment and ambiguity that was both appealing and enormously effective as a tranquilizer of enemies. He was no longer the victim of his bludgeoning first-person delivery. Instead, Mailer became his own most derisive critic as he observed his various personae—an aging, hungover activist in Washington, "the reporter" in Miami and Chicago, Aquarius in Cape Kennedy and Houston— pass through the postures of acute embarrassment, ineptitude, braggadocio, affectation, and occasional wisdom, hamming it up for the gallery or putting down a rival, but always finally being put down hardest by himself. The traits displayed by these personae had long been fixtures of Mailer's public character, but when he had displayed them in that character they had earned him little more than hostility. Now the writer in him had found a way of using them as material, and in the process he turned his worst vices into almost lovable virtues. The early Mailer committed the one sin Americans can never forgive: he took himself seriously. As a journalist, he began to laugh at himself—an action we prize even more highly than failure. In achieving these realignments Mailer can hardly be accused of cynicism. There is nothing to indicate that he was employing his skills as a politician, although they are recognized to be considerable. He seems rather to have passed into a new phase of personal and creative development in which he was able to engage himself and his material in fresh terms. By the late Sixties he had gained in wisdom as well as age, and he had also gained sufficient success to appease at least the larger hungers of his ego and give him a certain benevolent detachment. But that these things occurred at this particular time was immensely fortuitous, and so was the fact that he began just then to offer in his journalism a kind of material singularly appropriate to the historical moment and guaranteed to have a major impact particularly on the younger audience of the moment. It had been obvious for years to others, if not to Mailer, that if he expected, as he claimed, to have a revolutionary influence on the consciousness of the age, he would be unlikely to do so through the novel. The problem was not simply that his best talents were only erratically displayed in the novel, but that the form itself seemed inadequate to satisfy the needs of a generation who had grown to believe that the social realities of this world are far more important than imaginative fictions, and who were trying to relate to issues as the generation before them had tried to relate to ideas. Mailer's interests as a writer and those of his largest potential public thus nicely coincided, for it had been evident—perhaps even as far back as *The Naked and the Dead*—that his particular powers found their most intense stimulus in moments of social and political crisis, in apocalyptic confrontations between individuals and the massive forces of historical and institutional change. The march on the Pentagon, the riots in Chicago, the Presidential conventions of 1968 were all charged with apocalyptic portent. They were as beautifully suited to Mailer's temperament and style as if he had invented them himself—which, in fact, he might have done—and it so happened that all the seismic intruments agreed that these occasions demanded expression in precisely the form he and he alone could give them.

If he had come to envision himself as a symptomatic consciousness, mediating between his personal micro-hells and the major disasters of his age, he now had an audience desperately in need of someone on whom they could project their own more incoherent sense of being both agents and dupes of history, at once personally implicated in and collectively victimized by events. What they found in Mailer was a writer who could bring into focus the contradictory elements of this feeling, a spokesman able to express it in language and action more forcefully than they could or would have dared and, above all, a human being whom they could accept—as they had accepted no one since John Kennedy—for a hero because he epitomized in his humanness the ambiguities necessary to an acceptable heroism at that time. He was tough, brash, defiantly irreverent, a taker of unbelievable risks. But he was also—and openly admitted to being—vulnerable, uncertain, fearful of the impression he was making (on Robert Lowell, Dwight Macdonald, Eugene McCarthy, Sonny Liston), never completely convinced of the possibility that mere quaking guts might stand up to their monolithic self-possession.

Yet that exactly was the secret of Mailer's appeal, the very essence of his heroism, for he was guts at war with all his unmastered contradictions and fears, and he monitored them in battle with that deadly obsessiveness of the general who has never quite grown up to the courage of his command, brooding over the corpses of real men when he should have been figuring the cold statistics of killed and wounded. Such men as Lowell, Liston and McCarthy might be great poets, fighters, and politicians, but they could not be heroes, at least not in this time and generation, because they were too complete as personages, at once too intact in their fortitude and too remote from their mortality. Mailer was like the early characters of Hemingway, and he would like to have thought that he was more than a little like Hemingway himself. He was all blustering defense mechanism, the hairy fist clutching the fragile rose, bravery earned at the expense of panic, a mass of insecurities constantly in need of the challenge that would force him into at least the appearance of strength. He thus dramatized the antithetical impulses that underlay the protest movement and the psychology of the young. He expressed their strong mistrust of the pieties of the establishment at the same time that he forced them to confront their own even more pompous pieties. He embodied their sense of self-importance and of insignificance, their faith and their cynicism, their desire to make the grand gesture and their intuition that the grand gesture would probably have slight effect on anyone, least of all the blind course of history. Mailer, in short, was the perfect absurd white knight of their mighty, absurd crusade—the quixotic figure of fun, nobility, pride, self-derisiveness, and absolute honesty for a generation that had nothing to offer but its indignation, its idealism, and its preposterous nerve.

But one saw that these same qualities that made Mailer so attractive to the younger readers of his journalism also helped to ingratiate him with older readers and even former enemies. That developing note of self-derisiveness which came to characterize his treatment of his various personae was accompanied by an increasing tendency to equivocate about issues and people he at one time most probably would have demolished. Practically every portrait he drew of public events and personalities could be seen to have a dimension of meliorating ambiguity. If he put down liberals, one also noticed that he put down conservatives. He might show irritation over the fact that Ralph Abernathy had kept the press waiting forty minutes in Miami. He might even use the occasion to deliver one of his most agonized and eloquent perorations on the whole oppressive phenomenon of Negro rights: ". . . he [Mailer] was so heartily sick of listening to the tyranny of soul music, so bored with Negroes triumphantly late for appointments, so depressed with black inhumanity to Black in Biafra, so weary of being sounded in the subway by Black eyes, so despairing of the smell of booze and pot and used-up hope in the blood-shot eyes of Negroes bombed at noon. . . ."

He might even acknowledge the presence in "some secret part of his flesh [of] a closet Republican," yet the confession clearly costs him something in "dread and woe." Its impact is softened if not canceled by his so evident guilt, and that, it turns out, is not his loss but his gain, for he has registered his heresy in the very breath of denouncing it, and so may be said to have had it both ways—to have put into words our most vicious buried hatreds but purged himself and us with the detergents of self-disgust.

In the same manner one also saw him in *Armies of the Night* open an attack on his peers, yet with a sure instinct for the right one to destroy— Paul Goodman, lost to him anyway, but not Lowell, or Macdonald, who at that moment was known to be at work on a review of *Why Are We in Vietnam?* for the *New Yorker*. Again, it would be unfair to suggest that what has really happened to Mailer is that he has become a politician. Without doubt his vision has simply grown more dialectical, and he has found a way of dramatizing more completely his own intellectual and psychological contradictions. Nevertheless, one cannot deny that this often *appears* to be circumspection or that, deliberate or not, it has worked powerfully to his advantage. He now knows how little real profit there is in the self-indulgence of the direct attack, and how much potential risk. To allow oneself the exhilaration of trying with a single blow to kill off all one's literary competitors—as he very nearly succeeded in doing in "The Talent in the Room" and "Some Children of the Goddess"—is to take the chance of undermining one's whole campaign for the championship. Mailer did not dare to afford such luxuries now that he saw he had become the caretaker of a possibly major reputation and a talent for winning the large-scale approval he had fought for throughout his literary life.

The dangers for the public writer in achieving approval of this kind were all rehearsed for us in the sad example of Hemingway. Mailer began by envying Hemingway his reputation and, now that he has won something approaching its equivalent, he may be forced to suffer very similar consequences. If Hemingway finally found it more enjoyable to play at being the celebrity than to persist in the more arduous course of developing himself as a writer, Mailer may not be wholly exempt from the same temptation. Widespread attention is most easily won these days through performing in the mass media, and such perfomance is far less tiring than creativity. If in order to gain an audience for your important work you make yourself into a media performer, you must also know when to stop performing and get on with your important work. Otherwise, you may end by becoming nothing but a performer and, worse, you will begin to live for it as an end in itself. Mailer knows this better than most because he knows his own weaknesses better than anybody else. But it would appear to be time now for him to get back to work and begin to live out his fantasies through the creations of his mind and talent and not through such humiliating and disastrous exhibitions as his recent boxing match with José Torres on the *Dick Cavett Show*.

The two volumes devoted to representative selections from Mailer's work and to the views of his critics may serve as a reminder to him that he is indeed the caretaker, however careless, of a major talent and reputation, and they may also draw public attention away from his activities as a television pugilist and back to the real matter at hand. *The Long Patrol* contains an excellent sampling of his writings—both excerpted and complete—from *The Naked and the Dead* through *Of a Fire on the Moon,* and is intended, as the editor, Robert F. Lucid, says, to attract readers who may be discovering Mailer for the first time. The critical collection, also edited by Mr. Lucid, should surely win for Mailer both new and more respectful readers, for here are critics writing, whether in praise or condemnation, about a man whom they clearly consider a literary phenomenon of great importance. The book contains an extremely discerning and appreciative introduction by Mr. Lucid, Richard Foster's fine long study, which first appeared as one of the *University of Minnesota Pamphlets on American Writers*, the early and classic essays by Diana Trilling and by Norman Podhoretz, Elizabeth Hardwick's delightfully indignant and mostly uncomprehending review of *An American Dream*, as well as other pieces of varying quality and temper by such critics as Alfred Kazin, Richard Poirier, Tom Wolfe, Midge Decter, Leo Bersani, Jack Richardson, Gore Vidal, and Dwight Macdonald.

The two collections together testify to the size of Mailer's achievement and the solidity of his present reputation. That is what matters to us, and it should be all that matters to him. For now that he has proved that he can survive and triumph over failure, he has still to prove that he can survive his large success. To do this it would seem that he must learn again the lesson every successful writer has had to learn not once but many times: that it is necessary for him to become private once more because his real demons can never be confronted in the public limelight but only in the haunted personal dark. Yeats's lines addressed "To a Friend Whose Work Has Come to Nothing" may be even more appropriate to one whose work has come to a very great deal:

> Bred to a harder thing
> Than Triumph, turn away
> And like a laughing string
> Whereon mad fingers play
> Amid a place of stone,
> Be secret and exult,
> Because of all things known
> That is most difficult.

Monroe According to Mailer: One Legend Feeds On Another
[*Marilyn: A Biography*]
Ingrid Bengis*

I pick it up, I put it down, read 10 pages, pace, start to feel nauseous, read some more, dream about it, stare at the photographs, climb up on the roof of my house, start hammering nails into shingles with a vengeance, change from a bikini to the loosest shirt I can find, and then change back

*Reprinted from *Ms.* 2 (October 1973):44–47, by permission of Julian Bach Literary Agency, Inc. © 1973 by Ingrid Bengis.

again. I lose all sense of whether I am reading Monroe's biography, Mailer's autobiography, or my own. The pictures make me cry, the text makes me physically ill, as much when Mailer hits some psychic stratum which rings absolutely true as when he floats off into an absurd hypothesis which punctures on impact.

It will be this way perhaps for all those whose lives were profoundly affected, as mine was, by the fifties' attitudes, that made it possible for Marilyn Monroe to surface into fame and all, and helped edge her toward the suicide which Mailer, in one of his weakest and therefore most revealing moments, disputes.

I was 18 the year Marilyn Monroe died. She was not one of my favorites; I thought she was "vulgar," and, according to the single standard for which she was supposed to be appreciated, she did not measure up: Ava Gardner was much more beautiful, and sexier.

Yet the climate which shaped Monroe shaped me as well, and in retrospect I can see that as an adolescent I imitated her. Which is why *Marilyn* seems to demand such a special kind of personal confrontation.

Mailer's own approach to Marilyn is just such a personal confrontation, though whether with the real Marilyn Monroe or the Monroe of his own invention it is difficult to know. Direct evidence of the inner life, in biography, is almost impossible to come by, for letters, interviews, documents, even the words of the subject herself hold unlimited possibilities for distraction. No amount of evidence is ever sufficient to compensate for the deviousness with which human beings manage to conceal themselves, even in their most intimate relations—and what they do reveal in conditions of intimacy is not readily translatable into a public form.

What Mailer is after, however, is exactly the degree of intimacy which the conditions of biography would deny him. His strength is, and has always been, in his quick instinct for the raw edge of a thing, the hidden detail that reveals a personality otherwise obscure. Never having known Marilyn, he has to resort to buying a bottle of Chanel No. 5 in order to reconstruct what it must have smelled like on her body.

It is not just intimacy that Mailer wants. He wants Marilyn herself: the complete seduction of his subject. It sometimes seems that one is overhearing a conversation between Mailer and Monroe, and one becomes involved as one might become involved in a life-or-death issue. Will Norman Mailer be able to "save" (read "resurrect") Marilyn Monroe? Mailer has enough of a sense of the mystic and the occult to take seriously just such an attempt: imagination has always had powers of resurrection that no science can match. Reading *Marilyn* thus becomes an act of absolute attention, like listening in on the conversation of two lovers whose fate one cares about, while they are desperately trying to comprehend each other, and feeling that each failure involves the tearing of flesh.

One roots for imagination as a life force—hoping that it will have the power to succeed where analysis or mere understanding would fail: hoping, according to the great soap-opera tradition, that the hero will rescue the heroine. For soap opera, after all, is no small matter. The real dramas of life all resemble it, and one could count on Mailer to choose a subject which skirts the edges of disaster by bringing him close to the materials of gossip column: to public legend and private disintegration.

The question becomes this: Is Mailer the one to rescue her? Or is there a double tragedy to her life: first, the persistent bloodsucking thirst for more more more of that sexuality which she knew how to project and which was always "good box-office" (the pun is worthwhile); and second, the fact that literally everyone who became involved with other sides of her also became involved in a rescue myth—which, for those who consider themselves "more sensitive than the rest," retains a magical persuasiveness. But because human motivation is such a tangled thing, such a morass of self-interest masquerading as altruism, it always also has its destructive elements. And in Marilyn's case, they outweigh the constructive ones.

Where we become enmeshed, in reading Marilyn's biography, is a sort of unearthly dialogue between those who wished to seduce her and those who wished to save her. The lines between the two are perpetually blurring, and one is left with the exhausting thought that each led into the other; that saving and seduction were all too often the same thing. In fact, that saving could be, and usually was, far more seductive than outright seduction could possibly be.

That, I suppose, is part of what makes *Marilyn* so painful to read. Ultimately, one becomes an accomplice—whether seducer or savior—for after all, she is dead, and there remains the thought: If only she didn't have to be.

Yes, it was late already and the chips were all in. Yes, one knows that what might have saved her was being born into a different world or a different skin. One is struck almost overwhelmingly here by the shape which mere coincidence gives to our lives; the form that our bodies take, particularly with women, dictates more often than we wish it would, the form that a portion of our lives will take. Everyone wants to be loved (*but why must it be by everyone,* a part of me shouts) and everyone uses what they've got to get loved, disregarding in the urgency of need the forms that the "love" (read "attention") takes. Psychic starvation is a desperate business: one does not wait around for Baked Alaska.

Monroe it seems, died of precisely that psychic starvation, turning over and over again to the old temptations, the reliable things, when everything else had failed; turning to sex because it *worked,* it always worked when nothing else did. She was like an alcoholic who couldn't take just one drink. Like everyone addicted to some reliable habit of response, there was no way to simply "flirt" with it, no way to indulge yourself in a pinch. But Marilyn was always encouraged to do just that. "Show what you've got, baby." The day of her death, we have a photographer looking forward to the "final revelation" of what Mailer calls "that famous set of cheeks" in a

Playboy photograph. "To be naked before God and the world": *that* was what she wanted. What she got was "a famous set of cheeks." The difference was so vast as to be devastating. And was. How easy to imagine her thinking finally, "No matter what they say they want, that's what they really want. That's what I'm good for." The germs of self-love and self-hate are inextricably blended in a formula which ultimately proves to be toxic.

The trouble with Mailer here is that he loves the alcoholic in her. He is hypnotized by her body, by the quality of her sex. But that, in her case, is like being a social drinker who insists on his Saturday night bash with the alcoholic. It makes of an addiction a mere "attribute," or "pleasure." There are plenty of alcoholics who can be magnificent when drunk: it does not make them any less alcoholic. Every woman who has ever tried to be something larger than her sexuality should be shaken by the dilemma which Mailer makes palpable through his depictions of others and through his revelations of himself: the dilemma of Marilyn struggling to transcend her own performance, snatched at from every direction by those who wished to mold her in their own image, suck into that vortex of sexuality which we all, in some part of ourselves, *need*, but which can also be so poisonous.

Marilyn thus becomes a struggle for the possession of a soul. The reader is involved; Norman is involved. At one point Mailer writes that his "secret ambition had been to steal Marilyn [from Arthur Miller]. In all [Miller's] vanity, he thought no one was so well-suited to bring out the best in her as himself . . . a conceit which fifty million other men must also have had." One does not know for sure whether it is mere vanity at work here— a ritual seduction, Mailer proving that he can do it—or whether it is an authentic Existential Love Song. And of course, if Norman Mailer had been able to do it—well, a life is always worth more than the opinions one has of it.

Beyond that, I doubt that there is a woman in the world who doesn't secretly want to be brought "out" by *someone*, even if the someone turns out to be herself ("with a little help from my friends"). We are all so trapped in the half-visions we have of what we *might* be, while having to wallow around in what we actually are, that anyone who could make those half-visions alive and breathing would *have* to possess a power over us.

So Mailer plays to the gallery, plays to that desire for infinite self-realization that is in all of us, and one has to keep reminding oneself that "being brought out" is a *literary* exercise—just as it is an analyst's "job" to bring you out, and one must face that in real life he / she might not be able to do it at all.

But the literary and the personal in *Marilyn* always seem to be blurring. Mailer writes as if Marilyn were there the whole time, looking on, hovering over his project, demanding of him the most radical exertions of insight and comprehension, the fullest romanticism combined with the clearest reason, the greatest restraint with the greatest abandon, the largest practicality with the most extreme daring. All this by way of *proving* to her ghost that he is worthy of her. Mailer's Bitch Goddess, refined now through the mesh of some almost infinite personal regret, some final tenderness.

It is a strange cycle to get caught in. Has Mailer created a Myth of Marilyn in order to fall in love with it? Or did that Marilyn already exist? Mailer quotes Marilyn as having said, "I am always running into peoples' unconscious." That could probably be said of Mailer as well. But like everything about Marilyn (and one might say about Mailer, too), gifts have the capacity to turn treacherous. For running into other peoples' unconscious is all right if you have thick enough skin to sustain the collision. If you don't, it can be deadly.

The Bitch Goddess is, and always has been, the female equivalent of Mailer himself. The assumption that Mailer makes is that in real life, Marilyn is exactly that female equivalent. Everything else hangs on that assumption. Marilyn "working like a pearl diver for her legend" is Mailer working in the same manner for his. But there is one almost unbearably simple thing he fails to take into account in this cosmic communication he envisions. A Beast, even if it is only in the performance, has the advantage of a thick hide, or tusks, or fur. A Bitch Goddess or sex symbol, in her performance (one must accept that Mailer has chosen the Beast and Monroe the beauty, for their respective performances), has no such protection; she is instead *stripped* and achingly vulnerable. A *machismo* male is always defined by the toughness of his outer skin, and a sex symbol by the softness of hers. But what a difference. It can be the difference between a survivor and a suicide.

Of course, it is true that to be naked is not always to be vulnerable— though it usually is. But there is another element to consider: Mailer was in a position to choose his role; Monroe was not. Sex was the only thing she knew she had, the only thing she could count on. Every attempt to be something else was either a total failure or a half-failure. Mailer quotes we-don't-know-who quoting Monroe, "I guess they think [rudeness] is happening to your clothing." It is a desperate remark, the remark of a woman who was seen as all surface, who presumably didn't *have* an inner life susceptible to invasion; a woman who knows and finds it, ultimately, intolerable.

Over and over again, what we see is Marilyn not quite managing to be what people want her to be—except, that is, when she is being Beautiful. Jim Dougherty, her first husband, commenting on her separation from Joe DiMaggio, "attributed it to her inability to give a man a good meal . . . and recounted evenings when all [she] served were peas and carrots [because] she liked the colors." How many people marry a woman for her visual culinary aesthetics? She wasn't a good wife, dammit. That's what counts.

Then we have Andre Dienes, a photographer and early lover, returning to visit her in 1961. She is alone. It is her birthday. She is recovering from some female operation. The studio, says Mailer, has been trying to tell her she was insane. Dienes wants to make love to her. Mailer reports her saying, "Do you want to kill me? I have had this operation. You must not be selfish." Dienes' reaction is rage at being betrayed. By whom, or by what? What right did he have? But then what right did *anyone* have? The right never seemed to enter into things.

Mailer further reports (no sorting out truths from fiction here; rather, for the moment, just "suspension of disbelief") Marilyn getting a divorce from Dougherty who says he won't sign the decree unless she goes to bed with him again. Billy Wilder, who directed her in *Some Like It Hot*, remarks, "Flesh impact is rare. Flesh which photographs like flesh. You feel you can reach out and touch it." One is reminded of Maria Schneider's comment on Brando's body not being as beautiful as her own. But what about the *performance*, one asks. The goddamn performance? (Or even just the *person*.) As Mailer says, in his chapter on Marilyn in Hollywood, "Hollywood was built on the contemptuous principle that if an actor was nothing but a mouth, then what could an actress be?" And he seals the coffin only a page later with the words, "We never know which curses, evils, frights, and plagues are passed into another under the mistaken impulse we are offering some exchange of passion, greed, and sexual charge." Mailer is right. More than right. He has grasped the naked truth of it all.

Next we have her in love with her singing coach; a man who says to her that if he dropped dead, it would be bad for his son because, "Don't you see it wouldn't be right for him to be brought up by a woman like you." In Hollywood, she is branded "a freak, a sexual gargoyle, a tart who throws sex in your face. Yes, of course, she would pay for [her] walk in future years when executives would not believe she was a serious actress and cast her in roles which were slowly killing her." Mailer calls it a Faustian contract. And of course, it was. But what else could she have done? It is the absence of alternatives which makes the reader wail with despair.

As Mailer says, "She is probably deprived by these early films of the last chance to become a great artist and still have a little happiness for herself." Speaking of her in 1961 he says, "Whole parts of her psyche had been wounded, bruised . . . thickened and killed by then—and she may have been just a little on the other side of sex."

It is during this time that acting teacher Lee Strasberg, photographer Milton Greene, and playwright Arthur Miller are struggling for possession of her, as if she were a Ming vase, tearing her to pieces in order to save her. The vision of that struggle is one of the most grueling in the entire book: it is no longer a matter of the possession of her body, but of her mind. (Was there *anyone* as concerned with her as with the light she could reflect on their separate egos?) Mailer comments that the one thing Marilyn never knew how to express was anger. She retreated and became passive, the receptacle for everyone's fantasies. Mailer is aware of the enormity of all this. But, one is forced to ask, isn't he contributing to the same thing? Yes, but he thinks that because of his willingness to really "see" and accept her in all of her multiplicity, he is somehow different—and better. The truth is that no matter how much "better" he might have been, each of them thought they were "best" for her, too.

There is DiMaggio loving her but treating her as a trophy. Mailer describes him as feeling that "The highest prize in the world of men is the most beautiful woman available on your arm and living there, in her heart loyal to you." DiMaggio cannot cope with her ambition. There is Billy Wilder who cannot cope with her need to find her own painstaking way into a scene. John Huston, who directed her in *The Misfits,* cannot cope with her lateness, which he considers a "lack of professionalism." Yves Montand pontificates on her "childlike" qualities while delivering the most bitter condescensions. Miller extends his "experience" of life through her, using her as "literary food" (something every writer does, and Mailer knows it, though Mailer resorts to such petty viciousness in his characterization of Miller that he undermines one's willingness to consider the substance of what he has to say); Bobby Kennedy and Peter Lawford invite her to join them and "a couple of hookers."

The catalog of indignities is endless. And Mailer's antennae pick up the nuances of all of them. But even worse than the indignities, finally, is the inability of those who played some part in her life to sustain her "lapses"; to comprehend how desperate was her struggle to become, in that slow process which is the only one available to us, a human being in her own right. Everything was against her. Her weaknesses were as large as the forces which attempted to deny or obliterate her, but that is not at all surprising now. It was only surprising then. Marilyn's lapses were considered gargantuan. As for the world around her and its lapses—well, that's the way things were. There was no measuring rod to gauge the brutality of what was being done to her.

The photographs show her in every imaginable pose and frame of mind, living with her legend and outside of it, sometimes pitifully trying to "fit" her publicity, which Mailer thinks she thrived upon. It is only one example of the application of his own myth to her. I am inclined to believe instead that, since she could not escape them, she tried to use the deliberate mockeries of publicity for self-protection in the same way that a comic uses the joke on himself to both reveal and camouflage pain. It is the role of the Fool given a contemporary twist. And Mailer ought to know. For the real trap of fame is its irresistibility: once it has been taken on, every reaction against it is tinged with ambivalence—"I want to be loved. But no, not that way. No. But yes, that way, too."

Of course, the photographs cannot show her alone. And that is what Mailer has tried to do. In the end, he leaves us with a rather shallow hypothesis about her murder by right-wing government agents in an attempt to embarrass the Kennedys. It's as if he wants to weaken somehow all that he himself has said about the forces within and around her; as if he sensed finally that in the long run, he, too, would have become an accomplice. As if he knew that the temptation was simply too great.

The ending is a cheat. It reinforces the belief that he would have been part of the process which destroyed her. But even with all that, one has, finally, to respect the passionate effort of mind and feeling which he applies elsewhere to really knowing what it must feel like to be a woman; the care and tenderness that goes into the struggle to allow her, by clarifying her to herself, to live again.

"I Want to Go Ahead and Do It" [The Executioner's Song]   Joan Didion*

It is one of those testimonies to the tenacity of self-regard in the literary life that large numbers of people remain persuaded that Norman Mailer is no better than their reading of him. They condescend to him, they dismiss his most original work in favor of the more literal and predictable rhythms of The Armies of the Night; they regard The Naked and the Dead as a promise later broken and every book since as a quick turn for his creditors, a stalling action, a spangled substitute, tarted up to deceive, for the "big book" he cannot write. In fact he has written this "big book" at least three times now. He wrote it the first time in 1955 with The Deer Park and he wrote it a second time in 1965 with An American Dream and he wrote it a third time in 1967 with Why Are We in Vietnam? and now, with The Executioner's Song, he has probably written it a fourth.

The Executioner's Song did not suggest, in its inception, the book it became. It began as a project put together by Lawrence Schiller, the photographer and producer who several years before had contracted with Mailer to write Marilyn and it was widely referred to as "the Gary Gilmore book." This "Gary Gilmore book" of Mailer's was understood in a general way to be an account of or a contemplation on the death or the life or the last nine months in the life of Gary Mark Gilmore, those nine months representing the period between the day in April of 1976 when he was released from the United States Penitentiary at Marion, Illinois, and the morning in January of 1977 on which he was executed by having four shots fired into his heart at the Utah State Prison at Point of the Mountain, Utah.

It seemed one of those lives in which the narrative would yield no further meaning. Gary Gilmore had been in and out of prison, mostly in, for 22 of his 36 years. Gary Gilmore had a highly developed kind of con style that caught the national imagination. "Unless it's a joke or something, I

*Reprinted from the New York Times Book Review, 7 October 1979, 1, 26–27. © 1979 by The New York Times Company. Reprinted by permission.

want to go ahead and do it," Gary Gilmore said when he refused legal efforts to reverse the jury's verdict of death on felony murder. "Let's do it," Gary Gilmore said in the moments before the hood was lowered and the muzzles of the rifles emerged from the executioners' blind. Gary Gilmore's execution in 1977 was the first in the United States in ten years, and the last months of his life were expensively, exhaustively covered, covered in teams, covered in packs, covered with checkbooks and covered with tricks, covering to that point at which Louis Nizer was calling Provo in a failed attempt to add some class to David Susskind's bid for the rights, covered to that pitch at which the coverage itself might have seemed the only story.

What Mailer could make of this apparently intractable material was unclear. It might well have been only another test hole in a field he had drilled before, a few further reflections on murder as an existential act, an appropriation for himself of the book he invented for *An American Dream*, Stephen Rojack's *The Psychology of the Hangman*. Instead Mailer wrote a novel, a thousand-page novel in a meticulously limited vocabulary and a voice as flat as the horizon, a novel which takes for its incident and characters real events in the lives of real people. *The Executioner's Song* is ambitious to the point of vertigo, and the exact extent of its ambitiousness becomes clear at the end of the first chapter, when a curious sentence occurs, a sentence designed as a kind of Gothic premonition. Brenda Nicol, a forthright woman in her thirties who "hadn't gone into marriage four times without knowing she was pretty attractive on the hoof," has gotten a call from the penitentiary at Marion saying that her cousin Gary Gilmore was coming home—by way of St. Louis, Denver, Salt Lake—to Provo. "With all the excitement," Chapter One of *The Exeutioner's Song* closes, "Brenda was hardly taking into account that it was practically the same route their Mormon great-grandfather took when he jumped off from Missouri with a handcart near to a hundred years ago, and pushed west with all he owned over the prairies, and the passes of the Rockies, to come rest at Provo in the Mormon Kingdom of Deseret just fifty miles below Salt Lake."

Against the deliberately featureless simple sentences of *The Executioner's Song*, sentences that slide over the mind like conversations at the K-Mart ("Gary was kind of quiet. There was one reason they got along. Brenda was always gabbing and he was a good listener. They had a lot of fun. Even at that age he was real polite."), the relative complexity and length of this sentence at the end of Chapter One is a chill, a signal that the author is telling us a story of some historical dimension. Notice the intake of breath on the clause "and the passes of the Rockies," notice the long unbroken exhalation that ends in a fall on "just 50 miles below Salt Lake."

It is largely unremarked fact about Mailer that he is a great and obsessed stylist, a writer to whom the shape of the sentence is the story. His sentences do not get long or short by accident, or because he is in a hurry. Where he does or does not put the comma is a question of considerable concern to him: his revisions on *The Deer Park* are instructive in the extreme. Brenda Nicol may not have been taking into account that handcart, those prairies, those passes of the Rockies, but Mailer was, and, in that one sentence, the terms of the novel had laid themselves out: a connection would be attempted here, a search for a field of negative energy linking these events and these people and the empty melancholy of the place itself.

The Executioner's Song, then, was to be a novel of the West, and the strongest voices in it, as in the place itself, would be those of women. Men tend to shoot, get shot, push off, move on. Women pass down stories. "Well, I am the daughter of the very first people who settled in Provo," Gary Gilmore's mother, Bessie Gilmore, said once to herself when Gary was 22 and sentenced to 15 years for armed robbery in the state of Oregon. She said it again to herself on the July morning in 1976 when her niece Brenda and her sister Ida called to say that Gary was under arrest in Provo on Murder One, two counts. "I am the granddaughter and great-granddaughter of pioneers on both sides. If they could live through it, I can live through it." This is the exact litany which expresses faith in God west of the 100th meridian.

I think no one but Mailer could have dared this book. The authentic Western voice, the voice heard in *The Executioner's Song*, is one heard often in life but only rarely in literature, the reason being that to truly know the West is to lack all will to write it down. The very subject of *The Executioner's Song* is that vast emptiness at the center of the Western experience, a nihilism antithetical not only to literature but to most other forms of human endeavor, a dread so close to zero that human voices fade out, trail off, like skywriting. Beneath what Mailer calls "the immense blue of the strong sky of the American West," under that immense blue which dominates *The Executioner's Song*, not too much makes a difference. The place at which both Gary Gilmore and his Mormon great-grandfather came to rest was a town where the desert lay at the end of every street, except to the east. "There," to the east, "was the Interstate, and after that, the mountains. That was about it."

In a world in which every road runs into the desert or the Interstate or the Rocky Mountians, people develop a pretty precarious sense of their place in the larger scheme. People get sick for love, think they want to die for love, shoot up the town for love, and then move away, move on, forget the face. People commit their daughters, and move to Midway Island. People get in their cars at night and drive across two states to get a beer, see about a loan on a pickup, keep from going crazy. It is a good idea to keep from going crazy because crazy people get committed again, and can no longer get in their cars and drive across two states to get a beer. Nicole Baker, Gary Gilmore's true love, got committed the first time at 14. April Baker, Nicole's sister, had been "a little spacey" ever since she got bad-tripped and gang-banged when her father was on leave in Honolulu. "I am a split personality," April said when she was asked about the July night in Provo when she went to the Sinclair service station and the Holiday Inn with Gary Gilmore and he seemed to kill somebody. "I am controlling it pretty good today."

The Executioner's Song is structured in two long symphonic movements: "Western Voices," or Book One, voices which are most strongly voices of women, and "Eastern Voices," Book Two, voices which are not literally those of Easterners but are largely those of men—the voices of the lawyers, the prosecutors, the reporters, the people who move in the larger world and believe that they can influence events. The "Western" book is a fatalistic drift, a tension, an overwhelming and passive rush toward the inevitable events that will end in Gary Gilmore's death. The "Eastern" book is the release of that tension, the resolution, the playing out of the execution, the active sequence that effectively ends on the January morning when Lawrence Schiller goes up in a six-seat plane and watches as Gary Gilmore's ashes are let loose from a plastic bag to blow over Provo. The bag surprises Schiller. The bag is a bread bag, "with the printing from the bread company clearly on it . . . a 59-cent loaf of bread."

The women in the "Western" book are surprised by very little. They do not on the whole believe that events can be influenced. A kind of desolate wind seems to blow though the lives of these women in *The Executioner's Song*, all these women who have dealings with Gary Gilmore from the April night when he lands in town with his black plastic penitentiary shoes until the day in January when he is just ash blowing over Provo. The wind seems to blow away memory, balance. The sensation of falling is constant. Nicole Baker, still trying at 19 to "digest her life, her three marriages, her two kids, and more guys than you wanted to count," plus Gary Gilmore, plus Gary Gilmore's insistence that she meet him beyond the grave, reads a letter from Gary in prison and the words go "in and out of her head like a wind blowing off the top of the world."

Control is fugitive. Insanity is casual. The love-death seems as good a way of hanging on as any other. Gary and Nicole make wishes on a falling star and Nicole has "a rush of memories then like falling down in a dream." Gary's mother Bessie, sitting alone in her trailer in Oregon, gets a call about the murders from her sister Ida and she feels "vertigo at the fall through space of all those years since Ida was born." A sister-in-law of Nicole's thinks of sinking "right into the swamp of misery." A friend of the family is trying to sleep one night, when she hears Gary, whose visit she has declined, shatter her car window with a tire iron. "She let it go. It was just one more unhappiness at the bottom of things."

These women move in and out of paying attention to events, of noticing their own fate. They seem distracted by bad dreams, by some dim apprehension of this well of dread, this "unhappiness at the bottom of things." Inside Bessie Gilmore's trailer south of the Portland city line, down a four-lane avenue of bars and eateries and discount stores and a gas station with a World War II surplus Boeing bomber fixed above the pumps, there is a sense that Bessie can describe only as "a suction-type feeling."

She fears disintegration. She wonders where the houses in which she once lived have gone, she wonders about her husband being gone, her children gone, the 78 cousins she knew in Provo scattered and gone and maybe in the ground. She wonders if, when Gary goes, they would "all descend another step into that pit where they gave up searching for one another." She has no sense of "how much was her fault, and how much was the fault of the ongoing world that ground along like iron-banded wagon wheels in the prairie grass." When I read this, I remembered that the tracks made by the wagon wheels are still visible from the air over Utah, like the footprints made on the moon. This is an absolutely astonishing book.

In Pyramid and Palace
[Ancient Evenings]   Richard Poirier*

Until its final revision, *Ancient Evenings* carried the subtitle "The Egyptian Novel." It was a helpful hint that what was to follow was meant to be quite unlike the so-called "American novel" or the English, French, German or Russian novel. *Ancient Evenings* is indeed the strangest of Norman Mailer's books, and its oddity does not in any important way have to do either with its Egyptian setting or with the exotic career—exotic even by ancient Egyptian standards—of Menenhetet, its protagonist-narrator whose four lives, including three reincarnations, span 180 years (1290 to 1100 BC) of the nineteenth and twentieth dynasties (1320 to 1121 BC). What is remarkable here is the degree to which Mailer has naturalized himself as an ancient Egyptian, so that he writes as if saturated with the mentality and the governing assumptions, some of which he revises rather freely, of a culture in which the idea of the human is markedly different from what it has been in the West for the last 1,500 years or so. Mailer has never before tried anything so perilous, and the prodigious demands he makes on the reader are a clue to his ambitions. This is at once his most accomplished and his most problematic work.

Of the twenty-three books Mailer has written so far, only *Ancient Evenings* achieves the magnitude which can give a retrospective order and enhancement to everything else. Up to now it has been possible to think of him as perhaps a great writer, but one who had yet to write his major book. Many commentators have mistakenly credited him here, and in his last novel *The Executioner's Song*, with a new degree of self-effacement. Looking back from the new book one can see even more clearly than before that the central condition of nearly all his writing depends not on some prior

*Reprinted from the *Times Literary Supplement* (London), 10 June 1983, 591–92, by permission of the author and Times Newspapers Limited.

sense of self, the famous Mailer ego, but rather on self-fragmentation and dispersal. Even when, as is so often the case, Mailer is his own subject, he cannot be said to exist simply in the narrative that tells his story, but is to be found instead within a larger, expressive structure of which his voice is only one part looking for other parts. Just as it radically reduces his literary, let alone his personal identity, to assume that the voice of *Armies of the Night* refers us directly to the "real" Mailer, so it is equally mistaken to assume that because that voice is absent from *Ancient Evenings* he has thereby and suddenly become invisible.

Quite the reverse. The book comes into focus only when we are able to recognize the complicated way in which it is the most self-revealing of his works. Menenhetet, for example, carries out the implications of Mailer's more directly autobiographical writings because even as he tells stories about himself he is by that very process trying to put himself together from several different, remembered versions. This is also the case when Mailer writes about the march on the Pentagon or a championship fight. He treats the earlier Mailer who participated in those events as if he were already a soul or a spirit. The Mailer of the later time not only records but contends with earlier versions of himself, until the work is a record of the abrasions out of which will emerge, or so he hopes, a form he can call himself or his work or his career. The form his narratives achieve is what has survived of "Mailer" from the past, but the achievement is conditioned by a recognition that some of the many selves who make up a single person have been sacrificed to the making of form. Any form, especially for a believer in karmic roots, creates a longing for some possibly larger and more inclusive one. "Karma tends to make more sense than a world conceived without it," he remarks in a recent interview, "because when you think of the incredible elaborations that go into any one human being, it does seem wasteful of the cosmos to send us out just once to learn all those things, and then molder forever in the weeds. . . . There is some sort of divine collaboration going on."

Books of sustained visionary ambition—and this is true even of *Paradise Lost* or *Moby-Dick*—are bound to have stretches of tiresome exposition, phrasings that are ludicrous, whole scenes that, as Johnson remarked, should have been not only difficult but impossible. *Ancient Evenings* has Honey-Ball's scenes of spellbinding in "The Book of Queens." Nearly anything can happen here, and does, and what is remarkable is not that the American reviewers found things to make fun of, but that the risks usually pay off: moments of subliminal ecstasy, visionary descriptions of royal personages, of pools at sunrise and gardens which bring on a kind of sexual swooning, of floatings down the Nile. Mailer seems more at home in the writing than in any of his books except *Why Are We in Vietnam?* He luxuriates, sometimes to the limits of patience and beyond, in accounts of Egyptian low life, in the power put into play during a royal dinner party, in details of costume and what must have been at best a truly awful cuisine.

Near the beginning Meni calmly tells us what it feels like, moment by moment, to be eviscerated and embalmed, and there are equally confident accounts of the practice of magic and of the wholly chaotic polytheism of the Epyptians.

Mailer has imagined a culture that gives formal, and not merely anthropological sanction to what in his other works often seems eccentric or plaintively metaphysical, like his obsessions with "psychic darts" and mind-reading, with immortality, with battles of the gods (Liston and Patterson, it now seems, were later versions of the Egyptian gods Horus and Set), with villainous homosexuality, with magic and sorcery, and with excrement as an encoding of psychic failure or success. Having so often written as if the self had several versions, he is completely at ease with Egyptian names for the seven spirits of the self that continue to exist in different degrees of intensity after death.

Two spirit-forms that figure importantly in this book are the Ka and the Khaibit. The Ka, for which the term Double is a useful but inadequate substitute, is born with a person to whom it belongs and bears his exact resemblance; even after death it is that part of a person that requires the food and drink left for it in the tomb. It also requires sensual gratification. Thus, the Ka of, say, a third incarnation could encounter the Ka of the first and have sexual commerce with him—which means with himself—just as could a Ka with his own Khaibit, or Memory. In fact, Meni, who died mysteriously at twenty or twenty-one and thinks that he may have been one of the reincarnations of Menenhetet, finds himself, soon after the novel begins, kneeling on the floor of the Pyramid of Khufu with the elder Menenhetet's member in his mouth, and while it is an abhorrent experience he realizes that he may be coping, as it were, with himself and that the unpleasantness is a kind of preparation for his passage from the Land of the Dead through the horrors of the Duad to either the upper or the lower world. It is possible to assume that the two forms remain fixed in this position—the time, we can with difficulty work out, is roughly 100 BC—while they visualize the immensely long night of storytelling, the Night of the Pig, when any truth can be told without the fear of retaliation, a millennium back at the palace of Rameses IX.

Whether at the palace or at the pyramid, the scene of the novel is a scene of telling, of narration, of recollection. At the palace, where the reader mostly finds himself, Menenhetet and Meni are more decorously positioned than they are in the pyramid. The elder is telling the stories of his lives to the Pharoah, who hopes by listening and interrogation to become more closely identified with his great ancestor Rameses II, while the younger, his great-grandson then aged six, nestles between his mother, Hathfertiti (who is Menenhetet's granddaughter and, for many years, his lover) and the Pharoah (whom little Meni, using his powers of clairvoyance, knows to be his real father) while his reputed father (Hathfertiti's brother as well as her husband and Overseer of the Cosmetic Box) sulks to one side before eventually absenting himself.

The novel does not yield to summary or to any clear sorting out of family trees, and depends instead on the blurring of distinctions between persons or between historical events and visionary ones. Divided into seven books, possibly in obedience to the seven spirits or lights of the dead, it begins with the awakening of a Ka: "Crude thoughts and fierce forces are my state. I do not know who I am. Nor what I was. I cannot hear a sound. Pain is near that will be like no pain felt before." Some central themes are immediately announced: birth and rebirth, mystifications of identity and of genealogy, elemental dread. Once it has slithered out of the pyramid, the Ka walks through the avenues of the Necropolis in a vague search for the tomb of a friend named Menenhetet II. He finds the tomb, after some suitably macabre incidents, in one of the cheaper neighbourhoods and gradually realizes that he is himself the Ka of Meni II and that next to his partly exposed and deteriorating remains are those of the renowned Menenhetet I, moved from its own much grander resting place by the spiteful Hathfertiti.

After getting acquainted and finding their way into the great Pyramid of Khufu, they begin their recollection, which is also their attempted recollection of themselves. Even at the outset, and with only two figures in question, the effort to distinguish between them takes us into a thicket. And that is where we are meant to be. We are meant to understand that multiple identities, identities that in their passage through time come to blend with one another, are common among the fantastic array of Egyptian gods and therefore among those humans for whom the gods are a paradigm of mortal existence. Any Egyptian of high birth, for example, can consider himself an Osiris, the greatest of the gods (but not always), and can find a pattern for his own past life, or anyone else's past life, in the pains and indignities that were visited upon Him. It is therefore appropriate that Meni, in his bewilderment about himself, should ask Menenhetet to tell the stories that make up the long second book, "The Book of the Gods." The story of Osiris, Isis, and of the bitter, buggery-ridden battles between their son Horus and his uncle Set is a phantasmagoric version of much that happens to Menenhetet as his story unfolds in subsequent books.

Menenhetet, born the son of a whore, has an innovative skill as a charioteer which brings him to the attention of the extraordinarily beautiful and imposing Rameses II or, as he is called, Unsermare. At his side, and assisted by the Pharaoh's pet lion, Hera-Ra, Menenhetet helps turn disaster into victory against the Hittites at the battle of Kadesh. But he is then held responsible for the death of Hera-Ra, who sickened from eating too many amputed Hittite hands, and is exiled for fifteen years as a supervisor of a remote gold mine in the desert. It is there that he learns from a dying friend that a man may be born again by dying during the consummation of sexual intercourse. Bribing his way back into the court of Unsermare, he becomes the commander of troops and then Governor of the Secluded—which means that he supervises the Pharoah's "little queens" while being forbidden their sexual favors.

He breaks this interdiction with Honey-Ball in retaliation against Unsermare for having taken him by "both mouths" before Kadesh. And when Unsermare repeats this violation, this time in the company of some of the "little queens," Menenhetet is driven to the still more dangerous revenge of embarking on an affair with the most exalted of the queens, Nefertiri, who turns out to be one of Mailer's most engaging characterizations. Even as he is stabbed to death by the Crown Prince, he manages to leave within Nefertiri the seed of his first reincarnation. He thereby becomes his own father, though his and, above all, Nefertiri's parentage must be hidden from Unsermare, who is persuaded by Honey-Ball that he has begotten the child with her. And so it goes. The urgent exploratory stories told by Menenhetet and the others are accompanied throughout by an attendant detail so exasperatingly complete as to suggest now and then that Mailer, like Pynchon, cannot resist displays of his encyclopedic researches—said to have included a total absorption of the Egyptian funerary literature called the Book of the Dead.

Mailer has convinced himself that the book must be dense if it is also to be authentic. Thus Meni needs to be told the intricate story of the gods, the Pharoah needs to be told exhaustively about his ancestors. Menenhetet needs to rehearse his lives because each of them is convinced that only a person who can remember and explain his deeds when alive, or when he somehow partook of the life of another, can pass out of the Land of the Dead. And because of the endless mirroring of one life in another and in the lives of the gods, there is, for the anxious spirit, no limit to recollection, no ascertainable boundary.

While over the course of the seven books the various tales do manage to achieve some degree of narrative sequence and development—as they would have to do when all the characters are in search of some kind of teleology—each book also spirals out of and back into the scene of telling, and even that scene is set in a time when events have already become encrusted with centuries of re-telling and interpretation. No American reviewer of the novel has yet noticed the crucial admission by Menenhetet to Meni in the last chapter: that what might be called the Egyptian "gospels" in "The Book of the Gods" constitute an interpretation rather than an authentication of what they report. "If you think of the story of our Gods at the beginning of our travels, I will now confess that I imparted it to you in the way that these Romans and Greeks tell it to each other. That is why my tale was familiar yet different from what you know. For our Land of the Dead now belongs to them, and the Greeks think no more of it than a picture that is seen on the wall of a cave."

Ancient Evenings to some extent resembles Faulkner's *Absalom, Absalom!* or those novels of Conrad such as *Nostromo*, where, as Edward Said describes them, there is "evidence of a felt need to justify in some way the telling of a story." Faulkner and Conrad are more successful than Mailer in creating suspense and expectation within the stories, and among characters vividly differentiated; though *Ancient Evenings* is not lacking in suspense of this kind—it is there in the stunning account of the battle of Kadesh, or the intrigues between the rival Queens, Nefertiri and Rama-Nefru—the design of the book as a whole refers us finally to motives which are as vague as Mailer's or any novelist's motives for writing. Mailer offers none of the illusions so brilliantly sustained by Conrad, that there is something we want to know and that we will eventully know it, that a centre will be located in a wilderness of possibility, that the true shape of a person's life will emerge out of the mysteries that have shrouded it. The disaffection or impatience which many will feel with *Ancient Evenings* is likely to result from the fact that telling and listening have less to do with a desire to get somewhere (unless the reader is satisfied with being told that it has something to do with the saving of souls, and is meant to help Meni and Menenhetet pass through the Duad) but rather to get away from the loneliness, darkness, waste and dissolution which are, interestingly enough, the conditions Mailer has worried about since the mid-1950s as peculiar to the fate of the writer, especially the American writer, in the last half of this century.

It is in this context that one should consider his obsession with buggery. The obsession has in the past carried Mailer into a metaphysics of human biological creativity as a compensation for meaninglessness (the forty-six chromosomes in each cell of the body are, he tells us in *The Prisoner of Sex,* "a nest of hieroglyphics") and from there to a religion of artistic creativity (he had already observed in *The Armies of the Night* that these hieroglyphics are "so much like primitive writing"). Like the building of Hell in the nether regions by Milton's Satan, buggery for Mailer is a perverse response to God's invitation that we join him in the creation. For some centuries—long before Rojack in *An American Dream* refers to an evil girlfriend's backside as "Der Teufel"—buggery has been associated with the Devil's terrain. In nearly all his work Mailer at some point contemplates the significance of a juxtaposition concisely described by Lawrence when in "Pornography and Obscenity" he observed that "The sex functions and the excrementary functions . . . work so close together, yet they are, so to speak, so utterly different in direction. Sex is a creative flow, the excrementary flow is toward dissolution, decreation. . . . "

Though Menenhetet, like the Mailer of "The Metaphysics of the Belly" *(The Presidential Papers),* offers positive theories of scatology, the anus is mostly imagined as the site of evil. But there is also for Mailer a kind of art which is a trope for buggery. Writing about Genet he has referred to those aesthetic acts which "shift from the creation of meaning to

the destruction of it," offering as further examples "the therapy of the sur-
realist artist, of Dada, of Beat." And he continues, speaking now of his own
involvement in this dilemma: "jaded, deadened, severed from our roots,
dulled in leaden rage, inhabiting the centre of illness of the age, it becomes
more excruciating each year for us to perform the civilizing act of contributing to a collective meaning." *Ancient Evenings* represents such an attempt,
haunted by failure, to discover "collective meaning," to create spiritual
(and literary) genealogies that are as strong and mysterious as biological
ones.

Questions of origin soon become, for Mailer, questions also about originality and authorship. It is impossible to claim either of these, so the book
will tell us, without first accepting one's incalculable obligations to a mar-
vellous but murky antecedence. Mailer's (and our) debts to the past, it is
suggested, are enormous; they are also mysteriously entangled and un-
traceable. It is therefore a mistake to suggest, as some reviewers have
done, that because Menenhetet is given "that look of character supported
by triumph which comes to powerful men when they are sixty and still
strong" he is meant to represent Mailer, or that he is Hemingway, Mailer's
precurser. Mailer partakes both of Meni and Menenhetet, who at the end
are transformed into yet another dual figure: a triumphant Icarus-Daedalus.
In the final scene Menenhetet embraces and dissolves into the young man's
Ka as it tries to escape the destructive force of "the abominable onslaught
of offal" and to ascend the ladder of lights, knowing it will take not good-
ness to get to the top, but strength.

The joining has been made possible because Meni comes at last to accept all the stories he has been listening to, and, along with these, all the
burdens of the past. "The tales he has told our Pharoah, had been told for
me as well. It was I whom he wanted to trust him." He cannot disown any
of it because he cannot even know for sure that he did not somehow father
himself or father his own father, whoever that might be, as did Ra in Egyptian mythology. Way back in the book we were told that "The God begets
the God who will be his father. For the Gods live in the time that has
passed, and time that is to come."

Genealogies confound one another to create a future that can call on
the assembled strengths of Menenhetet, Meni, all the characters they have
loved, the Egyptian gods, along with their latest manifestations in Christian
mythology, and, not least, the now enriched figures of Mailer's earlier writings and earlier selves. The "I" in the last paragraphs is a composite of all
these but it is also the creative spirit with whom Mailer associates himself
in an apocalyptic vision that could anticipate either the coming of, in
Yeats's phrase, "the fabulous, formless darkness" of Christianity, or the last
phase of our own civilization:

> A pain is coming that will be like no pain felt before. I hear the scream
> of earth exploding. In this terror, vast as the abyss, I still know more
> than fear. Here at the centre of pain is radiance. May my hope of heaven

now prove equal to my ignorance of where I go. Whether I am the Second or the First Menenhetet, or that creature of our twice seven separate souls and lights, I would hardly declare, and so I do not know if I will labor in greed forever among the demonic or serve some noble purpose I cannot name. By this I am told that I must enter into the power of the word. For the first sound to come out of the will had to traverse the fundament of pain. So I cry out in the voice of the newly born at the mystery of my first breath, and enter the Boat of Ra.

This is, then, Mailer's "portrait of the artist as a young man," but it does not allow, as Joyce's does, for much distinction between that "artist" and the author of the book. If we are reminded of Joyce it is certainly not for the ironic reservations about Stephen implied in the last chapter of *A Portrait* and the first section of *Ulysses,* or even for the moment on the sea shore when Stephen imagines that "his soul had arisen from the grave of boyhood, spurning his graveclothes. Yes! Yes! Yes! He would create proudly out of the freedom and power of his soul, as the great artificer whose name he bore, a living thing, new and soaring and beautiful, impalpable, imperishable." This is a beautiful but forever embarrassing moment in the long history of the artist *exalte,* and Joyce meant to bring into question the prospects of anyone in the twentieth century who chooses to "enter into the power of the word." Mailer has always been frighteningly naive about this "power" and especially—as was revealed by his involvement with Jack Abbott—the privileges that should be accorded it, and he fully endorses Meni's grandiloquence. This is his most audacious book largely because behind it all is the desire, once and for all, to claim some ultimate spiritual and cultural status for the teller of stories, the Writer. Which is yet another ancient and perhaps pernicious story, though Mailer will always need to believe every word of it.

ESSAYS

Encounter with Necessity

Ihab Hassan*

Norman Mailer is a novelist of undeniable power. He is unpredictable, extreme, edgy, and disturbing in the genuine sense that his aim is always to get at the root of things, to impart the radical view of life. His stance, from the beginning, has been one of opposition. In a symposium sponsored by the *Partisan Review* on "Our Country and Our Culture," a chorus of deferential praise and criticism, Mailer spoke out: "Is there nothing to remind us that the writer does not need to be integrated into his society, and often works best is opposition to it? . . . I wonder if there has been a time in the last fifty years when the American artist has felt more alienated."[1]

We know Mailer in many guises: the young liberal who wrote a baleful novel on war, *The Naked and the Dead,* 1948; the revolutionary socialist of *Barbary Shore,* 1951; the hierophant of sexual mysteries and existential nihilism, in *The Deer Park,* 1955; and the new spokesman for Hipsterism, *Advertisements for Myself,* 1959. It is a serious critical error to identify his achievement with his first novel. His earlier interest in socialism has not prevented him from developing the more anarchic point of view of "The White Negro." For Mailer is a novelist of passionate and shifting ideologies, and his shifts are induced by a "capacity for seeing himself," in the words of Podhoretz, "as a battleground of history."[2] The shift from liberalism to radical socialism, and from the latter to anarchic existentialism also shows a determined effort to resist the call of *illusion* in America. This ruthless aversion to illusion, the false promise of hope, piety, and fashion, may be, as Geismar pretends, a central flaw in Mailer's artistic character.[3] More likely, it is the product of Mailer's peculiar demon which Geismar calls "juvenile malice," and which is juvenile only in the sense that it is perpetually protestant. Mailer's demon is obsessed, as all his novels in some way or other testify, with the meaning of *power:* the condition of vitality itself in

*Reprinted from *Radical Innocence: Studies in the Contemporary American Novel* (Princeton, N.J.: Princeton University Press, 1961), 140–51. Reprinted by permission of Princeton University Press.

the personal, social, and historical realms. Ideologies are merely the political foil of this radical awareness of life, as sex is its personal expression. This, in crude outline, is the logic of Mailer's development. It is what prompts him to write a novel—still unfinished—which is a "dissection of the extreme, the obscene and the unsayable," a tale of "heroes and villains, murderers and suicide, orgy-masters, perverts, and passionate lovers," aimed to "destroy innocence."[4] It is also what persuades him to open the novel itself, as a form, to "new moral complexities which I feel are more interesting than anything the novel has gotten into yet." Why not? God himself, as Mailer conceives him, is still on the make, still exists as a "warring element in a divided universe, and we are part of . . . His great expression, His enormous destiny."[5] Men still share God's battle for eventual omnipotence, and their fate is not a mean one. This heroic view of human destiny, however, is subverted by a conviction deep as it is implicit that men can do no more than hurl themselves against the iron walls of necessity. Rebellion and victimization, we see once again, go hand in hand in an apocalyptic battle for ultimate power. The demon-hero and the victim-hero are two personae of man caught in the process of realizing his *being*. Yet the inescapable fact about the process remains the fact of human frustration.

The Naked and the Dead presents a terrifying view of men at war, specifically the invasion of the Japanese-held island of Anopopei which the novel follows from the landing operations to the final mopping-up details. But the war, as we see it in this grinding, blundering campaign, is used as a mirror of vaster social and historical issues, issues that pertain to the kind of world men must live in when the battles are finally won or lost. The dramatic link between these areas of meaning in the novel are Cummings, the brilliant, power-crazed general who directs the campaign, and his staff officer, Lieutenant Hearn, a disillusioned and misanthropic liberal. The war itself is seen in a double focus. It is first observed from the impersonal vantage of staff officers playing a military chess game. This is the vantage of General Cummings and his servile, inept aid, Major Dalleson. But it is also observed from the individual point of view of the men who constitute a reconnaissance platoon headed by the ruthless and efficient Sergeant Croft. (The sole connection between these two areas of meaning—an unbridgeable gulf of prejudice and authority separates enlisted men from the officers—is Lieutenant Hearn who assumes command of the platoon on its final, fateful, and futile mission.) The discrete, personal view of the action, however, is linked again with the broader cultural implications of the novel by means of the "Time Machine," terse and highly suggestive portraits of the men involved, their dreams and background. The thematic structure of the novel is thus seen to be a series of points of view running full circle. At the dead center: an image of man, broken and harried.

The philosophy of history Cummings reveals to Hearn, in conversations charged with irony and silent antagonism, is one in which power looms dominant and unabashed. The future belongs to those exceptional members of the ruling class who can translate the potential of America into "kinetic energy"; the true aim of the war is to supplant the decadent fascism of the Old World by an authority more vigorous and cunning. Our century, as Cummings believes, belongs to the reactionaries; Hitler is our interpreter. The highest value men can achieve is not ethical or religious, as liberals think; it is rather to make men, oneself included, the instrument of one's policy. Men, therefore, must be controlled by hate and fear. And so Cummings lectures Hearn: "I can tell you, Robert, that to make an Army work you have to have every man in it fitted into a fear ladder."[6] This theory Cummings is ready to extend to society at large. The machine age requires the consolidation of power—and for that fear is required. Hence the inexorable conclusion of Cummings: "The natural role of twentieth-century man is anxiety." And again: "Only the innocent are healthy, and the innocent man is a vanishing breed. I tell you nearly all of humanity is dead, merely waiting to be disinterred."[7] This, indeed, is the impression readers take from the novel, though they may be hard put to reconcile Cummings' view with his statement: "There's that popular misconception of man as something between a brute and an angel. Actually man is in transit between brute and God."[8] What is puzzling here is not the apparent contradiction of the General's thought; it is rather the ambiguity in Mailer's vision. For sickness and anxiety are the historical facts which the novel dramatizes; the aspiration to omnipotence—in Croft, in Cummings—though dramatized too, is merely shown to be futile. Thus we sense that even if the divine ambition of the two men may have the illicit endorsement of the author, the explicit statement of the novel asserts defeat. Croft does not climb his mountain, and the General wins the campaign despite himself. Omnipotence, as private motive or historical destiny, gives way to impotence.

The campaign itself is successful. But in the over-all view of the war, absurdity prevails. It is the bungling Major Dalleson who mounts the decisive offensive while Cummings is away; the brilliant maneuver of the latter turns out to be quite pointless. Cummings, who likes to think the whole island is an ocarina on which he plays his tune, is driven to despair by the sudden, irrational lethargy which descends upon his troops. Entrenched in their foxholes and duck-walked bivouacs, they refuse to respond to his will—it is no wonder that the main section of the novel is entitled "Argil and Mold." The image of the invasion army, "like a nest of ants wrestling and tugging at a handful of bread crumbs in a field of grass," describes it all.[9]

The picture is not infinitely more promising when we move from the division to platoon level of action. Croft's platoon is one of the best in the invasion force; it responds to his efficient commands invariably. But there is no real community between the men, no love lost or friendship acknowledged—the relations between Croft and Martinez or Red and Wyman are really no exception. Racial prejudice and misogyny, self-interest and self-pity, and lust seem to be the only feelings most of the men share. The unvarying obscenities, stock attitudes, hair-triggered aggressions, weariness, resentment, and perpetual discontent of the soldiers define their emotional range. The platoon snarls or moans its way to boredom or death. The two men who come out best, in their human and bungling way, are Ridges and Goldstein—they carry Wilson on a stretcher through the jungle, though they could have easily abandoned him. Yet the two, a devout farm boy and a mildly paranoiac Jew, also carry the lowest prestige among their comrades.

Nor is the portrait of the men, taken individually, much brighter. They are all, in some way or other, caught, vexed, or defeated. Thus from Gallagher: "Everything turned out lousy for him sooner or later"; from Croft: "I HATE EVERYTHING WHICH IS NOT IN MYSELF"; from Red: "You keep rolling along and you never know what the hell the score is."[10] The few hopes and illusions they retain after the Depression are shattered by their war experience. And they have little to look forward to: "The months and years ahead were very palpable to them. They were still on the treadmill; the misery, the ennui, the dislocated horror. . . . Things would happen and time would pass, but there was no hope, no anticipation."[11]

The world of *The Naked and the Dead,* on all levels, is a dying world. Instinct rules it, power and fear; idealism makes but a weak, transitory show of itself in the person of Hearn or Goldstein. In the background is American society, the eternal betrayals of the American Dream. Mexicans, like Martinez, "breathe the American fables," but they can never become "white Protestant, firm and aloof"; Jews dedicate themselves to accept injury; and Swedes spend their puberty in coal dust.[12] Even the rich, like Hearn, must pay for their awareness in self-banishment: "A bunch of dispossessed . . . from the raucous stricken bosom of America."[13] In the foreground is the war. The stench of a Japanese corpse fills our nostrils, as it does Red's, and questions the meaning of human endeavor. "Is there really anything special about man?" Red cynically asks. The novel does not allow us to wonder much.

This is the world of the novel. Who, then, are its heroes? Excepting Hearn and Cummings, surely none of the officers. Or is it the enlisted men? Some of these, like Red Valsen, are eternal nay-sayers; some, like Roth, eternal victims; and a few, like Wilson, just average and sensual men. None manages to understand his experience or bring life to account. But it is Cummings, Croft, and Hearn who possess the richest personalities, and it is in their actions that the novel reveals itself.

General Cummings, we have already seen, nurses a vision of his manifest destiny. It is fed on sheer intelligence and power, sheer, that is, because it recognizes no human categories foreign to its aims. His character, nevertheless, is complex and contradictory, is compelling precisely because ruthlessness and sensitivity mingle in it. His consciousness of power is very nearly demonic; a mighty hunger chokes him. In trying to become God, his vision is constantly blunted by the resistance of men, and is constantly thwarted by its own peculiar form of corruption. The trajectory of an artillery shell, the curve of sexual excitation, the pattern cultures trace in their growth and decline—all manifest, as the General broods, the same sudden, sharp death. Against the harsh necessities of gravity or death, Faust can only rage. But Cummings' rage subsides into a shudder. The campaign he wins defeats his most exalted ambition.

Sergeant Croft is Cummings' earthy double. The General wants to mold the curve of human destiny, the Sergeant must climb Mount Anaka, highest peak on the island. Faust here assumes the shape of a Texan hunter—and criminal. For Croft shoots a man dead, though he is merely ordered to fire above the head of the rioters, and he murders a Japanese prisoner, after giving him a cigarette, simply for the sinister excitement of the thing. Croft's sense of his omnipotence, compared to Cummings', is primitive, almost feral. The mountain comes to represent for him everything he must know and conquer, the way to his own immortality. He is repelled and fascinated by it, views it with "awe and hunger and the peculiar unique ecstasy he had felt after Hennessey was dead, or when he had killed the Japanese prisoner."[14] The purity, the austerity, of its peak beckons him, and he contributes to the death of Hearn and goads his men to the breaking point so that he may plant his feet on its crest. But a nest of hornets explodes his purpose; in a scene of sheer horror, the hornets riddle Croft and his men in the last stage of their ascent, following them down the wild slopes like an avalanche of fire. Croft's hunger finds its limit:

> Croft kept looking at the mountain. He had lost it, had missed some tantalizing revelation of himself.
> Of himself and much more. Of life.
> Everything.[15]

Croft and Cummings, the two "demonic" heroes, are balked. Lieutenant Hearn stands between them, the natural enemy of both. But his defeat, though more final, has greater value. And his position in the novel is central from a dramatic as well as thematic standpoint. For Hearn is the dramatic link between the two other men who never meet. His humiliation by Cummings sends him to Croft's platoon, and it is Croft who plots the death of Hearn at the hand of the Japanese before the latter can fully redeem his earlier failure. Furthermore, Hearn shows a secret affinity with the Faustian impulse of the two men he must oppose. He, too, wanted to make the world in his own image and impose his will upon it: "Not a phony but a Faust."[16] But he does not have the passion or confidence or ruthlessness it takes; his intelligence is too skeptical, his disenchantment, like Red's, too thorough. Aloof and somewhat cold, he rebels first against his father and the affluent Chicago society his parents represent. He drifts through the literary circles of Harvard and, later, of New York, drifts away from the inadequacies of a liberal ideology, though Communist intellectuals reject him as a quixotic bourgeois. Faust, we see, is chained to Quixote in the person of Hearn who thinks of himself as an indolent seeker but finds nothing worthy of his acceptance. A rebel first, he becomes a drifter, an outsider, a spectator—till the war. But his contest with Cummings, and with Croft afterward, rescues Hearn from hollow disengagement—one of his mistresses calls him a mere shell. Defeated by the General, who forces Hearn in a symbolic gesture of subjugation to pick up a cigarette butt, and destroyed by Croft, Hearn, nevertheless, finds some dignity in the role of victim. He comes to understand why "it is better to be the hunted than the hunter."[17] The statement is a product of his crisis, the end of his encounter with adversity. It expresses the typical insight of the rebel-victim. In the case of Hearn, it is an advance over the philosophy which so far had shaped his life: " 'The only thing to do is to get by on style.' He had said that once, lived by it in the absence of anything else, and it had been a working guide, almost satisfactory until now."[18]

Hearn's belief in *style* stands in contrast with the belief of Cummings and Croft in *effectiveness*—the form of an action as against its results, the means versus the ends. But in all cases, the characters appeal to no standard outside of themselves, no objective ideal. They have in common the courage of meaninglessness. The demonic hero creates meaning by blindly asserting his will. The victim hero finds meaning in carrying his rebellion to the point of self-destruction. None of the "heroes" in the novel really succeeds in his search, though Hearn, the typical scapegoat—his brother officers think of him as the kind of man they *like* to see humiliated—Hearn comes closer than any other to redeeming the wasteland of Anopopei.

Given its kind of world and its type of heroes, it is not surprising to find that the structure of *The Naked and the Dead* exhibits most properties of the ironic form. The structure, in fact, can be construed as an ironic edifice to the nakedness and mortality of man.

For one thing, its vast sweep over the battlefield, and back in time into the lives of men, creates an image of controlled disorder. Chance, the very form of the book seems to say, is the necessity which controls men. The last section of the novel, and perhaps its weakest, focuses on the ineffectual Major Dalleson, and removes us from all the characters we have got to know intimately, from their trials and tribulations, as if they had all been lost in an absurd cosmic shuffle. From the first movement of the invasion, "Wave," to the last, "Wake," effort is wasted and purpose lost. The ending brings no resolution; the camera simply fades off leaving bubbles on a scarcely rippled surface.

The shifts of point of view, back and forth, from staff headquarters to platoon foxholes impress upon us not only the enormous distance between officers and men, but also the discrepancy between public policy and individual motive. The men are not simply lost in the great erratic shuffles of a military campaign; they are dwarfed by a grand design no one seems fully to comprehend. In the end, some men die and others live, but there is no real change in their outlook and no recognition. Even Hearn dies before he can restore himself in his own eyes or resign his commission. And the episodes Mailer calls "Chorus," a chorus of dissident, rueful, and sometimes bantering voices, manifest an ironic lack of awareness of what the total action means.

Again, the action of time is largely destructive. The "Time Machine" sections, which remind us less of H. G. Wells's science fiction than the vivid "Biographies" of Dos Passos' *U.S.A.*, reveal to us in clipped, poetic form how each character came to be what he is. Mailer's selection of crucial details or actions in these grim histories betrays his deterministic view of the American environment. The Time Machine is a machine indeed, an engine grinding men's hopes. Compassionate as Mailer wants to be, his tone strikes us with a secret sardonic note, as if the author were jeering at the stupid delusions of his characters. The ambiguity is there because the true sympathies of Mailer are divided between victims and oppressors alike. The "humility" of the author of which he speaks in the following confession is incomplete: "It took all of me to be at best a fair rifleman. No surprise then if I was a modest young man when it was all over. I knew I was not much better and I was conceivably a little less than most of the men I had come to know. At least a large part of me felt that way, and it was the part in command while I was writing *The Naked and the Dead*."[19]

The style of the novel reflects the same ambiguity. Cold and dispassionate, it pretends to be objective, naturalistic. Human agony is simply another phenomenon in the universe, mortality a fact of existence. The style brutalizes what it seeks to describe; it reduces the scope of our apprehension to the most common denominator. Yet it allows, despite all this, the straining quality of human life to come through. Here is a characteristic image of soldiers pulling guns through the jungle:

> Once or twice a flare filtered a wan and delicate bluish light over them, the light almost lost in the dense foliage through which it had to pass. In the brief moment it lasted, they were caught at their guns in classic straining motions that had the form and beauty of a frieze. Their uniforms were twice blackened, by the water and the dark slime of the trail. And for the instant the light shone on them their faces stood out, white and contorted.[20]

Rigid, even static, the surface of *The Naked and the Dead* conceals violent life underneath. It is the kind of life hard to disclose, difficult to dramatize, for it is blind and implusive. At best, it can be felt in moments of symbolic intensity—Croft killing the Japanese prisoner or brooding over his unattainable peak, Cummings thrilled by the fire of artillery, and musing over the trajectory of human destiny. (The very fact that sexual imagery is often used, in both cases, to evoke the latent content of their aspiration betrays the depth, the incoherence, of their motives.) Sometimes the pent-up life of the novel reveals itself, less successfully, in perverse gestures—Hearn bumping the General or dropping a map board on his feet, Croft squashing melodramatically a bird in his fist—gestures whose intentions far exceed their occasion. Even the monotonous exploitation of erotic fantasies in the novel may be seen as a clumsy attempt to bring into the open the unspeakable yearnings and frustrations, not exclusively sexual, of the men. It is as if Mailer, knowing that the spectacle of death is not drama enough, were constantly seeking to redeem it with tokens of life, a life he cannot quite define and which he can only express in clandestine ways.

The classic redeemers of death are scapegoats—people like Hearn, perhaps Goldstein. It is they who give to life some form. The form they give to fiction is ironic. If the structure of the novel does not highlight the sole fact of Hearn's victimization, it is because Hearn is sandwiched between two "demonic" characters, as Betsy was flanked by two "tragic" protagonists. Yet the book adapts itself, on the whole, to the existential pattern. Necessity rules the encounter of all. For Hearn there is no self-renewal.

Notes

1. Norman Mailer, "Our Country and Our Culture," *Partisan Review* (May–June 1952), p. 299.

2. Norman Podhoretz, "Norman Mailer: The Embattled Vision," *Partisan Review* (Summer 1959), p. 371.

3. Maxwell Geismer, *American Moderns* (New York, 1958), p. 179.

4. Norman Mailer, *Advertisements for Myself* (New York, 1959), p. 512.

5. Richard G. Stern, "Hip, Hell, and the Navigator: An Interview with Norman Mailer," *Western Review* (Winter 1959), pp. 104f.

6. Norman Mailer, *The Naked and the Dead* (New York, 1951), p. 152.

7. ibid., pp. 153, 276.

8. ibid., p. 277.

9. ibid., p. 41.

10. ibid., pp. 12, 142, 202.

11. ibid., p. 592.

12. ibid., p. 61.

13. ibid., p. 302.

14. ibid., p. 379.

15. ibid., p. 598.

16. ibid., p. 490.

17. ibid., p. 493.

18. ibid., p. 280.

19. *Advertisements for Myself,* p. 91.

20. *The Naked and the Dead,* p. 116.

On the Steps of a Zeitgeist

Jack Newfield*

A beginning in the form of a parody:

Mailer has always been Newfield's favorite writer. He dropped a half-dozen references to Mailer into his book on the New Left. He had gone to the same broken-down high school in Brooklyn as Mailer. Whenever he was bogged down writing a piece, he would use a little trick: he would stop, and read Mailer for an hour, and presto, the images would start flowing again, and his head would be filled with music.

Newfield's friends—writers and first-generation SDS types—were also aficionados of Mailer. Two years ago, Newfield, Paul Cowan of *The Voice*, Jacob Brackman of *The New Yorker*, and Paul Gorman, who is now writing speeches for Eugene McCarthy, went as a noisy claque to the 92nd Street Y to root for Mailer in his debate with those Establishment highbrows, Howe and Podhoretz. Newfield and his friends talked about Mailer all the time, and told each other how much Mailer was an influence on their writing and thinking, particularly in Mailer's fusion of personal, literary, and political radicalism (Cowan and Brackman had both written long, appreciative pieces on Mailer for the *Crimson* while they were still at Harvard).

But Newfield and Mailer did not enjoy much of a relationship. Once Mailer published a letter in *The Voice* rebuking Newfield for certain references to Mailer in a piece he did on the fighter Joe Shaw. Newfield bled. On another occasion, Mailer wouldn't let Newfield interview him on Channel 13. Newfield brooded.

But recently things were looking up. First of all, Newfield was no longer intimidated by Mailer. Second, Newfield once told Mailer he should listen to Bob Dylan because Dylan was an authentic poet. Mailer laughed, but a few months later admitted to Newfield that he was right about Dylan. Mailer also gave Newfield a mention in his nonfiction history of the Pentagon demonstration.

Newfield ached to review that book, but didn't feel confident enough. Then he went to see Mailer's debate-happening three weeks ago with Herbert Marcuse and Arthur Schlesinger. Marcuse is supposed to be "the philosopher of the New Left," and Schlesinger a philosopher for Bobby Kennedy. But Newfield identified with Mailer that night, as usual. When he saw all the New Left kids cheering Marcuse's antidemocratic rationalizations, while ignoring Mailer's shafts of warm wit and cold wisdom, he decided he must do something to rectify the New Left's romantic crush on Marcuse.

Newfield, for a while now, had been bugged with the New Left's faddish tinsel heroes. Debray. Mao. Marcuse. Leary.

*Reprinted from *Bread And Roses Too: Reporting About America* (New York: E. P. Dutton, 1971), 385–90. © 1968 by Jack Newfield. Reprinted by permission of E. P. Dutton, Inc. Originally published in the *Village Voice*.

And how could they not dig Mailer? Mailer, who preached revolution before there was a movement. Mailer, who was calling LBJ a monster while the slide rule liberals were still writing speeches for him. Mailer, who was into Negroes, pot, Cuba, violence, existentialism, bureaucratic depersonalization, and hipsters while the New Left was still a twinkle in C. Wright Mills's eye.

So Newfield, bored with writing about Kennedy, and too angry at the Columbia trustees and Lindsay's cops to be coherent, marched off to redeem Mailer's reputation with the New Left.

Last Friday was to be an archetypal Day in the Life of Norman Mailer, novelist, counterpuncher, filmmaker, mayoral candidate, stud, essayist, egomaniac, and successor to Whitman and Henry James as American Zeitgeist.

At 4:30 P.M., Mailer the Artist was finishing up the editing of his second home movie, *Beyond the Law*, at the Leacock-Pennebaker studio on West 45th Street. Mailer the Artist is quite intense and enthusiastic about his filmmaking.

"I've put six months of my life into this film," he said, which is longer than it took him to write his book on the Pentagon march.

Beyond the Law is described in that book as "a study of detectives and suspects in a police precinct," and it stars Mailer, his friend and actor Buzz Farbar, stockbroker Tom Quinn, welterweight contender Joe Shaw, former light-heavyweight champion Jose Torres, and Pete Hamill's younger brother, Brian. Mailer thinks it is not impossible that he had "divined and/or blundered into the making of the best American movie about police he had ever seen."

"I really wanted to call it *Fallen Angels*," Mailer the Artist said, "because everyone in it looks like an angel."

At 5 P.M. Mailer the Drinker entered a small characterless bar across the street from the film studio. Present were Jose Torres on crutches, with his brother and trainer, Pete Hamill and his brother, Farbar, and Tom Hayden, the revolutionary. Hayden began to discuss revolution with Mailer.

"I'm for Kennedy," said Mailer the Drinker, "because I'm not so sure I want a revolution. Some of those kids are awfully dumb." Hayden the Revolutionary said a vote for George Wallace would further his objective more than a vote for RFK.

But quickly, Mailer and Hayden found two pieces of common turf. Hayden was there because, like the rest of the world, he wanted a small piece of Norman Mailer. He wanted Mailer to help out a movement project geared toward reaching soldiers bound for Vietnam. He wanted Mailer to speak to GIs at a coffeehouse in Columbia, South Carolina. Mailer easily agreed.

But Mailer also discovered he wanted something from Hayden. He wanted to go to Cuba and spend a week with Fidel Castro.

"I want a guarantee," he said, "man to man, that I can see Fidel. Or else, fuck him. I'm not taking any chances of going there and then not seeing him. My time is valuable too."

Hayden said he thought it could be arranged.

At 6:30 P.M., Mailer the Rebel arrived at Dwight Macdonald's apartment on East 87th Street for a fund-raising party for the Columbia University student strikers. They wanted a piece of Mailer too.

Mark Rudd was there with three comrades. The guests included George Plimpton, Art D'Lugoff, Bob Silvers, Frances FitzGerald, plus Mailer's eclectic entourage, which still included Torres, who is rather skeptical about the whole New Left.

While Mailer the Rebel drank bourbons, an SDS kid named Steve made a plea for an immediate $3400 as a down payment for a co-op loft on Wooster Street into which the SDS regional office could move. He explained how SDS had been mysteriously evicted from three offices in the last year. He also explained how SDS sent out a fund-raising letter by Macdonald last week, and had not received any mail since, even letters mailed to themselves as a test. Mailer, the metaphysician of conspiracies, listened. He ended up giving SDS $100 in cash, plus loan of $900 against the receipts of a benefit showing of his first film, *Wild 90*. "I can do this because I'm in debt," he explained.

Then Rudd, who faces six years in jail for his activities at Columbia, began to speak. Mailer the Rebel looked into his open unfinished face.

Rudd said that the fires at Columbia last week were set by police provocateurs dressed as plainclothesmen after the students had left the buildings. Rudd also said that "plainclothesmen began the anticop slogans that started the violence on the sundial. They falsified evidence too."

Mailer the Rebel, nursing his fifth bourbon, interrupted to say, "I'm sure you're telling me the truth in general. About particulars, I don't know. I want the facts. What walls did you paint? What walls did the police paint? You've got to put the police on the defensive. I know that cops create evidence. They've done it to me. All cops are psychopathic liars. Your fight is to show that the people who run the country are full of shit. You've got to come up with the hard evidence of what the cops did. . . . If you win, then America will be a little different place."

Rudd then said something about needing money to pay for lawyers' fees.

Mailer the Rebel, punching his left palm with his right fist, interrupted, leaning forward in his six-button vest.

"Most lawyers are corrupt and filled with guilt. That's the liberal middle-class game, lawyers and fund-raising parties and more bureaucracy. Why don't you kids defend yourselves? If you're cool, and telling the truth, you're better off without lawyers. Let totalitarian America judge each one of your faces."

"We're too ugly," Rudd said, and Mailer mentally gave him that round.

"We need lawyers," Rudd continued, "also to allay the fears of the mothers."

"You have the mothers come to court, too, if you've got the balls," barked Mailer the Rebel, in his Mafia–W. C. Fields voice.

Before he left Macdonald's, Mailer had to remind Steve of SDS that he had not yet written out his promised check. The SDS kid, who had liberated university buildings, said he didn't want to seem presumptuous by pestering Mailer.

As he left, Mailer the Rebel said, "I don't agree with SDS. I gave them the money because they are an active principle. They are taking chances, and they just might be right. I have some sympathies with them, but not intimate agreement. I'm not a Left hard-on. I'm a Left conservative."

Mailer the Celebrity, in a playful, puckish mood, was a few minutes early for the taping of the Merv Griffin television show. So, wearing his pancake makeup, he went off to Smith's proletarian bar on Eighth Avenue, for another drink.

Did he believe what Rudd said about the police?

"One chance out of a hundred some crazy SDS kid set the fires. But one hundred chances out of one hundred some cop did it. I know cops."

Suddenly, a tall, hip Negro faggot aproached Mailer, recognized him, and said he had gone to Choate.

Mailer the Celebrity looked at the man, who had a long knife scar on his face, thinking perhaps of Shago Martin or Sonny Liston, and offered to bet him $100 that he did not go to Choate.

They traded a few verbal jabs, Mailer, in his own judgment, having "to work for my draw," and then split for the television studio.

A little tight, Mailer walked out to face an audience that looked like it was bussed over from the Crimmins murder trial. Empty, pinched faces. They were mindless television fanatics, and Mailer was quite aware that the last time he had been on Griffin's show, he criticized the Vietnam war and was booed by the yahoo audience. But Mailer was up for this one; just before walking out, he had been throwing loving overhand rights that stopped just short of Pete Hamill's smiling face. "Not hitting you, Pete, takes something out of my character," he barked.

"Norman Mailer is one of the leading spectator sports in America," Griffin said, and Mailer swaggered out of the wings, hunching up his shoulders like Carmen Basillio coming to Ray Robinson.

They shook hands and Mailer the Celebrity announced, "My hands are cold because I've been holding drinks for the last two hours."

A current of panic shot through Griffin's all-American face, fearing that Mailer was wild drunk.

"How has the mood of the country changed since you were here last?" Griffin asked, sounding like a Sunday robot-panelist.

"The instances of faggotry have gone up in the country," Mailer said.

"That means more smoking, folks," quipped Griffin.

Griffin then asked Mailer about the Presidential election.

"If Humphrey runs against Rockefeller, I will take the year off and go to Coney Island. . . . Humphrey may slip through because he is a whale who moves like a snake on the way to the hog trough."

Mailer then tossed off passing references to the film *Marty* and Machiavelli, which the yahoo audience did not seem to understand.

"Is this the idiot row?" Mailer barked.

"What is your image of yourself?" Griffin asked.

"An activist."

Suddenly, stand-up comic Morey Amsterdam, a walking file of one-liners, said, "I've come here to learn something, and I'm still waiting."

The audience, finding its spokesman at last, cheered wildly.

Mailer, quite sober by now, then revealed his secret weapon—self-depreciation. "Morey," he said, "once again you've inherited the problem of a landslide."

At 9:30 Mailer the Counterpuncher arrived at Madison Square Garden to see the light heavyweight championship fight between Dick Tiger and Bob Foster. Walking through the smoke-haloed ringside toward his seat, the former welterweight contender, Billy Graham, warmly embraced Mailer, as if he were actually an old fighter. Indeed, Mailer is not built unlike Jake LaMotta, who was standing next to Graham.

Mailer the Counterpuncher wanted Tiger to win, even though Tiger had twice defeated his buddy, Torres. But like any detached professional critic, Mailer was properly impressed by Foster's crunching left hook, which dropped Tiger for the count in the fourth round.

Later, after midnight, Mailer the Zeitgeist traveled up to Columbia and climbed over a fifteen-foot fence to talk to a twenty-year-old named Mark Rudd.

The Prisoner of Sex   Diana Trilling*

[On April 30, 1971,] . . . I participated in a meeting in New York at which Norman Mailer proposed to defend his recently published book, *The*

*Reprinted from *We Must March My Darlings: A Critical Decade* (New York: Harcourt, Brace, Jovanovich, 1977), 199–210, by permission of the publisher.

Prisoner of Sex, against the criticisms of a panel of four women. . . . In a subsequent speech on feminism and women's liberation, not reprinted in this volume, I described the second evening as follows:

In the spring of 1971 a curious, highly publicized and much-attended event—tickets twenty-five dollars in the orchestra, ten dollars in the balcony—took place in Town Hall in New York: Norman Mailer, the celebrated author of a recent book called *The Prisoner of Sex,* his statement on the theme of women's liberation, undertook to defend his views against a panel of women variously critical of the beliefs he developed in that volume. It was no less than a confrontation, though it also turned out to be something of a happening; and it was appropriate that it took place in Town Hall because by imaginative extension the evening might, I suppose, be regarded as a present-day version of an American town meeting: it offered opportunity for the fullest possible exercise of our democratic right to free opinion and expression. I was a member of the panel that evening, the last of the four women speakers on the platform, but there were times in the course of the meeting when it seemed as if everyone in the audience was, if not a speaker, a highly vocal, often inexplicably angry participant in the goings-on. It would be difficult to exaggerate the disorder of the evening: the raucousness, the extreme of polemic, invective, obscenity. Although it was 1971, the spirit was far more that of the sixties than the seventies; and it may be, in fact, that it required an event like this to put a seal on the previous decade of violent demonstration and disruption. The Theater for Ideas, sponsor of the meeting, had, I was told, invited several women to be members of the panel who had either refused outright or backed away at a late moment on the ground that it was an indignity to be chaired by a male, worst of all by the black-souled author of *The Prisoner of Sex.* It seemed to me that objections such as these overlooked the fact that Mailer offered a fair *quid pro quo:* he would chair the evening and in return his female panelists could attack him, his book, and his ideas as freely as they wished. Actually it is the single instance I know of in which the moderator of an evening has wittingly doubled as its victim.

But as it turned out, Mailer was little moderate; it would have been impossible that he should be inasmuch as, from the moment the curtain rose, he was under most intemperate assault from the women in the audience. He of course gave as good as he got in the way of insult and dirty talk, and I found myself glad of this—when I had consented to join the panel I had not contracted to be present at a symbolical slaughter. Still, his working posture, half boss-man and half Old World gallant, was not well contrived to please or subdue: the ambiguousness of being the unwanted chairman of a gathering at which he would manifestly have preferred to play the generous host to his female adversaries made something of a mockery of his customary charm.

And one must surmise that he was thrown off base by Germaine

Greer. Miss Greer was the star attraction of the evening, sufficiently confident of herself to accept with generosity her place as second speaker. This
put her at Mailer's right at the table. She had made public announcement
of the reason why she, unlike others of the sisterhood, had consented to be
on the panel: she wished to meet Mailer and go to bed with him. This was
probably heady stuff even for him. When I arrived in the Green Room of
Town Hall the two of them were already there, together with Miss Greer's
team of BBC television reporters who, much like Mailer's TV retinue on
his Pentagon march, had been pertinaciously attendant on Miss Greer's
tour of America. Mailer and Miss Greer were being photographed together
by a score of cameramen with Mailer holding up, not his own book, but
Miss Greer's recent volume, *The Female Eunuch*, for the cameras. If an
old-line feminist like myself expected an audience of militant women to
take it amiss that one of their foremost agitators publicly grasped the educa-
tional occasion as an opportunity to forward her personal ambitions, both
sexual and commercial, I obviously failed to appreciate the distinguishing
contemporary fact that by being so overt about her desires Miss Greer had
scored a victory for our sex: transcending reticence, she had transcended
traditional femininity and moved all of us up a notch in the scale of male-
female equality. Throughout my speech, friends in the audience later informed me, Miss Greer behind me passed little notes to Mailer, an upstag-
ing technique for which she had already become known from various public
appearances: if it was perhaps not an entire success in diverting the audience from what I was saying, it must have been distracting enough for the
chairman. At any rate, it is so that I account for his sharply calling time on
me in the middle of what I am afraid was the only admiration he was to
receive that evening for the poetic force of some of his writing on the relation of the sexes.

   But the fact that I was permitted to give my speech at all was remarkable: a plan to disrupt the meeting just before I spoke failed. Jill Johnston,
columnist for the *Village Voice* and a leader of the Radical Lesbian group
which had recently announced its imperial role in women's liberation, was
the third speaker of the evening. At the conclusion of her talented remarks
two of her young women friends, like herself dressed in well-patched jeans
and boy's shirts, rushed to the stage and the three of them, locked in embrace, having lost their balance, rolled on the floor, hugging and kissing.
It was a miscalculation to have thought that a Lesbian exhibition could
break up a meeting like ours—in New York City, 1971, no curtains were
rung down, no one was outraged unless it was Mailer; it was he who demanded, in what must surely be the nicest malappropriateness of the era,
"For heavens sake, Jill, act like a lady!" To make ostentatious perverse love
in the sight of an audience which, with the best will in the world, finds
itself unable to be shocked is bound to be deflating, and soon, in some embarrassment, Miss Johnston and her friends slunk away.

   But apparently it was not alone in addressing Jill Johnston that Mailer had used the word "lady." At some point in the discussion he seems to have referred to me, in all apparent neutrality of intention, as a "lady writer," or it may have been a "lady critic," and now, when it came to the question period, a member of the audience inquired of me whether I didn't object to this designation. The question was so mild that I took it to be a mere formality of friendly participation from the floor. I replied that perhaps I ought to object but actually I didn't. My answer was careless, in the mood of the moment. At a meeting in which all sexual differences were being wiped out not merely on behalf of equality for women under law and in the world of work but for all purposes of life itself; in the context of an evening in which one half of the human race, man, was being treated as expendable, I felt the need to separate my position from that of the other women panelists and their audience and, at any cost, to put myself on the side of sexual duality. It was only when the dust of the evening had settled and I was no longer moved to counter the extremity of opinion and behavior which had characterized the discussion that I let myself see that the question was of course not an expression of concern about the genteel connotations of the word "lady"; it had seriously to do with professional condescension to women. It was addressed to the pejorativeness in the mechanical sexual differentiation Mailer had indulged in, and its point was not negligible: to be a lady writer, a woman writer, a female writer is not the same as being a writer. It is a professional value judgment; implicitly, a *de*value judgment, analogous to the implied condescension with which one speaks, say, of a male nurse: no nurse is a lady nurse, she is *a* nurse. No man is a man writer, he is *a* writer. The unqualified professional category, the literary profession itself, is apparently the property of the ruling sex, and women who enter it require identification tags, like visitors at an army installation. . . .

It was in this context that I delivered the speech which I reprint here.

When, some weeks ago, I was first asked to join the discussion this evening, I of course already knew that women's liberation represented no single movement, no single point of view about the condition of women, but that it probably had as many definitions as there were women attracted to the idea of changing their lives or men aware of the mounting tides of female unrest in our society. I knew that there were those for whom it provided a new strategy of personal assertion, those for whom it offered a new occasion for cultural and institutional assault, those for whom it meant a long-delayed revivification of the women's rights movement which once went under the name of feminism, those for whom it was a prophetic vision of an erotic utopia, and those for whom it was Thurber's war between men and women as it might be formulated, twenty-five years after he had created *his* fancy, in the darkest imagination of the Pentagon. What I did not know, and learned only as I heard that one woman speaker after another was refusing to participate in the occasion, as if under penalty of some special ingenuity of female torture should she submit to the presence of a male chairman, in particular this male chairman, was that women's liberation was an authoritarianism already notably advanced in purpose and efficiency. Here we have accomplished virtually nothing on behalf of women other than perhaps to open a first outer door on grievances which we have either suppressed or lived with in loneliness: are we already so sure we can name the enemy and get him into our gunsights? To me, such certainty—certainty as virulent as this—would seem to suggest that among women no less than among men the energies we have most ready to us are the energies of rage and imposition, we who are supposed to be so contemptuous of governments, or sexes, that rage and impose.

Well, I am not at all sure that I am able this easily to identify the enemy of my sex. But much as I dissent from some of the attitudes which inform Norman Mailer's recent book about women, I am fairly certain it is not Mailer. Knowing him, I know he will forgive me for saying that, big as he looms on the modern literary scene—and I long ago put myself on record as considering him the most important writer of our time—he is not *that* big. He is not as big as biology, for instance, or culture. Certainly he is not as big as the combined forces of biology *and* culture.

Although, as I recall, Mailer makes little or no explicit mention of biology in *The Prisoner of Sex,* the concept of biology permeates it. Indeed it is biology which provides the chief determinant of Mailer's view of the relation of men and women. This cannot come as an entire shock to anyone acquainted with his work: one could have deduced much of his present position from his old and continuing rejection of birth control. Still, I doubt that we could have been entirely prepared for this degree of biological emphasis in a writer who, in so many areas other than that of the relation of the sexes, has been so pre-eminent a spokesman for the unconditioned life: an unconditioned culture and an unconditioned politics. After all, was it not Mailer who, for our time and far more immediately than D. H. Lawrence, made the conjunction—it is no minor one—between social-political revolution and a revolution in personal consciousness? Nothing, surely, puts a more terrible shackle upon unconditioned selfhood, nor more effectively weakens the metaphors by which we undertake to make a revolution in personal consciousness, than to introduce into our imagination of life, as Mailer does in *The Prisoner of Sex,* the stern determinisms of nature.

And in fact one has only to turn from Mailer's piece to another current statement on the situation of the sexes, Germaine Greer's *The Female Eunuch,* to recognize how great is the breach which an emphasis, like Mailer's, on the biological determination of life makes between, on the one hand, a willingness to confront this fundamental condition of our sexual being and, on the other hand, the dominant mood of our radical times. As whoever has read Miss Greer's book must recall, biology is finally the vanquished villain of *The Female Eunuch.* (Psychology is also defeated but in 1971 this takes fewer pages—seven and a half to be exact.) Miss Greer's

vision of female transcendence starts nowhere if not in the need to rid ourselves of biology other than in a single manifestation, that of female sexual
desire. It would appear that in the service of sexual impulse anything is
well lost for Miss Greer: love, motherhood, the nurturing instincts, even
the pleasures of a developing relation with the same lover. For Miss Greer
sex is not sex unless it is *only* sex, a triumphant refusal of any other of the
forms in which libido may present itself. *The Female Eunuch* is said to be
a book about feminism. I find this misleading, as if we were to say of Norman O. Brown's *Life Against Death*, with its celebration of the polymor-
phous perversity of infancy, that it is a book about what we have always
wanted to know about children but were afraid to ask. Actually Miss
Greer's book is its own call to a new order of consciousness in which the
fullest possible unhindered release of female sexual impulse will alter our
way of personal feeling and, in consequence, alter the way in which we
conceive society.

In fact, it is perhaps not to Mailer but to Miss Greer and the Radical
Lesbians, to all the strange contradictory voices which make the present-
day chorus of radical female protest that we should attend if we are to hear
our latest message of a society altered by a revolution in consciousness. But
this is not to say that Mailer cedes his rule of the kingdom of metaphor
without a last flourish of trumpets—for in a world as crowded and desperate as ours, what is it except a figure of speech, a discordant one, to ask for
the constant apotheosis of sex in parenthood? Even as he professes the
stern actualities of biology, Mailer reveals his attraction to what I would
call the *poetry* of biology, and in so doing takes his place in line with those
major male writers of our century who, like him, are so vulnerable in terms
of social reality and with whom he is linked in the attack upon him by militant women—D. H. Lawrence and Henry Miller were similarly concerned
with the body as the gateway to heaven.

And yet, much as my own taste runs to prose in matters which have
to do with the proliferating—and starving—populations of the world, and
vigorously as I oppose myself to the dangerous poetic excess of Mailer's
stand against contraception, I as vigorously disincline to join his current female opposition. For the plain fact is that I prefer even an irresponsibly
poeticized biology to the no-biology-at-all of my spirited sisters. I think the
former proposes, at least where life is supportable, not only more but better life.

But even as I reject the antibiological views of the extreme female liberationists, I also disincline to join any attack upon them which has at its
source the wish to protect the sexual culture in which we now live. Mailer
accepts little of our general culture, but he does accept much of our sexual
culture as given, in particular that part of it which has to do with the relative status of the sexes. Where I separate from most of the radical liberationists who are winning the facile assent of women understandably troubled by their present sexual situation is that women's liberation seeks a

culture which will invalidate the biological differences between men and women. Where I separate from Mailer is that, while honoring biology, he implicitly acquiesces, as I do not, in the intolerable uses which culture has made of the physical differences between the sexes.

In this, Mailer, who I know thinks of himself as in remorseless disagreement with Freud, in actuality gives support to Freudian doctrine precisely where I believe it to be most absolutist and questionable. Freud's use of the words "activity" and "passivity," male activity, female passivity, have recently come under hostile examintion by women concerned with women's role in society; and justifiably so. Almost unavoidably the words themselves, in our culture, imply a value judgment, favorable to "activity" as being energetic, positive, productive; unfavorable to "passivity" as being lax, inert, uncritically receptive to whatever may be socially given. Even as a description of male and female roles in mating the words suggest what is unacceptable, the man is the seeker and woman the yielder or object. For an active woman to be told that hers is the other, the passive role, activity being the prerogative of men—surely this must seem the very negation of spirit. And applied to the conduct of the sexes in coupling it suggests the denial to women of their full freedom of initiation and participation.

But in anatomical fact the distinction between the active and passive sexual roles is an ineluctable condition in nature. Granted that there can be sexual pleasure for both men and women which is attained without activity on the part of the male; sexual union cannot be achieved without it, nor the propagation of the species. It is nevertheless one thing to accept this irreversible condition in nature and yet another to carry it beyond its biological confines as Freud did when he said that men were the makers of culture and that women mustn't interfere with man's life in culture. In a paper she wrote a few years ago, Dr. Phyllis Greenacre, an eminent woman psychoanalyst—it was she, by the way, who discovered that babies are often born sucking their thumbs, thus releasing mothers from yet one more blame for the terrors of the race—conjectured that perhaps the reason why men have made the major artistic and intellectual contributions to civilization lies in their possession of a thrusting assertive inquisitive external genital; and in something of the same speculative spirit Dr. Erik Erikson speaks of the existence in women of something he calls "inner space" by which they define their sense of themselves and their gifts. It is not my impression that either of these talented clinicians is undertaking to put limits on the capacity of women to employ and enjoy their fullest possible range of activity outside the home. But Freud unhappily is undertaking exactly this and so I think is Mailer though he doesn't put it as bluntly as the middle-class Viennese physician. It is required, then, that we remind Mailer that just as there are men who make no thrust toward the new and untried, there are women who refuse to be imprisoned in inner space even though their sense of themselves may in some important degree be conditioned by it. I defer to none in my regard for Freud. But I take from him only that which affirms and adds to life, discarding from his work, as from the work of anyone, including that of Mailer, including that of the female liberationists, whatever is impoverishing or absolute.

And among those efforts of the women's liberationists which I find most impoverishing, most absolutist, is the doctrine now being promulgated on the female orgasm. I find it remarkable that the same people who properly criticize our society for its hard treatment of homosexuals have no hesitation in dictating to women—and it *is* dictation, make no mistake about that, especially when it is directed to the young—where they are to find their presumably single path to sexual pleasure. I am talking, of course, about the campaign now being mounted to persuade women that there is no such thing as a vaginal orgasm, and that they therefore might just as well dispense with men even in bed. This is one-dimensional neurological map-making falsely representing itself as psychophysiology in depth, and it takes meanest advantage of the endemic ignorance about our bodies, perhaps especially in their sexual uses, which still persists into our present day of supposed enlightenment. So swift and strong, indeed, is the effect of anything which offers itself as scientific sexual information that we may have already reached the stage where whoever would wish to increase rather than thus narrow the range of women's sexual responsiveness will be thought to be boasting an unnatural advantage. Nothing in the sexual culture of recent decades has been more justifiably attacked than the idea that there is a single definition of what is or is not normal in sexual desire and response. As an added benefit of our deliverance from a presumptuous and even tyrannical authority in our choice of sexual partners or in our methods of pursuing sexual enjoyment, it would be good if we could also be free to have such orgasms as, in our individual complexity, we happen to be capable of, without having to consider whether they are of a kind and source which further the politics of sex.

If, however, I find it sad and dangerous that the nature of the female orgasm has now been brought into the realm of sexual politics, I find it appropriate that a political attitude be brought to bear on many matters in which the personal impulses naturally take a public form. Mailer makes the assumption—and here I am moved to charge him with disingenuousness since his experience must necessarily have demonstrated the opposite—that not just a few but most, perhaps even all, women are wholly fulfilled in love and motherhood and that unlike men, they have no unused libido which presses for sublimation in art or in work. He fails to confront even the fiercely practical fact that women often have to support themselves and the babies he recommends to them in such abundance and that in consequence they require not only equal opportunities with men and equal rewards but also special protections demanded by the special biology which he celebrates. These are indeed political concerns and proper issues for public agitation. I have just come from Harvard in Cambridge, Massachusetts. At Harvard at this moment there are twelve women assistant professors together with a few dozen female tutors and teaching assistants. Harvard is Mailer's university; does he know these figures? These women carry a man-sized share of the teaching duties of Harvard but they will achieve faculty rank and tenure only when there will be enough political agitation to shake the men who rule the university out of their complacent superiority. Otherwise, as things stand, there is no rank or tenure for women at Harvard.

Biology is all very well, Norman. All these women have biology and they might be happy to celebrate it with you. But they have, as well, a repressive, life-diminishing culture to contend with. Your book *The Prisoner of Sex* has your always-beautiful intention of life enhancement and also, in its own particular way which is your particular way, a splendid imagination of women: I suppose we could describe it as the imagination of women in love. It nonetheless fails in its imagination of the full humanity of women, and this is a charge which no one would be impelled to level against your imagination of men.

Norman Mailer and the City of New York: Faustian Radicalism   Martin Green*

As announced above the mind of Dr. Faustus was fain to love forbidden things, after which he hankered night and day, taking unto himself the wings of an eagle in order to search out the uttermost parts of heaven and earth; for his forwardness, lawlessness and wantonness pricked and goaded him to such a degree, that the time came when he decided to try out and put into action certain magic words, figures, characters and conjurations in order to summon up the devil before him.

And this apostasy was nothing more nor less than his pride and arrogance, despair, audacity and insolence, like unto those giants of whom the poets sing that they carried the mountains together and were fain to make war on God, yea like unto that evil angel who opposed God, and was cast off by God on account of his arrogance and presumption.

Quoth Faustus ragingly, I will know, or I will not liue, wherefore dispatch and tell me.[1]

MAILER AND POLITICS

The city of New York is itself a Faustian temperament; in its buildings, in its street scenes, in its racial and political tensions, in its social harsh-

*Excerpted from *Cities of Light and Sons of the Morning: A Cultural Psychology for an Age of Revolution* (Boston: Little, Brown, 1972), 58–59, 62–67, 75–78. Reprinted by permission of the author.

ness, it contains a series of violent reachings toward power, and excessive and forbidden power; which a visitor, even if he arrives from another of the world's metropoles, can feel on his nerves as a dangerous stimulant and challenge. It is no wonder that now, at the climax of the city's world-career, a group of writers are to be found who express it, take its temperament as their subject, reenact that in their style and sensibility. And it is no wonder, though it could not have been predicted, that the genius among them should be the one who expresses his city, relates to it, represents it, in the most various ways—including straight political representation.

In 1969 Norman Mailer ran, with a Left Conservative program, as candidate for the Democratic nomination as mayor of New York. He offered the policy of making the city into the fifty-first state, and analogously, of giving power to its neighborhoods so that they could design community life-styles, each for itself. Some could be integrated, some segregated; some could make church attendance compulsory, some could practice free love. Financing would be made available so that slum areas could be re-built room by room, to the occupier's taste and with the occupier's participation. Once a month every machine except those absolutely necessary would be stopped for a "Sweet Sunday." There would be a monorail around Manhattan and a free jitney bus service. There would be craftsman training and pollution control, legalized gambling and neighborhood cable TV, vest-pocket neighborhood colleges and weekend wrestling jousts for adolescents in the public parks.

The idea of Mailer as mayor was a comic one for several reasons. The one most relevant here is that Mailer is a writer; and I mean that his ideas on political subjects and his performance in political affairs are those of a literary man. In *Armies of the Night* his theories of the Vietnam War, and of the march on the Pentagon, are in the style of D. H. Lawrence while his behavior over the weekend was in the style of Dylan Thomas or Brendan Behan. Both his principles and his practice are governed by a highly literary sense of what constitutes style and what constitutes authenticity, of what is offensive and absurd, and when things become boring, and which is the step you absolutely refuse to take. That is why it was funny for most of us to think of his becoming mayor. But it did not mean that his politics were invalid. He was running seriously in his own opinion, and by any objective standard of seriousness the other candidates had quite as much against them as he had. I at least found his proposals admirable; and if we couldn't imagine the voters taking them seriously, that could have caused sadness rather than laughter.

So the striking thing is that we should find the idea of a writer becoming mayor comic. It is true that Mailer is also, in his words, an egomaniac; which always gives rise to a certain amount of nervous laughter from others. But that brings us back to the same point, for only an egomaniac writer *could* run for mayor of New York. Anyone else would "realize" that he "shouldn't." And it is typical of Mailer's services to literature that he should break through such inhibitions, which are inhibitions with plenty of common sense and common sensibility to them, to be broken only with much expense of adrenalin and sweat and hot flushes of shame and rage.

But I don't want to deplore the sheepishness of our profession. My own voice is too close to a bleat to be a proper vehicle for that particular truth. I want to reflect on the special case Mailer presents, of a writer oriented toward the city he lives in, feeling a mission to save it, a radical and political mission. It is rare, surely, to find an important writer who is concerned about the political workings of his own city or country with the same passionate concern as he brings to his writing. Such a writer needs a range of gifts that goes beyond the strictly literary; and he must be aiming at being a great man. As Rousseau said, "Although it is not impossible for a writer to be a great man, it is not by writing books, either in prose or verse, that he will become one." In most of the writers we call great, as in Mailer, we can trace the effects of a Faustian bargain. But even among that group Mailer stands out as the one most directly related to politics. Lawrence and Tolstoy, though men with an immense range of gifts, are not comparable from this point of view. Neither had, for instance, Mailer's gift—so rare among literary men—for public political speaking.

Nor had Goethe, but it is Goethe I offer as the great predecessor and contrast for Mailer. (In fact as a young man Goethe *was* told by a phrenologist that he was born to be a public speaker; but this only alarmed him—or so he says—as meaning that all the professions he was actually considering would be wrong for him; because there was in Germany then no political career open to him in which he could have used those talents.) For more than fifty years Goethe took a hand in governing the city and the state of Weimar, and during the first ten he was in many ways the chief minister. He too might have described his political philosophy as Left Conservatism, and when he first came to office he was distrusted for the wildness of his personal behavior. He had opted, before he reached Mailer's age, for a much more conservative style than Mailer. But that was partly because there was an aristocracy for him to belong to—except under ducal patronage he would never have reached public office. And if there were an aristocracy to join today, would not Mailer join it?

The contrast between them—the standard images of the two men could hardly be more different—derives largely from Goethe's determination to cultivate other temperamental potentialities, to cancel the Faustian bargain and to abide by the standard civilized and cultural contract. Most notably when he abandoned Sturm und Drang for Weimar, but again and again later, he decided to live by the values of society and knowledge and culture. Mailer has always refused to do that. Though a man of learning and a leader of opinion perforce, he has established his identity in his acts of dissent and dissociation from everything established. But because there was an element of the daimonic in Goethe's conservatism, and an element of the conservative in Mailer's Faustianism, the two have some interesting similarities nevertheless. Neither man has any significant traces of a Calvinist or party-ideological temperament. The elements of radicalism in their politics are due much more to their Faustianism, which makes them both hostile to liberal moderation. One sees that in their fascination by great men, power-figures, as well as in their own performances. Take for instance Goethe's fascination with Napoleon; his identification with the imperial adventurer's cause as against that of the German liberals and nationalists. In Mailer's case, take his fascination with Lyndon Johnson and with Barney Oswald Kelly (of *An American Dream*). In both writers this fascination is a natural extension of their feeling for striking personalities and against worthy causes—for Karl August and Byron in Goethe's case, for Sonny Liston in Mailer's case, against liberal enthusiasms in both cases. Both men study power in other personalities in order to acquire it for themselves; though they normally present themselves as powerful, in relation to someone yet more so they portray themselves as strikingly naïve.

Wilhelm Meister is the story of a young man acquiring power of personality by this kind of study in the world of the theater. (The theatrical profession, because it teaches men how to appropriate powerful meanings to their bodies, is a vocational arena for transacting the Faustian bargain.) In Mailer's case, take his imaginative relation with Hemingway, or Sergius O'Shaughnessy's relation to his tutors in *The Deer Park*. (You see the same thing in Kingsley Amis, a similar temperament; the heroes of his early novels habitually oriented themselves toward older, masterful men, in apprenticeship; for instance Patrick Standish in *Take a Girl Like You*.) The left elements in their politics derive not from any radical ambition to reform the world—any general uniformity of salvation would disgust them—but from an Erasmian-humanist decency. These elements are therefore not very emphatic.

POLITICS AND LITERATURE

One day no doubt Mailer will give us an account of his adventures in politics, whether or not he ever takes office. And that is likely to make a very good book, because the subject matter is well suited to the form he has made his own, and has made the characteristic literary form of our generation, the autobiographical narrative in which different voices and genres play against each other as well as playing together. His two most brilliant successes in this genre are *Advertisements for Myself* and *The Armies of the Night*, though *Presidential Papers* and *Cannibals and Christians* are also interesting books with brilliant things in them. In *Advertisements for Myself* the contrast in voices and forms is most obviously a contrast between on the one hand the essays and fiction he is reprinting, and on the other the present-tense reflective narrative that connects them. In *The Armies of the Night* we have first the "History as a Novel" and then "The Novel as History." The discontinuity of forms is less striking, but there is the same thematic contrast between the outrageously indiscreet and personal, and the powerfully insightful and reflective. That contrast is primary because this is a Faustian form; in formal terms the contrast rehearses the Faustian bargain; by being outrageous one makes oneself insightful. The artistic success of the genre lies in the connection made between those two, the way they feed each other and stimulate each other and interact. This is what makes it possible, approaching literature even from the point of view of form, to call Mailer the most important writer of his time. He recognized *our* form; Mary McCarthy achieved her best book, *Memories of a Catholic Girlhood*, by virtue of that form. Mailer made something marvelous out of it.

His political style has a similar combination of the willfully indiscreet and the solemnly prophetic. That style marks the influence of his literariness on his politics; and the influence of his political engagement on his writing accounts for some of that substantiality which makes him superior to most people writing today. He has been more serious and more responsible in his relation to his city and his country than most of them have, than most of us. But Faustian is the crucial interpretive term here too; there are strong elements of nihilism and anarchism in his political outlook. One need only remember "The White Negro," still one of his most powerful and authentic pieces, to be convinced of that. Against his *New York Times Magazine* piece for May 4, 1969, "Why Are We in New York?" which opened his mayoral campaign, we must set something reported in the daily *Times* of March 4. This was a Theater for Ideas discussion of "The End of the Rationalist Tradition?" with Peter Gay and Jean Malaquais defending rationalism, and Mailer and Fiedler attacking it. Mailer's opening statement declared that the logical end of rationalism was the present pollution. "The only way to end smog is for the citizens to get muskets, get on barges, go to Jersey, and explode all the factories." And he insisted that this was not the fault of capitalism—that socialism would do exactly the same. It was not a matter of politics but the consequence of rationalism, of the Western *mind*, no matter what its political persuasion. Fiedler is reported as recommending a return to myths and to "the power of positive unthinking." "The new irrationality is not directed at building something where nothing was, but it is directed against the city, the university, against the antiseptic, therapeutic church. . . . Reason, although dead, holds us with an embrace that looks like a lover's embrace, but turns out to be a rigor mortis. Unless we're necrophiles, we'd better let go."

Clearly, neither man was at his most considered or serious in this debate. But then neither man sets great store by being considered or serious; they hope to reach significant truth rather by being excited and paradoxical. They are, as they say, irrationalist. It is a central part of Faust's bargain with the devil, according to Goethe, that he will give up the use of reason, inasmuch as it has to do with ratio and proportion; that he will exceed all bounds and limits in reaching for mysterious truths and powers. There is a fairly widespread school of such thinking today; Norman Brown and McLuhan are other representative names. So it is fair, I think, to take what they said seriously, and to note that even just before his mayoral campaign Mailer was ready to represent—only temporarily and fragmentarily, no doubt but vatically—forces that defined themselves as hostile to the city, along with the university and the church.

Fiedler I want to associate generally with Mailer in this discussion, because I think he represents the same forces, the same temperament of mind, and represents it in the field of literary criticism and scholarship. By associating the two, I can exemplify the operation of that mind in literature as a whole much more variously. Fiedler projects the same overweening egotism—"I have heard from time to time reports of friend separated from friend or lover from lover by arguments over one or another of my essays" (*No! In Thunder*)— and is equally irrationalist. In *Waiting for the End*, for example, he predicts the end of the novel, on the grounds that the form cannot live any longer than that eighteenth-century faith—now dead—in the power of writers to subdue the unconscious to reason. Nowadays we know that the unconscious is much the more powerful of the two. The form that succeeds the novel will be nonliterate, he predicts, and with the end of literacy and rationalism will come the end of conscience, moral individualism, and all of liberal culture. He sees the white Negro as the child of the love match between Huckleberry Finn and Nigger Jim, and endorses this orgiastic chiliasm as a solution to American society's ills.

Mailer and Fiedler are among the most scathing of all rejectors of liberalism. This is natural, since liberals are essentially men of reason and men of the city. That is why these two are the men my argument must immediately engage with, in order to show where it stands, how it defends itself, in calling itself liberal. From several diatribes by Mailer, let us take an early example, from the 1962 *Esquire* piece on the Patterson-Liston fight.

> I could even wonder . . . whether the entire liberal persuasion of America had rooted for Floyd in the same idle, detached fashion as myself, wanting him to win but finding Liston secretly more interesting, in fact, and indeed, demanding of Patterson that he win only because he was good for liberal ideology. I had a moment of vast hatred then for that bleak gluttonous void of the Establishment, the liberal power at the center of our lives which gave jargon with charity, substituted the intolerance of mental health for the intolerance of passion, alienated emotion from its roots, and man from his past, cut the giant of our half-awakened

arts to fit a bed of Procrustes, put Leonard Bernstein on the podium, John Cage in silence, offered a National Arts Center which would be to art as canned butter is to butter, and existed in a terror of eternity which built a new religion of the psyche on a God who died, old doctor Freud, of cancer.

Practically all of Mailer's case against liberalism gets mentioned there, its hostility to passion, to the arts and to religion, and its worship of mental health—its anti-Faustianism, its Erasmianism of temperament. It is true that there is a moral puritanism in the original self-condemnation; that he, as a liberal, had supported Floyd in an "idle, detached fashion"; he had not scrutinized his motives with sufficient severity. But honesty with oneself is only one half of his remedy against the fault, and the other half is less reassuringly old-fashioned; a commitment to the life of the senses and to those emotions not preprogrammed and preguaranteed by the superego. That is the Faustian remedy, and dangerous enough.

· · ·

SOME HISTORICAL BACKGROUNDS

Mailer has always been interested in the occult, in magic and alchemy and drugs. His theories, of cancer and the nature of God and the tendency of the universe, all bear the stamp of mysticism in the loose sense. And his city, New York, is a city of the occult, though also of technology. The two things complement each other and blend in a certain sort of city, which I want to call the metropolis; a great, brutal, discordant city, full of race, creed, and class conflicts, crudely lacking in both moral and intellectul integrity, hideously unlike either the city of faith (Jerusalem) or the city of culture (Athens) and yet much more the template of subsequent Western cities than either of the two officially touted models. An apt emblem of this sort of city, and its worship of the-occult-and-technology, is the mechanical theater of Hero of Alexandria, which gave performances of "The Apotheosis of Dionysos" in the second century A.D. This was a religious mystery in which the altar moved and burst into light, by means of hydraulic machinery, and Dionysos came to life before the audience-congregation's eyes, gestured, spoke, poured liquids from his goblet and thyrsus, and cymbals clashed and Bacchantes danced, all by machinery. The audience could appreciate the technical ingenuity while they underwent the religious frisson, and could remain all the time radically uncommitted. The Egyptians had long been fascinated by animated statues. It is said that already in the third century B.C. there was a Dionysos in Egypt who could pour wine from a goblet. And the Hermetic manuscripts make much of the secret rituals by means of which statues could be built by men and yet acquire divine life and prophecy—after the right incantations, the right music, the burning of the right herbs, etc.

The great world-prototype of this sort of city is Alexandria, the city, like New York today, of Jews in exile and cultural eclecticism; of Cabbalism, gnosticism, magic, alchemy, of every exotic religious doctrine and practice. It was a great center of commercialism-and-gnosticism, a factory of dissociated sensibility. And in all its main outlines New York belongs to this Alexandrian type of city. *An American Dream*, Mailer's rendering of New York in fiction, is an Alexandrian novel, full of machines and magic, full of telephone conversations with the moon and with the wind. It is a compendium of superstitions, incantations, irrationalisms, a compendium of gnoses. It portrays a city where, as one character puts it, there is a maniac buried underground who runs the communal mind of the eight million citizens, and sets up the mad coincidences of its life.

The citizens of Alexandria were mostly Greek, and the language was Greek, but there were large Egyptian and Jewish (and many other) minorities, and of these the Jews were the most active in intellectual affairs. It was the greatest Jewish city in the world, and the center of Jewish learning, where the Septuagint was translated into Greek, and where Philo and his followers interpreted the Old Testament by elaborate allegorical methods, to make it yield intuitive, mystic, and Hellenic meanings. When one reads of the Museum, an academy where learned men of every description were maintained at the state's expense, one is bound to think of New York's universities and of the allegorical interpretations being developed around American literature—by, for instance, Fiedler—in those classrooms. The library is said to have contained seven hundred thousand volumes at its height, and the white marble lighthouse of Pharos stood four hundred feet high; but the city was full of racial and social conflict, and its streets were frequently the scenes of mob battles between religious and ethnic groups. The character of Alexandrian poetry is suggested by the name of Theocritus, and of its science by Ptolemy and Euclid. It is to be contrasted with Athens at *its* height of development in much the way New York is to be contrasted with Emersonian Boston; for both the elaborated and sophisticated ingenuity of its intellectual products, and the brutal racial conflicts within its social substance.

Imperial Rome was another of the great wicked metropoles. And so—despite its smallness—was Elizabethan London. The latter's brilliant Renaissance styles of individuality at court, in dress, in theater, in food, in sex, in conspicuous consumption, everything that made the Puritans hate men like Raleigh, remind us of New York. The Puritan style was plain of speech, methodical, purposive, ordered, disciplined. This is what Mailer conjures up in the figure of Teague the Marxist in *The Armies of the Night*, and it is plain that Mailer, like Raleigh, represents opposite qualities. He belongs to New York, the wicked city to which he is yearning to return all through the weekend.

THE BODY AND THE CITY

I defined the Faustian pact before as a way of coming into imaginative possession of one's body. There is something similar in Mailer's way of coming into imaginative possession of his city. He knows his body in extraordinary sensual detail, in an extraordinary series of sensual epiphanies and hallucinations—its sexual life, its intestinal life, its excremental life, every secretion of every gland, even the life of individual cells is dramatically vivid to his imagination. In this he just goes further than writers like Updike, Roth, Bellow, and Fiedler; the modern novel is suffused in body odors and body sensations, in body; it is because Salinger won't join them in that enterprise—and because that enterprise is crucial these days to a writer's temperamental contract—that he is silenced. But Mailer is more individual in the way in which he knows his city—which is by the same mode of knowledge. He knows its smells, he knows its secretions, he knows its shames, he knows its fevers. He knows its sexual life, he knows its intestinal life, he knows its excremental life. In both *An American Dream* and his movie *Beyond the Law* he portrays on the one hand the city of the Mafia and the police, and on the other the city of Andy Warhol and Susan Sontag's "Notes on Camp." In both cases it is the underground city, the city of the night. Of course he knows the above ground city too; he knows everything, but his mode of knowledge is to be characterized as bringing out, giving relief to, the underground and the night truths.

This is no doubt because Mailer's whole life-style is imitative of New York's life-style. No writer has ever been more of the moment and of the scene. No one before ever wrote *Advertisements for Myself;* advertising not only his own personality, but the fact of his imitation of Madison Avenue, his desertion of the ivory tower for the most contemporary and commercial of circus stands. Few writers have had such acquaintance with a city's jails and asylums, its precinct offices and gang rumbles, its divorce courts and rich parties. He has lived the life of the city in the sense the newspaper editors give to that phrase—the headlines are his natural habitat. Most writers' lives suggest to some degree pastoral retreat and innocence. Wordsworthian quiet, a primrose by a river's brim, or at least the quiet of a library and a study. Mailer's suggests the opposite; rich, overspiced, overbourboned food in overexpensive restaurants; punching policemen, stabbing a wife, delivering drunken and obscene speeches in theaters and public parks. He has in some sense incorporated into himself the forces of his city, imaginatively appropriated and mastered them by imitating them.

Notes

1. E. M. Butler, *The Fortunes of Faust*, Cambridge, 1952.

The Formulation Expanded:
Mailer's Existentialism   Robert Solotaroff*

Although the hipster hero celebrated in the 1957 essay "The White Negro" is not quite as dated as Mailer's 1958 claim that "there's a great danger that the nihilism of hip will destroy civilization," this vintage of the existential hero is nonetheless by now a very improbable figure. One wonders if ten, five, or any of them ever really existed. We would still do well to look at "The White Negro" closely. The extraordinarily well-written essay is of considerable interest in itself, and, whether by addition, revision, or rejection, the larger part of Mailer's later work follows from this first sustained attempt to formulate his existential positions. If "existentialism is based upon the supposition that to exist is to face up to the conditions of life which generate . . . anxieties about our very being . . . to exist is to realize man can be nothing,[1] then the essay's opening considerations of the causes of our intimations of absurdity are stunning yet orthodox:

> Probably, we will never be able to determine the psychic havoc of the concentration camps and the atom bomb upon the unconscious mind of almost everyone alive in these years. For the first time in civilized history, perhaps for the first time in all of history, we have been forced to live with the suppressed knowledge that the smallest facets of our personality or the most minor projection of our ideas, or indeed the absence of ideas and the absence of personality could mean equally well that we might still be doomed to die as a cipher in some vast statistical operation in which our teeth would be counted, and our hair would be saved, but our death itself would be unknown, unhonored, and unremarked, a death which could not follow with dignity as a possible consequence to serious actions we had chosen, but rather a death by *deus ex machina* in a gas chamber or a radioactive city; and so . . . in the middle of an economic civilization founded upon the confidence that time could indeed be subjected to our will, our psyche was subjected to the intolerable anxiety that death being causeless, life was causeless as well, and time deprived of cause and effect had come to a stop.[2]

Confronted with this collapse of nerve forced upon all of us by the lessons of the last few decades, that newly arisen, practical philosopher from the underside of society—the hipster—emotionally apprehends that

> if our collective condition is to live with instant death by atomic war, relatively quick death by the State as *l'univers concentrationnaire*, or with a slow death by conformity with every creative and rebellious instinct stifled . . . if the fate of twentieth-century man is to live with death from adolescence to premature senescence, why then the only life-giving an-

*Excerpted from *Down Mailer's Way* (Urbana: University of Illinois Press, 1974), 89–99, by permission of the author and publisher. © 1974 by the Board of Trustees of the University of Illinois.

swer is to accept the terms of death, to live with death as immediate danger, to divorce oneself from society, to exist without roots, to set out on that uncharted journey into the rebellious imperatives of the self.[3]

Embracing the fact that a more real life begins only on the far side of the acceptance of death[4] the hipster insists that the way to this life is through growth; the animus to become more than one was, to accumulate more energy and perception, provides the only springboard to value in an otherwise absurd world. He, of all men, must accept the possibility of death, for to grow he must let himself be driven by those imperatives, and the most rebellious one—the need for violent adventure—is dangerous. The intuitive hipster thus stands in extreme contrast to the more reflective conformist who has been numbed as much by the perception of his own murderous desires as by the imminence of death. The hipster, in Mailer's fond view, is instead a philosophical psychopath, totally committed to the gratification of his own desires and totally indifferent to the societal mores which forbid these gratifications. Such characteristics are common to all psychopaths, but Mailer argued that the hipster differs from the conventional psychopath—if such a term may be used—in his "narcissistic detachment of the philosopher, that absorption in the recessive nuances of one's own motive which is so alien to the unreasoning drive of the psychopath."[5] He seemed also to argue that the hipster's superior capacity for intellectual and emotional detachment enables him to grow more than his unreflective counterpart. I say "seemed" because Mailer was finally unclear about the ways in which the hipster differs from the conventional psychopath and the possibilities of either one actually changing for the better.

Mailer never completely surrenders any of his idea complexes. They simply turn up later in a different context, in combination with other ideas. For example, in the opening paragraph of "The White Negro," Mailer implicitly argues that the meaning of Marxism has collapsed before the onslaught of the absurd. If it is no longer possible for one to believe that human happiness can be achieved by "mastering the links of social cause and effect," then we can no longer hope to reveal the historical importance of a period by discerning how much progress was made toward eliminating economic contradictions. Yet the historicity of Marxism, the emphasis placed upon historical process and the way that time accelerates or decelerates—to the Marxist inasmuch as it carries us toward the economic resolution—turns up later in "The White Negro" linked to a theory of individual possibility which is founded upon the workings of the nervous system. Grounding dynamic growth-time and deadening clock-time in biological and historical processes, the 1957 Mailer claims that we would be better able to realize ourselves in the horrific society in which we live if we did not possess historically antiquated nervous systems. They are antiquated because they were formed in our infancy and thus carry in the style of their circuits the very contradictions of our parents and our early milieu. Therefore we are obliged, most of us, to meet the tempo of the present and the future with reflexes and rhythms which come from the past. It is not only the "dead weight of the institutions of the past" but indeed the inefficient and often antiquated nervous circuits of the past which strangle our potentiality for responding to new possibilities which might be exciting for our individual growth.

Through most of modern history, "sublimation" was possible: at the expense of expressing only a small portion of oneself, that small portion could be expressed intensely. But sublimation depends on a reasonable tempo to history. If the collective life of a generation has moved too quickly, the "past" by which particular men and women of that generation may function is not, let us say, thirty years old, but relatively a hundred or two hundred years old. And so the nervous system is overstressed beyond the possibility of such compromises as sublimation, especially since the stable middle-class values so prerequisite to sublimation have been virtually destroyed in our time, at least as nourishing values free of confusion or doubt. In such a crisis of accelerated historical tempo and deteriorated values, neurosis tends to be replaced by psychopathy, and the success of psychoanalysis (which even ten years ago gave promise of becoming a direct major force) diminishes because of its inbuilt and characteristic incapacity to handle patients more complex, more experienced, or more adventurous than the analyst himself.[6]

Perhaps the most remarkable stance in "The White Negro" is not Mailer's argument that the hipster might break open the concrete surface of Eisenhower America or even the partial defense of "two strong eighteen-year-old hoodlums . . . beating in the brains of a candy-store keeper"[7] by a man who had sympathetically characterized Joey Goldstein. Rather, it might be the possibility that the attempt "to divorce oneself from society"[8] can actually be achieved. So much of Mailer has always believed that any individual alone on a desert island would bring with him the residue of all that family and society at large have inflicted upon him that he never asserted that the hipster could totally divorce himself. Rather, the hipster tries to become as freed from social imperatives as Marion Faye; how he tries is considered, and the possibility of success is forgotten or quietly buried.

Mailer has always been such a complicated man that one cannot bluntly assert that he celebrated the hipster because he unequivocally hoped to become one himself. Certainly the author, who could not explicitly endorse the hipster solution, was much less rebellious than the hero of the essay. And Mailer's need to turn out a first-rate piece of work was related to, but not identical with, the implicit celebration of rebellion in the essay. Rather, it would seem that most of him hoped (among other things) to so rebuild his own nervous circuits that he could fend off the threats and rewards of society much more easily than he had. Since he continued to want so many of these rewards, *Advertisements for Myself* is rebellious in a curiously opportunistic way, but what is more to our concern here is Mailer's obvious attempt to project the hipster as a kind of personal absolute who might exert a pull upon his own psyche to bend it toward the rebellious, the antisocial, the primitive, the creative.

More and more the essay seems to be a highly creative fiction—again, did any of Mailer's hipsters exist? Thus the claim for the diminishing success of psychoanalysis seems to be bluff as does (judging from what psychiatrists have told me—but of course they are suspect!) the replacement of neurosis with psychopathy. "Not a phony but a Faust," Hearn said. The claims might be "stretchers," but the fascination with force, whether as power in social spheres or energy in more individual ones, has been there throughout. Mailer wrote in *Of a Fire on the Moon*:

> If there is a crossing in the intellectual cosmos where philosophical notions of God, man, and the machine can come together it is probably to be found in the conceptual swamps which surround every notion of energy. The greatest mystery in the unremitting mysteries of physics must be the nature of energy itself—is it the currency of the universe or merely the agent of creation? The basic stuff of life or merely the fuel of life? the guard of the heavens, or the heart and blood of time? The mightiest gates of the metaphysician hinge on the incomprehensibility yet human intimacy of that ability to perform work and initiate movement which rides through the activities of men and machines, and powers and cycles of nature. [9]

These are gracefully posed questions; the 1957 ideologue, hammering out the foundations of his system, tries (as Mailer might say in one of his early-sixties poems) to drive to the short hairs: Just how does energy work, how might more of it be freed? Look to the absolute, to the philosophical psychopath for the way out of the emotional impasse in which Mailer claims we all find ourselves and out of which no psychiatrist can help us. With fanatic singleness of purpose, the hipster sets about making a new nervous system for himself. But how does it work? A year earlier, in one of his *Voice* columns, Mailer wrote that growth was finally a greater mystery than death. Here is an attempt to solve the mystery, to explain how sex might be time and time might be the connection of new circuits:

> The psychopath is notoriously difficult to analyze because the fundamental decision of his nature is to try to live the infantile fantasy, and in this decision (given the dreary alternative of psychoanalysis) there may be a certain instinctive wisdom. For there is a dialectic to changing one's nature, the dialectic which underlies all psychoanalytic method: it is the knowledge that if one is to change one's habits, one must go back to the source of their creation, and so the psychopath exploring backward along the road of the homosexual, the orgiast, the drug-addict, the rapist, the robber and the murderer seeks to find those violent parallels to the violent and often hopeless contradictions he knew as an infant and as a child. For if he has the courage to meet the parallel situation at the moment

when he is ready, then he has a chance to act as he has never acted before, and in satisfying the frustration—if he can succeed—he may then pass by symbolic substitute through the locks of incest. In thus giving expression to the buried infant in himself, he can lessen the tension of those infantile desires and so free himself to remake a bit of his nervous system. Like the neurotic he is looking for the opportunity to grow up a second time, but the psychopath knows instinctively that to express a forbidden impulse actively is far more beneficial to him than merely to confess the desire in the safety of a doctor's room. The psychopath is ordinately ambitious, too ambitious ever to trade his warped brilliant conception of his possible victories in life for the grim if peaceful attrition of the analyst's couch. So his associational journey into the past is lived out in the theatre of the present, and he exists for those charged situations where his senses are so alive that he can be aware actively (as the analysand is aware passively) of what his habits are, and how he can change them. *The strength of the psychopath is that he knows (where most of us can only guess) what is good for him and what is bad for him at exactly those instants when an old crippling habit has become so attacked by experience that the potentiality exists to change it*, to replace a negative and empty fear with an outward action, even if—and here I obey the logic of the extreme psychopath—even if the fear is of himself, and the action is to murder. [Italics mine.][10]

One of the most interesting struggles that runs through Mailer's career is his attempt to ground the intuitive in the factual, the mystical in the phenomenal, the psychic in the biological and the apocalyptic in the historical. If "incompatibles have come to bed"[11] in hip thought, not the least incompatible of these matings is the explanation of the magical, expanded moments during which a man can change and become better than the society he lives in, in terms of the Freudian assumption that the Oedipus complex is finally the source of human neurosis—with the psychopath undergoing a far more radical cure than any the sternly moral Freud suggested. Mailer did not follow through and offer us the details of the marriage, but we can easily fill them in for ourselves. Presumably, the successful sexual act symbolically represents the possession of the mother, and the successful violent act works as a substitute for the killing of the father figure who stands in the way of incestuous gratification. Most of us have absorbed the father figure—who, of course, eventually extends to include the edicts of society—by identifying with him and thus creating the superego. Precisely because he has never made the identification, because he has no superego, the extreme psychopath does not have to overcome guilt as he nerves himself to perform his violent act. With the emphasis placed on raw animal courage, we are once more back to Croft, fighting his fear of the unknown as he tries to scale Anaka. (We also look ahead to the protagonists of *An American Dream* and *Why Are We in Vietnam?* as they nerve themselves to climb their respective Anakas. Although the celebration of sex and violence decreased considerably as Mailer's career progressed, the great concern with the courage of his characters and of himself continued unabated.)

Mailer added to the primordial linkage between hatred and love. The infant hates the father who blocks the path toward total gratification, but the psychopath also hates himself; he

> murders—if he has the courage—out of the necessity to purge his violence, for if he cannot empty his hatred then he cannot love, his being is frozen with implacable self-hatred for his cowardice . . . .
>   . . . At bottom, the drama of the psychopath is that he seeks love. Not love as the search for a mate, but love as the search for an orgasm more apocalyptic than the one which preceded it. Orgasm is his therapy—he knows at the seed of his being that good orgasm opens his possibilities and bad orgasm imprisons him.[12]

New energy is the goal, the possibility which both the hipster and the unreflective psychopath seek. (The former also seeks perceptions which will give him further energy and which seems to distinguish him from the latter, though Mailer was not clear on this issue.) But how does this relate to the symbolic incest and orgasm? Does the value of a particular orgasm lie in its ability to serve as a surrogate for the incest so that the mixture of frustrated desire and fear which is blocking the energy is eliminated? Or does the symbolic passage through the locks of incest enable the orgasm which—following Wilhelm Reich's theory—sets free the dammed-up energy?

Mailer tacitly chose the Reichian alternative; in fact, he has been so influenced by his reading of that much maligned and very impressive thinker that we would do well to pause here to consider Reich's explanations of the workings and nature of that sweet the hipster seeks: energy. For Reich, energy is a bioelectric force in man. Its basic unit is the orgone, eventually derived from the sun and present in every organic cell and in some organic materials—a concept which surely had a good deal to do with the formation of Mailer's later theory of man's containing many "beings," some languishing, some perishing.[13] This energy seeks release in orgasm, and when that release is blocked, the energy is then fixated upon infantile conflicts. Consequently, the psychoneurosis of the Oedipus conflict is now charged with the misdirected energy. Thus strengthened, the neurosis further inhibits sexual release, damming up still more energy as the victim is plunged into greater anxiety and the emergence of different physical maladies. For when energy is not released through the workings of what Reich calls the genital-sensory system, it is transformed into aggression and moves to the cardiac system, where the aggression is felt as anxiety. Aggression is thus explained not in Mailer's terms as anger towards one's parents or toward one's own cowardice, but more basically as the first new form that energy takes when it cannot find sexual relief.

Since Mailer by and large denies psychotherapy any real efficacy,[14] he prescribed in "The White Negro" the savage cure of acting out the anger as totally as possible. Reich's therapy has much more benign social consequences. Because of our fear of the dangers which the release of the aggression will bring upon us, we encase it in character armor. This armor is both physical and psychic in nature—physical in that it manifests itself as rigidities in different parts of the body as a defense against freeing that part in the orgasm which we have been taught is wicked, and psychic because it is caused by the erroneous ideas about sexuality given to us by repressive parents and society at large. Through physical and psychic therapy, the physician gradually cracks the armor, freeing the anger to express itself in socially harmless ways. (Hence Henderson's bellowing exercises in Bellow's *Henderson the Rain King*.) As the anger is dissipated, he encourages the patient's sexual activities, for orgasm is the cure for both the anger and Oedipus complex. With the body finally fulfilling its *natural* function of discharging accumulated energy, there will be neither the crippling anger (and consequently anxiety) which resulted from the lack of release nor the Oedipus complex, which drew its strength from the same source.

If Mailer disagreed with some of Reich's theories, he accepted enough to argue that orgasm sets free the dammed-up energy. For the hipster feels that

> to be with it is to have grace, is to be closer to the secrets of that inner unconscious life which will nourish you if you can hear it, for you are then nearer to that God which every hipster believes is located in the senses of his body, that trapped, mutilated and nonetheless megalomaniacal God who is It, who is energy, life, sex, force, the Yoga's *prana*, the Reichian's orgone, Lawrence's "blood," Hemingway's "good," the Shavian life-force; "It"; God; not the God of the churches but the unachievable whisper of mystery within the sex, the paradise of limitless energy and perception just beyond the wave of the next orgasm.[15]

(So wide are the differences among the thinkers mentioned in this sentence that a number of readers have misunderstood Mailer. His lover's quarrel with Reich should be pursued here, though, and I offer in the notes at the end of the book a long note which treats the problems created by lumping together Lawrence, Shaw, and Hemingway.)

We must remember that Mailer, who said a year before he wrote "The White Negro" that if he were to go to an analyst he would go to a Reichian one, wrote that the orgasm which the hipster sought was "unachievable . . . just beyond the wave of the next orgasm." I have already referred to Mailer's claims that *he* is peculiarly qualified to ferret out the secrets of the self, and there was no chance of his reducing himself to a mere epigone, devoting his energies to restating or amplifying another man's system. But what follows from "natural" is far more important. In reply to the question of whether the orgasm serves as a surrogate for incest, Mailer accepts the Reichian schema enough to believe that the working out of the

Oedipus complex is the means towards the end of freeing energy through improved orgasm. But precisely because Mailer also believed that total orgasm is unattainable, Reich's basic sexual theory is—within the vastly smaller world of "The White Negro"—subjected to a reinterpretation as radical as the transformation of Marx's theory of social upheaval by Mao's doctrine of permanent revolution.

It might be argued that the life views of both Reich and the Mailer of "The White Negro" are biological monisms. Reich posits a monism which acts best (or most naturally) in a circular manner—the energy builds up, is released, and the process then repeats itself. Mailer's monism (in its ideal or natural movement) describes a spiral—a man grows by freeing energy, but this energy must be put to the task of freeing still more energy. To make the same point in a way which better suggests its ethical implications, Mailer has liked to call himself a dialectician for some time, and, in fact, he has always been one. To the hipster (and Mailer), "incompatibles have come to bed, the inner life and the violent life, the orgy and the dream of love, the desire to murder and the desire to create, a dialectical conception of existence with a lust for power, a dark, romantic, and yet undeniably dynamic view of existence for it sees every man and woman as moving individually through each moment of life forward into growth or backward into death."[16] Reich also sees each man and woman as growing toward the ability of having orgasm or dying away from the possibility. But the total orgasm is not only achievable, it is natural. The man or woman who cannot have it is unnatural. In terms of the circular process, the orgasm is the point at which the circle is closed. One is left wholly satisfied and ideally retraces the same course of accumulating energy and discharging it as economically as possible.

For Mailer one's nature is best expressed in the quest for the unattainable. It is worth repeating that we are describing the difference between an essentialist who can finally ground the value of a man's activities and thought in his ability to realize a fixed biological nature and a romantic existentialist who claims that man's nature is precisely to create new natures. The ethical problems of Mailer's 1957 position can be seen if we perceive that what makes his dialectic of growth so different from Plato's, Hegel's, or Marx's—all obvious differences admitted—is its endlessness. Not endlessness in time, for that comes with a particular individual's death, but in terms of a fixed goal which reached down to provide meaning and value to earlier, lower stages of the dialectic. There is in all four dialectics an emphasis on transcendent movement as there is not in Reich's. The movement in all but Mailer's is toward a conclusion—a realm of ideas, or the Prussian state, or the classless society—all of which argue (as does Reich's biological functionalism) for a basis by which an action, a state of consciousness, a historical stage, and so on, can be objectively evaluated. The fixed end permits an appeal to something outside the individual. In Mailer's endlessly spiraling dialectic, there is only the quest for the infinite ("the universe . . . being glimpsed as a series of ever-extending radii from the center")[17] which is of course an infinite quest ("the hip argument . . . would claim that even in an orgasm which is *the most* there is always the vision of an outer wider wilder orgasm which is even more *with it*").[18]

And the endlessness deepened as Mailer's career proceeded. Whether or not an individual's "time" ends with his death became an open question as the author's commitment to an afterlife began to emerge in 1958. Although the ethical imperatives of energy, God, and afterlife were grounded in his conception of Being, this Being is precisely something which tries always to grow into more Being. The attempts to explain systematically the workings of Being stopped after 1965, but, as I suggested, the fascination with energy continued, and the celebration of the endless romantic quest continued as well. Did not "immediate reflection" tell Mailer that the Apollo 11 moon-shot was a step toward expanding the holdings of God or the Devil out into the universe—toward the other planets, toward the stars? But let us return to that 1957 Vulcan on pot and the considerable heat that he generates as he hammers out his system.

Notes

1. Carl Michaelson, *Christianity and the Existentialists* (New York: Harper & Row, Publishers, 1956), p. 10.

2. Norman Mailer, *Advertisements For Myself* (New York: G.P. Putnam's, 1959), p. 338.

3. *Advertisements*, p. 339. Mailer also places "the square's" terror of self in historical context: "The Second World War presented a mirror to the human condition which blinded anyone who looked into it. For if tens of millions were killed in concentration camps out of the inexorable agonies and contractions of super-states founded upon the always insoluble contradictions of injustice, one was then obliged also to see that no matter how crippled and perverted an image of man was the society he had created, it was nonetheless his creation, his collective creation . . . and if society was so murderous, then who could ignore the most hideous of questions about his own nature?" (ibid., p. 338).

4. The idea is familiar one among existential thinkers. To place Mailer in heavier company, Karl Jaspers has said that "to philosophize is to learn how to die" (*The Way to Wisdom*, tr. by Ralph Manheim [New Haven: Yale University Press, 1951], p. 53), and Heidegger has urged us to rush towards death, to make our lives more authentic than the abstracted, second-hand ones of the mass of men by accepting the individuality of our deaths and basing the authenticity of our individuality upon the acceptance. The latter even defines man's being as *Sein-Zum-Tode* (being towards death).

5. *Advertisements*, p. 343.

6. *Advertisements*, pp. 345–46.

7. *Advertisements*, p. 347.

8. *Advertisements*, p. 339.

9. Mailer, *Of a Fire on the Moon* (Boston: Little, Brown and Company, 1970), p. 189.

10. *Advertisements*, pp. 346–47.

11. *Advertisements*, p. 342.

12. *Advertisements*, p. 347. This is the seed of Mailer's idea that one should only love that which offers growth.

13. In *Of a Fire on the Moon*, Mailer grounded the hexes, intuitions, and whammies which abound in his work of the sixties in the claim that we emit electricity charged psychic forces. Could this also have been derived from Reich?

14. "In practice, psychoanalysis has by now become all too often no more than a psychic blood-letting. The patient is not so much changed as aged, and the infantile fantasies which he is encouraged to express are condemned to exhaust themselves against the analyst's nonresponsive reactions. The result for all too many patients is a diminution, a "tranquilizing" of their most interesting qualities and vices. The patient is indeed not so much altered as worn out—less bad, less good, less bright, less willful, less destructive, less creative. He is thus able to conform to that contradictory and unbearable society which first created his neurosis. He can conform to what he loathes because he no longer has the passion to feel loathing so intensely." [*Advertisements*, p. 436.] This is the first attack upon the technique of psychoanalysis. All of the earlier and most of the later criticisms are *ad hominem* thrusts at the cowardly, conformist, middle-class psychiatrist. Mailer will later write that "life seems to come from a meeting of opposites" (Norman Mailer, *Cannibals and Christians* [New York: The Dial Press, 1966], p. 281), and it would follow that if psychoanalytic techniques are indeed as he describes them, there would not be the kind of opposing forces which would enable the emergence of new psychic life.

15. *Advertisements*, p. 351. A long note—The breakneck speed which the sentence develops is impressive, but the problems created in the easy equation of a univocal "good" for markedly different views are quickly evident even for the reader who has made no attempt to unearth the bases of Mailer's positions. For example, Reich's orgone belongs in its human manifestations to a closed system with an inner final cause, the satisfaction of *our* needs. Shaw's life force is transcendent, and its end lies outside the individual in the creation of a higher biological organism. As Mailer gradually extended his transcendent positions he, for example, agreed with Shaw that sex primarily exists for reproduction and did not regard reproduction (as Reich did) as a by-product of our sexual needs.

We seem to have here the statement that the ultimate reality, the *nature* of man, is a mighty instinctual lover of pleasure and power. It is buried within us and we can best realize our nature by freeing this trapped God and experiencing the benefits of power, pleasure, and perception He would bring to us. (This metaphorical immanent God is not to be confused with the literal, transcendent God who plays such an important role in Mailer's post-1957 thought. Although this latter God manifests part of himself in our unconscious, it is precisely a part—he is far more than one person's instincts.)

Although His nature cannot be fully liberated, it is still the fixed core of our being, and inasmuch as we are not acting to free it we are unnatural. This regaining of our immanent, primal essence seems to me to be what Lawrence urged (and Eitel sought to achieve), and were this clearly and simply Mailer's only position, those critics would be justified who have called him a romantic primitivist—an essentialist and not an existentialist at all. But later in "The White Negro," Mailer asserted the familiar existentialist position that a man's nature is not a set entity, but that with every action he creates a new self and a new truth about what it means to be a particular human being. When Mailer writes that in Hip "each man is glimpsed as a collection of possibilities" (*Advertisements*, p. 354), he is stating an existential view of man as surely as Heidegger was when he stated that possibility is higher than and prior to actuality or as Sartre was when he claimed that man is the future of man.

George Schrader has claimed that Mailer was an essentialist who advocated having "orgasm over and over again, each time more than the last and with no devleopment" and that "he seeks to live only in the *instant* which is unchanged in being repeated" ("Norman Mailer and the Despair of Defiance," *Yale Review*, Vol. 51 [December, 1961], p. 274) when Mailer's emphasis was on how unattainable the ultimate orgasm and perpetual instant was. What Schrader attributed to Mailer was something very close to Eitel's noble savage theory, one which Mailer never really accepted and certainly did not in "The White Negro." Schrader correctly accused the latter of being a romantic but said that "European existentialists have been considerably opposed to all varieties of romanticism" (*ibid.*, p. 270). Mailer's romanticism centers not in his belief that perfection can be achieved only in the art object—he has too didactic a view of art for that—but in his emphasis upon the quest for an ever-receding goal. In contrast to Schrader's claim of the existential opposition to romanticism, this quest bears a strong resemblance to Sartre's description of the inevitably futile attempt to fuse the *en-soi* and the *pour-soi* except that for Mailer the quest is a less "romantically" hopeless one. If it is argued that Sartre objects to this inevitable romanticism and Schrader's claim is thus still valid, we might turn to the obvious comparisons that might be drawn from William Barrett's acute comments on the quest for Being in Wordsworth (William Barrett, *Irrational Man* [Garden City, N.Y.: Doubleday and Co., Inc., 1962], pp. 125–26; and Heidegger: *Being and Time*, tr. by John Macquarrie and Edward Robinson [New York: Harper & Row, Publishers, 1962], pp. 304–11). As the discussion of Mailer's later writings proceeds, we will see the hipster's desire to grow fused with a quest for Being, though from what I can make out of *Being and Time*, Mailer's conception of Being is much different from Heidegger's.

16. *Advertisements*, pp. 342–43.

17. *Advertisements*, p. 352.

18. The quotation is found in Mailer's reply to a criticism of "The White Negro" by Ned Polsky, both of which were printed in the Winter, 1958, *Dissent* and collected in *Advertisements* (p. 369).

Awesome Men: *The Fight* and *Genius and Lust*
Philip H. Bufithis*

In his nonfiction Mailer has written so insightfully about the people and events of our national life that now at any new development in our culture, we find ourselves asking the question, "What would Mailer say about it?" We want to know.

However much critics may dispute the merits of his novels, most of them would agree that there is no better journalist in America. *The Fight* would not change their view. The book describes Muhammad Ali's fight with George Foreman in Zaïre (formerly the Congo) to regain the heavyweight championship of the world. Mailer immerses us first in the political and social ambience of the fight. He portrays President Mobutu, iron-willed leader of a new nation, as a mysterious unapproachable potentate, a man determined to bring the dubious gifts of progress to his people while at the same time making them ever mindful of their—and his—vital connection with the magical energies of tribal traditions. If Ali, messianically proclaiming his Muslim message for the salvation of the black race, is the "Prince of Heaven," Mobutu is the chieftain of fecund darkness.

Kinshasa (Formerly Leopoldville) is a city rife with nepotism and poverty. The municipal buildings, aswarm with bureaucratic inefficiency, and

*Reprinted from *Norman Mailer* (New York: Frederick Ungar Publishing Co., 1978), 121–29, by permission of the publisher.

the streets, winding through clusters of dusty hovels, are watched over by Mobutu's soldiers and police. Nonetheless, there is a growing sense of unity and hope in Zaïre where black power is a formidable reality. The people believe in it, more so than ever as Ali comes to town.

The Fight is built around Ali. He lives within it as a pulsating presence. When he speaks his seriocomic patter arrays the page:

> "If I," said Ali, "give the enemy some of my knowledge, then maybe he'll have sense to lay back and wait. Of course I will even convert that to my advantage. I'm versatile. All the same, the Mummy's best bet is to stand in the center of the ring and wait for me to come in." With hardly a pause, he added, "Did you hear that *death* music he plays? [somber orchestral music piped into the P. A. system at Foreman's training camp] He *is* the mummy. And," said Ali chuckling, "I'm going to be the Mummy's Curse!"

Ali seems a version of Mailer himself, which may explain Mailer's fascination with him for fifteen years. If Mailer were less subtle and more loud, he would resemble Ali more than a little. And if we recall Mailer's other living hero, Henry Miller, the three personalities suggest an unmistakable unity. Each man is the embodiment of loquacious defiance. They are romantic individualists in an age of growing collectivism, and they both have an inflammable sense of personal honor. It may not be at all wrong to see them as sympathetic to the values of the past. How agreeable for Mailer, then, that this book takes him to the living past, to Africa, where, if technology and trade are to succeed at all, they must be wedded to tribal tradition.

Reading *Bantu Philosophy* by Father Tempels, a former missionary in the Belgian Congo, Mailer brightens with the discovery that the philosophy of African tribesmen is close to his own. A basic premise guides the book: whereas the American mind subjugates or sublimates primordial instincts, the African mind allows itself to be informed by them. At the core of Bantu philosophy is the belief that the human being is more than the result of environmental and genetic influences. A man is also the reflection of how he lived his previous lives. A man is not merely a socio-biotic entity with his own individual psyche but, paraphrases Mailer, "a part of the resonance, sympathetic or unsympathetic, of every root or thing (and witch) about him." To be strong he must catch and cultivate this "resonance."

Mailer argues that the American black, though he may not describe his life in this way, lives it in this way. Bantu philosophy is his heritage, and in its light Mailer tries to understand Ali. The role of heavyweight champion of the world has a potent spiritual existence of its own. Not to seize it constitutes, in Western terms, an ego loss. Ali is the exemplar of the American black consciousness that, cut off from African tradition and transplanted to America, is trying to reconnect with *kuntu*, the creative, potent flow of forces that permeate the primeval elements of the universe.

Bantu philosophy is fascinating enough, however, without Mailer trying to demonstrate it with spiritual feats of his own. The book becomes silly when he attempts magically to transfer his courage to Ali by stepping around the parapet between his hotel balcony and the adjoining one. A lot of unnecessary spooking goes on in *The Fight*. He imagines the Ali and Foreman camps vying for all available stock on a fluctuating *kuntu* market. Father Tempels would be bemused.

Mailer's narrative is far more effective when it excludes the transempirical and attends to the concrete realities at hand. He visits Foreman's camp; he watches Ali work out with his sparring partners; he runs with Ali; he trades quips with promotion men, managers, and trainers; he is with Ali in his dressing room before and after the fight; at the Dakar airport on his return trip to New York, he helps a stewardess assuage a mob of Africans who, convinced that Ali is aboard the plane, rush across the runways and insist on seeing him. Whatever scene Mailer describes, we are right there with him because his observations wholly delight us. At fifty-two he has reached that stage where a rueful, earned wisdom has seasoned his rebel ire and a sense of common humanity has tempered his brashness.

Mailer's observations are sly, remarkably perceptive, and always pushing toward those boundaries of experience beyond which language cannot go. When he crosses those boundaries, his prose naturally falters. But such risk taking keeps us reading. His style is suspenseful. We watch him perform entrechats of language. Sometimes he slips, as exemplified by his decription of the teeming cricket and locust life of the African night: "Were insects a part of the cosmos or the termites of the cosmos?" The more we think about such a thought the less it means.

But who could do what Mailer does with Ali's knockout blow to Foreman's head? Invoking metaphors very few writers would ever imagine and none would dare use, he gives us a description of unforgettable, unaccountable rightness:

> Foreman's arms flew out to the side like a man with a parachute jumping out of a plane, and in this doubled-over position he tried to wander out to the center of the ring. All the while his eyes were on Ali and he looked up with no anger as if Ali, indeed, was the man he knew best in the world and would see him on his dying day. Vertigo took George Foreman and revolved him. Still bowing from the waist in this uncomprehending position, eyes on Muhammad Ali all the way, he started to tumble and topple and fall even as he did not wish to go down. His mind was held with magnets high as his championship and his body was seeking the ground. He went over like a six-foot sixty-year-old butler who has just heard tragic news, yes, fell over all of a long collapsing two seconds, down came the Champion in sections and Ali revolved with him in a close circle, hand primed to hit him one more time, and never the need, a wholly intimate escort to the floor.

Mailer does here what he does throughout *The Fight*. He harmonizes disparate modes of discourse into one original voice. He chronicles, poeticizes, observes, and analyzes. He works his combinations, much like Ali himself. *The Fight* is the perfect marriage of style and subject. The literature of sport has never seen a better book.

With *Genius and Lust*, an anthology of the works of Henry Miller, Mailer turns full-fledged literary critic. There are about 500 pages by Miller and about 100 pages by Mailer, who early in the book has this to say: "Miller at his best wrote a prose grander than Faulkner's, and wilder— the good reader is revolved in a farrago of light with words heavy as velvet, brilliant as gems, eruptions of thought cover the page. You could be in the vortex of one of Turner's oceanic holocausts when the sun shines in the very center of the storm." This is impressionistic criticism carried to extravagance, but at bottom, like most of Mailer's assessments in this book, it is quite discerning. The curious thing, however, about this passage is that the honors Mailer ascribes to Miller are the very ones he imagines should be accorded to himself. In 1956 with his columns for *The Village Voice*, Mailer transformed his style, cutting free from the influence of Hemingway, from those direct sentences of studied dispassion, and shifted his allegiance to the stylistic tradition of Miller. His prose became gusty, dense, exhortative, eloquently cadenced; it purposively flew in the face of "literature." He abandoned Hemingway's clean, well-lighted camp by the side of the river and entered the river itself. "I am the river, he [Miller] is always ready to say, I am the rapids and the placids, I'm the froth and the scum and twigs—what a roar as I go over the falls." When Mailer rhapsodizes over Miller, he is idealizing himself.

Genius and Lust can be read not only as its subtitle states, as "a journey through the major writings of Henry Miller," but as an overview of Norman Mailer the writer, for Mailer shares practically the same strengths and defects as Miller. Yet it should be established at the outset that in some significant respects these two men can hardly be called literary brothers or, as a proper regard for time would dictate, father and son (Miller is 86 and Mailer 55). Miller is the last of the buoyant anarchists, a novelist of hearty diabolisms who has always written as he pleased, remaining all but deaf to the world's censure. Trophies, adversarial or admiring critics, and fat royalties have been to him very much beside the point. Mailer, on the other hand, has been working since the mid 1950s at the impossible task of disturbing people and then coaxing them to adore him. He is a creature of topicalities, consistently choosing as his subject matter the events, the celebrities, the issues that the nation itself, for reasons he is always trying to divine, has chosen. It is hard to imagine Miller, an unregenerate bohemian sequestered from the clamorous world in his hermitage at Big Sur, appearing on TV, negotiating for movie rights, making big-time deals with publishers, and meeting deadlines.

Still, the arresting fact remains that the work of Miller and Mailer coalesce at some very important points. If it has been Miller's Promethean aim, as Mailer says, to "alter the nerves and marrow of a nation," it has been Mailer's to effect "a revolution in the consciousness of our time," as he states in *Advertisements for Myself.* The quiet old satyr of California would probably deem Mailer's estimation of his novelistic purpose a bit inflated. And it is inflated if we view Miller's work as a whole. But his early novels—*Tropic of Cancer, Black Spring, Tropic of Capricorn* (excerpts from which compose over half this book)—did very much intend to drastically reshape the mind of man, and in so doing necessarily set out to remake literature by destroying it. Almost immediatley in *Tropic of Cancer* Miller says: "This then? This is not a book. This is libel, slander, defamation of character. This is not a book, in the ordinary sense of the word. No, this is a prolonged insult, a gob a spit in the face of Art, a kick in the pants to God, Man, Destiny, Time, Love, Beauty . . . what you will." In his own defiant idiom, Mailer made a similar avowal in *Advertisements for Myself* when he wrote that his artistic intention was to "mate the absurd with the apocalyptic," to merge "the extreme, the obscene and the unsayable," "to attempt an entrance into the mysteries of murder, suicide, incest, orgy, orgasm, and Time."

Miller and Mailer are inveterate renegades who share a common enemy. The great noise, let us call it, that seems to Mailer to be getting louder and louder with every passing year—the noise of government, technology, advertising, and of every clamorous need of the bourgeois for regulation, conformity, and security. Such a cultural condition militates against the American artist—and, by extension, the thinking, imaginative man— and turns him into a rebel or a victim.

Mailer shares obsessions with Miller as well as defiances. Both show a symbolic connection between sexual transgression and moral freedom. Their books are testimonies to the proposition that a life of sexual vagabondage can be as worthwhile and as honest as many another life. When Miller was writing in those four decades before the 1970s, he did not have to justify this proposition to women. In 1971, with *The Prisoner of Sex,* Mailer did and enlisted Miller to run interference for him against the attacking new feminists. If Miller degrades women in bed and uses them as carnal fodder, Mailer wrote in that book, it is because he is in awe of their life-bearing powers, their mysterious alliance with the gestating energies of the cosmos, and so he feels he must, perhaps out of some kind of deeply envious wonder, cut them down, debase them. This is as stupendous a piece of illogic as Mailer has ever committed. In *Genius and Lust* he commits it again when he says that Miller's "dread" of women's intimate closeness to the source of all creation makes him "revile them, humiliate them . . . do everything to reduce them so that he might dare to enter them and take pleasure of them." Nonetheless, Mailer's claim for Miller's greatness cannot be denied: he was the first writer to break down the inhibiting walls of American fiction and introduce the sex act as a subject for serious novelistic treatment.

When it comes time for Mailer to discuss Miller's later and lesser works and to include excerpts from them (*The Rosy Crucifixion, The Air-Conditioned Nightmare, Sunday after the War, Big Sur*), he admits to Miller's defects without being too particular to name them. He says only that "There is not one Henry Miller but twenty, and fifteen of those authors are very good." His reticence about the weaknesses of Miller's writing may spring from the possible fact that in elucidating the master, the pupil finds himself looking into a mirror which reflects his own blemishes. He is not too eager to make a case of them. Yet it remains that both writers lapse on occasion into what one might call "word drunkenness"—amorphous, onrushing displays of private philosophy and phantasmagoria. And they tend at times to substitute discourse for drama, to tell when they should be showing.

But such criticism of writers the like of these serves only to show the obverse side of their greatness. At their best they possess the kind of rebelliousness that at once outrages and fascinates. Their work begins in defiance but ends in discovery. Their backs are up, but they seem all the while to be dancing. More significantly for Mailer, however, there is a certain strategy for survival expressed in *Tropic of Cancer* that he has taken as a major lesson to be learned and incorporated into his own work. Henry Miller, down and out on the foul streets of Paris, stays alive and happy by dissolving his ego in identification with the chaos around it. It is a perilous strategy, but one that has the potential of winning for him the opportunity he desires as an artist, the opportunity to deeply know the world. He takes in and controls, by the power of the creative imagination, forces in the world that would otherwise destroy him. Mailer dramatizes this maneuver in his characterization of Stephen Rojack in *An American Dream* and with D. J. Jethro in *Why Are We in Vietnam?* "Man learns more about the nature of water . . . if he comes close to drowning," Mailer once said in an interview.[1] This statement lies as close to the heart of his philosophy as any statement he has ever uttered. We can hear the voice of Miller behind it. If the task Mailer set himself in *Genius and Lust* was to gain a wider public prominence for the work of Henry Miller, it was also to pay back a long outstanding debt.

Note

1. Raymond A. Sokolov, "Flying High with Mailer," *Newsweek*, 9 December 1968, p. 87.

An American Dream: "Hula, Hula," Said the Witches   Judith Fetterley*

An American Dream is saturated with images of massive male power conglomerates. There is the Mafia, the C.I.A., the police force, the institutions of government and big business, the media networks, the university establishment; and behind them all, ensconced in his phallic tower, is Barney Kelly, the empire builder, the ultimate symbol of conglomerate and institutional power. The book is saturated as well with images of individual men enacting violence on women: Rojack's murder of Deborah; the marine who smashes his wife's head with a hammer; Henry Steels, who "shacks up with a fat broad in Queens" and "six weeks later he kills her with a poker" (*An American Dream* [N.Y.: Dell, 1965], p. 81); Roberts, who beats up his wife; Cherry's murder. Power, it would seem, is definitely male and in the hands of men. Yet, Rojack's thesis about human, by which he means male, nature is that "magic, dread, and the perception of death" (p. 15) are the sources of motivation and that cowardice is the root of neurosis—hardly a thesis one would expect from someone in a position of power. Indeed, *An American Dream* can be read as an elaboration of the same male fantasy that generates the critical interpretation of *The Bostonians* and that is the opposite of the social reality James presents in his novel. Mailer's fantasy of female power and male powerlessness is remarkably similar to the phallic critics' mythology of an embattled male, suffused with fear, fighting off the malign influence of witchy, bitchy women. The function of this mythology is nonetheless clear: it serves to disguise and hence to perpetuate the very reality it inverts.

Our first view of Rojack is emblematic: he is hanging from the balustrade of a balcony ten stories above the street, only the tenuous grip of the four fingers of his right hand between him and the itch to jump. A sense of precarious existence is Rojack's primary self-definition. Everything he experiences in the course of his thirty-two-hour dream / nightmare is seen as a test whose passing will once again establish for a brief period of time the fact of his existence. The climax of the book is the most elaborate expression of the precarious nature of Rojack's identity and existence. His trip around the parapet of Kelly's balcony is strikingly metaphoric, presenting the image of someone delicately poised between life and death and alternately threatened and supported by forces outside himself. Rojack's existence is never a given; rather, it is something that must be continually proven, asserted, created. In the simplest terms he belongs to those who must become, as opposed to those who simply are.

In Rojack's obsession with death we feel the full force of his self-defini-

*Excerpted from *The Resisting Reader: A Feminist Approach to American Fiction* (Bloomington: Indiana University Press, 1978), 164–78, by permission of the author and the publisher.

tion. It is not accidental that the memory that precedes his initial dangling is that of four Germans under a full moon, dying at his hand. The vision behind the eyes of the fourth soldier which plunges Rojack into a "private kaleidoscope of death" is not simply that death is "a creation more dangerous than life," but that he, Rojack, is an agent of death and that death alone is his mode of creation and source of power (p. 14). Rojack's paradigm of self is after all, "I was: murderer," and it is this vision of himself that sets him to walk the streets of Harlem at night in search of a death that will accord with it (p. 123).

Rojack does not, however, simply fear a definition of the self as an agent of death. More significantly, he fears that he may in fact be already dead: "Instinct was telling me to die . . . 'You can't die yet,' said the formal part of my brain, 'you haven't done your work.' 'Yes,' said the moon, 'you haven't done your work but you've lived your life, and you are dead with it.' 'Let me be not all dead,' I cried to myself" (p. 19). The evidence on the side of the moon, though, is frightening, for Rojack is permeated by a sense of emptiness at his center, a conviction that his personality is "built upon a void" (p. 14). Overwhelmed by the feeling of not belonging to himself but of being moved in on and possessed by forces outside of and distinct from himself, he comes to believe that his mind and body are in fact the agents of some alien power.

Barney Kelly elicits this fear acutely. No matter where Rojack goes, he discovers that Kelly has been there first and has in effect displaced him; and he comes to feel that he is simply acting out Kelly's desires and is being manipulated by him. The sense of displacement dominates the events surrounding his murder of Deborah. What began as a private act, born out of the imperatives of the self, rapidly becomes a public one involving the intricacies of international espionage, the relations of TV program producers to network establishments, and the internal politics of universities. When Rojack leaves his apartment building, he is surrounded by newspaper reporters; when he enters the police station, his individual act becomes lost in the power games being played there. His final release from the police has nothing to do with him or his vision of the meaning of his act but is instead a result of behind-the-scenes manipulation stemming from Kelly's belief that Rojack has done a job for him.

It is women, however, who most clearly and consistently elicit Rojack's sense of himself as marginal, threatened, and given over to death. The voice that speaks to him from the moon and tells him he is already dead is female; and it is this same voice that urges him to give himself up, confess to the murder of Deborah, and die. It is in the presence of Cherry, on the edge of their first lovemaking, that he thinks, "when I was in bed with a woman, I rarely felt as if I were making life, but rather as if I were a pirate sharpening up a raid on life, and so somewhere inside myself—yes, *there* was a large part of the fear—I had dread of the judgment which must rest behind the womb of a woman" (p. 115). In killing Deborah he fulfills his worst fears about himself; and the evil eye of her mangled corpse throws back upon him a frightening judgment. Women also confront Rojack with the fear that he has no center and is not in possession of himself. The impulse to kill Deborah begins in his sense that she has "opened a void": "I thought again of the moon and the promise of extinction which had descended on me . . . . I was now without a center. Can you understand? I did not belong to myself any longer. Deborah had occupied my center" (p. 32). Later, he has a similar experience with Cherry: "And that sensation of not belonging to myself, of being owned at my center by Deborah—that emotion which had come on me not five minutes before I killed her—now came back" (p. 166).

This ability in women to elicit such a vision of the self has its source in the belief that women are ultimately more powerful than men. Rojack is convinced that the real power behind those institutions which dominate the landscape of *An American Dream* is, in fact, female and that the ultimate manipulations are carried out not by men but by women. It is Mrs. Roosevelt who is mentioned as Stephen's mentor and entré into the world of politics; and it is Deborah and her coterie of female friends who, on being rebuffed by Shago Martin, determine his fate by making sure that he is "no longer in danger of developing into a national figure" (p. 172). On reading the list in the society-page obituary of the organizations to which Deborah belonged, Rojack reflects on "that endless stream of intimate woman's lunches into which she disappeared every perfumed noon over the years— what princes must have been elected, what pretenders guillotined, what marriages turned in their course. . . . What a garroting must have been given my neck by the ladies of those lunches, those same ladies or their mothers who worked so neatly to make me a political career all eighteen years ago" (p. 129).

Even Kelly, that ultimate symbol of conglomerate male power, is seen by Rojack as living under the shadow of the power of women—not simply in relation to Deborah and her posthumous capacity to embarrass him with the consequences of her amateur games of espionage, but, more significantly, in relation to Ruta, who alone seems to have the kind of knowledge that can control Kelly's behavior. This vision of the relationship between male and female power is registered for Rojack, appropriately enough, as he enters the Waldorf Towers on his way to see Kelly: "The street outside the side entrance was decked, however, with three limousines double-parked and a squad of motorcycle policemen stood at the door. . . . in the foyer . . . still another eight, each man more than six feet two, handsome as a prize herd of test-tube bulls. . . . some woman of huge institutional importance was about to descend" (pp. 193–94). The image of men as superstuds lined up in attendance on the demands of women, who represent and possess ultimate power, is central to the mythology of *An American Dream*.

This view generates Rojack's attraction to Deborah. Rojack sees Deborah, as Gatsby sees Daisy, not as a person but as a status symbol and a way into power. The need to establish his own credentials in relation to her is immediately apparent and reflects that precarious sense of identity, an identity on the make, which characterizes Rojack. And it is equally apparent that one of the ways in which his identity gets made is by his "making it" with powerful women; the "success" of the evening depends not simply on accomplishing the seduction but on who it is that one has seduced. What makes Deborah a worthy conquest and the evening "fair" is the fact that she is rich and powerful, she is Barney Kelly's daughter and a Caughlin Mangaravidi to boot, and she is sophisticated to the point of being bored by the offerings of even such extraordinary males as Jack Kennedy and Scott Fitzgerald. In seducing her Rojack proves that he is a very special "sword" indeed.

Throughout their relationship Rojack views Deborah through the lens of the status he gets from his relation to her and the power to which she provides access: "I had . . . become the husband of an heiress"; "I finally had been the man whom Deborah Caughlin Mangaravidi Kelly had lived with in marriage, and since she'd been notorious in her day, picking and choosing among a gallery of beaux . . . she had been my entry to the big league"; "I had also the secret ambition to return to politics . . . . With her beside me, I had leverage, however, I was one of the more active figures of the city—no one could be certain finally that nothing large would ever come from me" (pp. 15, 23, 23–24).

But it is not simply that Deborah represents institutional power or provides access to political power. She is also connected intimately to Rojack's capacity to realize personal power. She is the "armature" of his ego, and he fears that he does not have the "strength to stand alone" without her: "when she loved me . . . her strength seemed then to pass to mine and I was live with wit, I had vitality, I could depend on stamina, I possessed my style. . . . The instant she stopped loving me . . . why then my psyche was whisked from the stage and stuffed in a pit" (p. 24). Rojack accords Deborah complete control over his sense of who and what he is; he sees her as able to make him or break him, able to free him into power or reduce him to nothing. That Deborah possesses the key to his self-image is made clear from the start of their relationship: " 'You're not Catholic, are you?' 'No.' 'I was hoping perhaps you were Polish Catholic. Rojack, you know.' 'I'm half Jewish.' 'What is the other half?' 'Protestant. Nothing really.' 'Nothing really,' she said. 'Come, take me home.' And she was depressed" (p. 37). While Rojack later attributes this depression to Deborah's conviction that he lacks a sense of grace, it seems more likely, given the way he records the interchange, that he believes her depression stems from his failure to live up to her conception of somebody interesting, from her sense of him as nothing. In contrast to her rich identity as Deborah Caughlin Mangaravidi Kelly, her efforts to get an identity out of his name result in "nothing really." It is this view of himself as nothing that Deborah continually aggravates by saying he is nothing but a bully or nothing but a coward, by reminding him that he is not her father or her first husband or her real lover. The potential for murder in Rojack's relation to Deborah is thus double: she both represents his way of becoming something and confirms his sense of being nothing.

The attribution to women of power over male self-image structures Rojack's relation to Cherry. He seeks in her, as he did in Deborah, some image of the self that will give him power and control. It is his desire to look good in Cherry's eyes and to live up to what he thinks she sees in him that enables him to resist the temptation to give in to the police and thus confirm that sense of self he fears. Cherry is directly responsible for his "salvation," as Deborah is for his damnation. But the point is still the same; Rojack needs from Cherry exactly what he needed from Deborah and killed her for not providing. His identity and his power are inextricably connected to women. Women are the arbiters of his fate.

What fuels Rojack's conviction that women are in control of his life is a mythology which pervades *An American Dream* and which posits as its central premise the belief that women, as a result of being women, are in possession of an elemental power of which their institutional, political, and personal power is but a sign. *An American Dream* is grounded in the mystique of women as "psychic." Good, blonde Cherry is psychic enough to know who is going to win at the gambling tables of Las Vegas, and she is able to beat out a Mafioso by playing on his fear that she will haunt him. Herself a potential killer, Cherry has acquired the kind of power that can get people killed. Possession of psychic power is central to Kelly's Bess: "Each time we got together I felt as if I were an open piggy-bank: had to take whatever she would drop into me; her coin was powers. My nose for the market turned infallible" (p. 228). The connection between women's possession of psychic powers and their access to institutional, political, and personal power is revealed in Bess, for it is her psychic powers that put her in a position to control not only the stock market but also Kelly: "I was in her damn grip. Intolerable. I was afraid of her. More afraid of her than I'd been of anybody" (p. 228).

Rojack and Deborah double Kelly and Bess: "She had powers, my Deborah, she was psychic to the worst degree, and she had the power to lay a curse" (p. 27). Deborah's possession of psychic powers defines her as it defines Rojack's relation to her, creating his sense of being in her control, of acting in response to impulses, messages, and commands from her, a puppet on the end of her invisible strings. What Deborah's witchcraft controls, though, is not just Rojack's behavior: "Yes, I had come to believe in grace and the lack of it, in the long finger of God and the swish of the devil, I had come to give my scientific apprehension to the reality of witches" (p.

38). Deborah's power is great enough and Rojack's precariousness great enough that she has, in effect, taken over his mind.

This mystique of women as psychic has its roots in a biological mythology that is central to the drama and the politics of *An American Dream*. According to this mythology, women's power derives from their possession of a womb, that "mysterious space within," that "purse of flesh" in which are "psychic tendrils, waves of communication to some conceivable source of life, some manifest of life come into human beings from a beyond."[1] Behind "that woman's look that the world is theirs" is the fact of their biology, which, by providing a ligature between themselves and elemental sources of power, shapes the nature of their identity (p. 48). Women have the power that derives from a fixed and stable identity, a conviction of existence, an assurance of being on the side of life. It is understandable, given this myth of biology, that Rojack's sense of his existence as precarious and of women as having power in themselves and over him should emerge most clearly in his sexual relations with them. Rojack's vision of the way women use sex is that of the "considerable first night" (p. 186) offered to a second lover as a comment on the first. Thus, the man they are in bed with is of less importance than the man they are humiliating through the gusto of their infidelity, and the male comes off a loser no matter what his role: "Now I could know again why women never told the truth about sex. It was too abominable when they did" (p. 186). But the abominable truth that women have to tell through sex is nothing other than the fear that persistently plagues Rojack—the fear that there is nothing inside him, no center to his being; the fear that he is irrelevant and hence nonexistent; the fear that he is an agent of death rather than life. Contemplating Deborah's infidelity exposes the hollowness at his center and makes him want to jump, just as Deborah's saying she doesn't need him any more sexually sets off the murderous impulse in him.

In his relation with Cherry, Rojack articulates most clearly the connection between the nature of his sexual experience with women and his fears about his own identity: "The possibility that what I felt, when we made love, was a sensation which belonged to me alone, left me murderous" (p. 166). Behind this fear that male and female sexual experience are separate and distinct, behind the fear that he can never know whether what *he* experiences is what *she* experiences, is the fear that he is not necessary for women's sexual pleasure. The face of this fear is revealed when Cherry tells him that with him she has had for the first time an orgasm with a man inside her. Although presented as a testament to his powers, her remark has the effect of reminding him how rarely men give sexual pleasure to women and therefore of eliciting the fear that she may be lying to him and that he, like all the other men she has been with, is unnecessary for her pleasure. Only in the context of this fear can one understand the crucial importance of the vaginal orgasm in Rojack's sexual mythology.

Rojack's sense of irrelevance which produces in him the fear of being an agent of death who may be already dead is not limited to his questions about his role in women's sexual pleasure. He is further terrified by the thought that he is not necessary for creation. The belief that women have the capacity for self-generated reproduction has long been a phantom of the male imagination, appearing in modes as disparate as the elaborate mythology surrounding the Virgin Mary and the slang phrase, "she's gotten herself pregnant." What gives weight to this fear is the inescapable fact that no man can ever know for certain that he is the father of any woman's child; paternity is at best a hypothesis. Rojack's obsession with paternity—his hatred of devices of contraception, his refusal to make love to Cherry until she has removed her diaphragm, his horror at the idea that she aborts her child because she does not know whether the father is Shago or Tony— both points to this fact and seeks to compensate for and overcome it. In this fact are the origins of that quality of mystery which Rojack feels to be women's nature, and which makes him hate and fear them, for all other unknowings are avatars of this one: "he said, 'Did you know she did some work for us?'—said it in such a way I would never know for certain, not ever, there was something in his voice I could not for certain deny" (p. 246).

The sexual dimension of the paradigm that men become and women are reinforces the biological context of the myth of woman's power and man's powerlessness. In *An American Dream*, an identification is made between the precariousness of male existence and a precariousness in male sexuality. This connection is dramatized through the structure of Rojack's thirty-two-hour dream nightmare. The series of tests he undergoes serves as metaphor for the supreme sexual test. The metaphor is literalized in the final test, where the question becomes, Can I get up? Rojack's walk around the parapet is a thinly veiled analogue for an erection. *The Prisoner of Sex* provides a useful gloss on the attitudes toward male sexuality in *An American Dream*. In *The Prisoner of Sex* Mailer locates a major source of his hostility to the Women's Movement in its failure to realize "that a firm erection on a delicate fellow was the adventurous juncture of ego and courage," and in its "dull assumption that the sexual force of a man was the luck of his birth, rather than his finest moral product."[2] The same vision informs Mailer's remarks about D.H. Lawrence: "he had lifted himself out of his natural destiny which was probably to have the sexual life of a woman, had diverted the virility of his brain down into some indispensable minimum of phallic force—no wonder he worshipped the phallus, he above all men knew what an achievement was its rise from the root, its assertion to stand proud on a delicate base."[3]

This analysis of Lawrence, however, suggests another dimension to the precariousness of male sexuality: one's struggle to become male is an attempt to avoid one's natural destiny, which is to be female. The numerous references in *An American Dream*, in one form or another, to male homo-

sexuality indicate its significance for Rojack. Yet, what is crucial here is not
the degree to which Rojack may or may not have homosexual desires, but
rather what he thinks it means for a male to give in to those desires. The
clue is given early in Rojack's account of his killing of the German soldiers:
"a great bloody sweet German face, a healthy spoiled overspoiled young
beauty of a face, mother-love all over its making, possessor of that over-
curved mouth which only great fat sweet young faggots can have when
their rectum is tuned and entertained from adolescence on, came crying,
sliding, smiling up over the edge of the hole" (p.11). For Rojack, as for
Mailer (note his remarks on Genet in *The Prisoner of Sex*), the identifying
act of male homosexuality is anal intercourse and the male homosexual is a
mother's boy who becomes sexually female. Male homosexuality is not seen
as an equal sexual relation between two men but rather as a situation in
which one man is used as a woman by another man. This attitude is, of
course, the inevitable consequence of Mailer's concept of sex as solely a
function of power; yet, its implications are deeper than this. In all his comments on the subject, Mailer's focus is on the man who is made a woman.
Becoming female is for Mailer the essence of homosexual desire, because
what male homosexuality represents for him, and consequently why it must
be resisted, is the tendency in men to be women. Behind Mailer's view of
male homosexuality is a conviction that the ur-state of human sexuality is
female and that male sexuality is something created. Males must continually fight their way out of this state and must continually create themselves
sexually as male. Achieved against the grain, male sexuality is always in
danger of ceasing to exist, "defeated by the lurking treachery of Freudian
bisexuality, the feminine in a man giving out like a trick knee at a track
meet."[4] Male homosexuality takes its peculiar significance from the fact that
it proves the validity of the paradigm of female being and male becoming,
and keeps alive the fears that are its result. The male homosexual is a man
who has given in to the tendency to be female and who has as a result
ceased to exist.[5]

   That Rojack fears in himself the tendency to be sexually female and
that this fear is partly the source of his dread of nonexistence are suggested
in a number of ways. Consider, for instance, his predilection for analingus,
an experience in which he is penetrated and hence "female." No wonder
Rojack becomes murderous when Deborah reveals she has shared this
practice with other men.[6] Or consider his peculiar susceptibility to being
moved in on and possessed and his particular horror upon confronting this
susceptibility in himself or other men. When Kelly describes himself as a
piggy bank open to receive the coin of Bess's powers, he is presenting an
image of the male as a "purse of flesh." Or consider the extraordinary violence and the nature of Rojack's attack on Shago Martin, Cherry's faintly
effeminate black lover: "I took him from behind . . . and we ended with
Shago in a sitting position, and me behind him on my knees, my arms
choking the air from his chest as I lifted him up and smashed him down,

and lifted him up and smashed him down again" (p. 181). A metaphor for homosexual rape, the attack has the function of exorcizing Rojack's fear of being female by forcing someone else to act out the homosexual possibility. In seeking to annihilate Shago, Rojack seeks to annihilate the woman in him. Significantly, it is Shago's refusal to capitulate and his final taunt that Rojack has merely "killed the little woman in me" that reopen the floodgates of dread in Rojack (p. 183).

Rojack's fear of being sexually female provides a key to understanding his mythology of women's power. If their sexuality is a given while his is something that must be continually created against it, then they have both the power which derives from simply being and the power which derives from his needing them in order to become. And it is just possible that in making love to a woman the impulse to be female is as strongly elicited as the desire to become male, so that women have at their disposal as well the power that derives from their representing his deepest, most secret, and most feared desire—to be them.

Notes

1. Norman Mailer, *The Prisoner of Sex* (New York: Signet-New American Library, 1971), p. 47.

2. Ibid., pp. 35–36.

3. Ibid., pp. 111–12.

4. Kate Millett, *Sexual Politics* (New York: Doubleday, 1970), p. 327.

5. Mailer's work clarifies the political function of the culture's obsession with homosexuality. By keeping the image of the "faggot," the male as woman, in the forefront of cultural consciousness, he is able to justify ever greater excesses of masculinity as requisite antidotes for this induced fear.

6. That analingus is the practice at issue between Rojack and Deborah is made clear from Mailer's commentary on *An American Dream* in *The Prisoner of Sex*: "Still, there is a story they tell of Kate Millett when the winds blow and lamps gutter with a last stirring of flame. Then, as the skirts of witches go whipping around the wick, they tell how Kate went up to discuss the thesis at her college and a learned professor took issue with her declaration that the wife of the hero Rojack . . . had practiced sodomy with her husband and lovers. 'No, no,' cried the professor, 'I know the author, I know him well, I have discussed the scene with him more than once and it is not sodomy she practices, but analingus. It is for that she is killed, since it is a vastly more deranging offence in the mind's eye!' " (p. 71). That Deborah does it to Steve is made clear from her comment, as she informs him she will never do it with him again, that "the thought—at least in relation to you, dear sweet—makes me brush my gums with peroxide" (*An American Dream* [N.Y.: Dial Press, 1965, p. 34).

Mailer's Cosmology
J. Michael Lennon*

Ever since it was concluded that Yeats' system of cycles and gyres was not a matter of personal belief but an imaginative construction designed to buttress and justify his poetics, it has been difficult for any contemporary author to receive a fair hearing on his cosmology. Norman Mailer is a good example. Although he has introduced the "conception of God as an embattled vision which had terrified him from the hour he first encountered the thought"[1] in almost every one of his works from *The Deer Park*[2] (1955) on, most critics have either ignored his belief or slighted it,[3] even though Mailer has stated unequivocally that "every other one of his notions had followed from that [conception]" (*Fire*, pp. 409–10). My intent in this essay is to delineate Mailer's cosmology, which he says "is obviously the most ticklish, dense, incomprehensible and for most readers perverted part of my thicket."[4]

Mailer has described himself as an existentialist for over twenty-five years but I cannot conceive of any figure in the mainline, Sartrean school who would take as "a working stance" the notion "that life is probably good—if it isn't good, then our existence is such an absurdity that *any* action immediately becomes absurd."[5] Sartre and his followers, "alienated beyond alienation from their unconscious" and its "enormous teleological sense," and disbelieving in what Mailer calls "a mysticism of the flesh,"[6] can only begin with the premise of Sartre's Roquentin that "really there is nothing, nothing, absolutely no reason for existing."[7] Yet if Mailer's fleshy intuitions convince him of purpose in the cosmos, he is just as unwilling as Sergius O'Shaugnessy, the hero of *The Deer Park*, to believe that "the universe is just an elaborate clock." Such a mechanistic assumption, O'Shaugnessy says, is unacceptable, because then one must agree with W. Somerset Maugham that "nobody is any better than he ought to be" (*Deer Park*, p. 88).

Mailer's universe is neither clock nor chaos; his first premise is the exact opposite of Roquentin's, yet in several ways Mailer still must be considered an existentialist, and some aspects of existential thought must be considered if we are to grasp all the implications of his belief. But if we hope to enter the most confusing patches of his cosmological thicket, we must consult the American Romantics' vision of a dynamic universe in which each fact resonates with analogical meaning, man more than any other fact because he alone mirrors the entire design of the universe.

The most concise statement of Mailer's belief comes in *St. George and the Godfather* (1972); "The world's more coherent if God exists. And twice coherent if He exists like us."[8] Mailer's most profound intuition, however, is of "a charged and libidinous universe," a universe he compares to a com-

*Reprinted from *Modern Language Studies* 12 (Summer 1982):18–29, by permission of the author and the journal.

plex and recalcitrant lock whose "key was metaphor rather than measure" (*Fire*, pp. 201, 413). Unlike atheistic existentialists who see the extramental world as neutral, gratuitous or indecipherable, like the forehead of the White Whale, Mailer senses meaning in the cosmos. In *Of a Fire on the Moon* (1970) he says, "It was in the complacent assumption that the universe was no majestic mansion of architectonics out there between evil and nobility, or strife on a darkling plain, but rather an ultimately benign field of investigation which left Aquarius in the worst of his temper" (pp. 101–02). Mailer is here closer to Emerson than Melville (who like Ahab wondered if there was "naught beyond" the appearances of reality) for he cannot, even for the sake of argument, believe the universe lacks meaning.

But insofar as Mailer believes that God "exists like us," that "He is imperfect in the way we are imperfect,"[9] that "He too can suffer from a moral corruption" (*Advertisements*, p. 351), his position is not incompatible with that of Melville who also conceived of the possibility that frailty and evil could exist on a cosmic scale. Faced with a world of "abysmal idiotic disproportions," Mailer says, "it becomes too difficult to conceive of an all-powerful God who is all good" (*Playboy* Interview, 72). Melville brooded over that notion of Zoroastrianism which (like Manichaeanism) postulates a cosmic struggle between good and evil.[10] Mailer also takes seriously the Manichaean-Zoroastrian belief in the division of power throughout the universe, but, as the following quotation demonstrates, he is as undogmatic on the subject as was Melville. What distinguishes Mailer's theomachy, or war of the gods, from Melville's is that it is existential. Zoroastrian belief calls for good to prevail at the end of time. Mailer's God, like man, cannot know his final destiny.

The first full statement of Mailer's beliefs came in a 1958 interview with Richard G. Stern:

> MAILER: . . . I think that the particular God we can conceive of is a god whose relationship to the universe we cannot divine; that is, how enormous He is in the scheme of the universe we can't begin to say. But almost certainly, He is not all-powerful; He exists as a warring element in a divided universe, and we are a part of—perhaps the most important part—of His great expression, His enormous destiny; perhaps He is trying to impose upon the universe His conception of being against other conceptions of being very much opposed to His. Maybe we are in a sense the seed-carriers, the voyagers, the explorers, the embodiment of that embattled vision; maybe we are engaged in a heroic activity, and not a mean one.
>
> STERN: This is really something.
>
> MAILER: Well, I would say it is far more noble in its conception, far more arduous as a religious conception than the notion of the all-powerful God who takes care of us.
>
> STERN: And do you take to this conception for its perilous nobility, or do you take to it because you believe in it?

MAILER: I believe in it.

STERN: You believe in it.

MAILER: It's the only thing that makes any sense to me. It's the only thing that explains to me the problem of evil. You see, the answer may well be—how to put it?—that God Himself is engaged in a destiny so extraordinary, so demanding, that He too can suffer from a moral corruption, that He can make demands upon us which are unfair, that He can abuse our beings in order to achieve His means, even as we abuse the very cells of our own body (*Advertisements*, p. 351).

Three linked strands run through this cluster of ideas: First, Mailer sees the universe as process, a cosmic dialectic with the final synthesis unwritten; second, there is an extraordinary emphasis on man's free will, his ability to rough-hew not only his own destiny but to affect God's as well. "The moral consequences of this," Mailer says in the same interview, "are not only staggering, but they're thrilling; because moral experience is intensified rather than diminished" (*Advertisements*, p. 351). Finally, there is a pronounced Pauline-Calvinistic sense of evil which is associated both with the imperfections of men and God and the actions of a powerful, wily Devil. In almost every one of his discussions of cosmology,[11] these three beliefs are mentioned. In his darker moments Mailer has also entertained the thought that "the ardors of His [God's] embattled voyage could have driven Him mad" (*Fire*, p. 138). Melville's Ahab considered the same possibility. For both writers the exact nature of the *anima* behind the pasteboard masks of reality is uncertain.

D.J.'s statement in *Why Are We in Vietnam?* (1967) that "if the center of things is insane, it is insane with force,"[12] and his hallucinatory vision of God as "some beast of a giant jaw and cavernous mouth with a full cave's breath and fangs, and secret call: come to me" (p. 217), is surely equivalent to Ahab's obsession with "that inscrutable thing" of "outrageous strength with an inscrutable malice sinewing it"[13] that Moby Dick either represents or is. Yet I do not believe either creature-image reflects the central belief of its creator. It has been claimed that D.J.'s vision is the heart of Mailer's cosmology,[14] but I believe that it can be established that a noble but imperfect God struggling with a principle of evil, with the outcome unknown, is Mailer's deepest belief. Here again Melville is instructive. The White Whale energizes Ahab in the same way that the bestial deity D.J. sees in the electric Alaskan night generates the destructive erethism needed for him to declare in the last words of the book, "Vietnam, hot damn" (p. 224). "Evil, be thou my good," is the implicit, blasphemous prayer of Ahab and D.J.

The reason why Melville and Mailer are willing to give their heroes license to try on the barbaric and court the demonic lies in their belief that the quintessential human activity is the quest. The fact that the actions of the moral nihilist may be negative is "irrelevant," Mailer says. The important thing is that "they are concerned with the forefront of experience."[15] Movement must precede morality, and "the message in the labyrinth of the genes," Mailer insists, is that "violence was locked with creativity, and adventure was the secret of love" (*Pres. Papers*, p. 40). The peril to life and soul of violence and nihilism is not only known to Mailer and Melville, but sought. The attraction is not for evil itself but for its defining power as a benchmark in the cosmic war. The measure of such "extreme situations" for Mailer is their ability to burn "out the filament of old dull habit" (*Pres. Papers*, p. 198). Stasis and silence are the worst sins. Stubb is a "mechanical" and the morality of Mailer's Sam Slovoda has neither a positive nor a negative charge.[16] "The essence of biology," Mailer says, "seems to be challenge and response, risk and survival, war and the lessons of war" (*Pres. Papers*, p. 167). And the most important lesson of this dialectic, though costly, is finally not too dear. It is the self-knowledge necessary for growth. Writing of Hemingway soon after his death, Mailer says, "If we are ill and yet want to go on, we must put up the ante. If we lose, it does not mean we wished to die" (*Pres. Papers*, p. 105). So Melville's Ahab cries, "my topmost greatness lies in my topmost grief,"[17] and Mailer explains (in his preface to a collection appropriately entitled *The Saint and the Psychopath*) that the beauty inherent in violence almost drove Kierkegaard mad "for he had the courage to see that his criminal impulses were also his most religious."[18]

Melville asserted in *White-Jacket* that "I have a voice that helps to shape eternity; and my volitions stir the orbits of the furthest suns. In two senses, we are precisely what we worship. Ourselves are Fate."[19] His statement approximates Cherry's in *An American Dream* (1965) that "God is weaker because I didn't turn out well."[20] Melville's line also parallels D.J.'s belief that "we are all after all agents of Satan and the Lord" (*Vietnam*, p. 27), and the possibility that Barney Kelly, like Fedallah, may be "a solicitor for the Devil" (*Dream*, p. 221). For Mailer and Melville human psychomachia both partakes of and parallels the struggle between the Lord and the Devil. This is the existential deck of cards Mailer says all his work is dealt from (*Playboy* Interview, 84), and the reason moral experience in this context is "staggering" and "thrilling." I do not believe Melville could accept without qualification Rojack's belief that "God was not love but courage. Love came only as a reward" (*Dream*, p. 191), but surely he would subscribe to Mailer's espousal of "a life committed to the notion that the substratum of existence is the search, the end meaningful but mysterious" (*Advertisements*, p. 315).

From all information it appears that Hawthorne did not feel Melville's urge to strike through the mask. He could not have accepted Mailer's belief that "creativity is always next to the verboten" (*Errands*, p. 112), and unlike Melville he consciously avoided some of the darker corners of human experience. Melville, who loved "a deep diver," would share Mailer's belief that investigation of themes like racism, cannibalism, incest and monomania could provide what Mailer calls "the inelectable ore of the authentic" (*Errands*, p. 153) as well as the exemplars of hagiology. I think Melville would agree with Mailer that the saint and the psychopath "were united to one another, and different from the mass of men. They were closer to existence" (*Errands*, p. 190).

Melville leaves Hawthorne at the door to the forbidden and plunges into the "blackness of darkness;" Mailer too explores the abyss but the desperation of his attempt does not, as with Melville, preclude a return. Ishmael does not go to the pit and so is saved. After gaining a Lear-like knowledge of himself and the universe Ahab goes under; Pierre dies in confusion; Bartleby does not speak. Life for them was an incurable sickness. But for Mailer "acute disease is cure" (*Pres. Papers*, p. 7). There is even a "curious happiness" from "a wound in that period when we do not know which flesh is severed forever and what is recuperable." Unlike Hemingway's "unreasonable wound" which brings chaos, the wound Mailer speaks of may bring change, and "change," he continues, "may give life" (*Fire*, p. 117). Committed to the necessity of quitting the lee shore for the endless sea, Melville had small hope that voyaging out could accomplish more than the romantic satisfaction of refusing to surrender to inevitable defeat. Ishmael alone among Melville's heroes is able to balance the lure of the masthead, the haven of the lee shore and the fascination of the fire. For the rest, for Ahab, Vere, Pierre, Bartleby and the narrator of *The Confidence-Man*, the answer is that there is no answer, just a knowledge of what Melville called the "fusion indistinguishable" of good and evil.

Mailer attempts a cosmological synthesis more sweeping than Emerson's because it gives evil equal play, and he criticizes Sholom Aleichem, as Melville criticized Emerson, for "a determined inability to confront evil in intimate forms" (*Errands*, p. 81). He refuses, however, to accede to easy righteousness. In a 1972 letter he says that the war of God and the Devil "is no longer a simple combat and each are capable of subtlety in their methods. Then the difficulty in comprehending the authority of the senses is that it often becomes rarefied to a point which the flesh simply can't make. So in our most existential moments we can't know if we are saints or demons, or put another way, agents of white or black magic. So the war may prove like many wars that it proves nothing."[21] The choices are hard, but as Rojack says and Mailer believes, it is always "better to choose" (*Dream*, p. 191).

Choice for Mailer is the forward edge of the quest, existential because it is a foray of unknown strategic value in the war between God and the Devil, yet absolutely necessary because the alternative is entropy. Choice and movement are never purposeless because they provide definition. Mailer believes it is crucial to allow *all* thoughts and feelings to come to the surface. "Growth," he says, "cannot be understood without going into the nature of waste" (*Pres. Papers*, p. 270). If society stifles an individual, smothers him in conformity, then he cannot act in any moral way. Stultified by the homogenization of technological society, man's first impulse should be to escape—escape first, assertion of self first, change first—then morality, then self-discipline, then harmony, community, love. This is the basic argument of Mailer's 1957 essay "The White Negro,"[22] a brilliant delineation of the impoverishment of the romantic spirit in America. It also offers a prospectus for a new hero—the hipster, an urban adventurer seeking new energy in the wild west of American night life. The hipster, or White Negro, whatever his shortcomings, is at least in motion and so accumulating a body of experience to react to later.

It is not a world of trouble that Mailer sees—that would be welcome—but instead a stagnation of all possibility. A few years after WWII, he says, America took on "a collective odor which was reminiscent of a potato left to molder in a plastic box" (*Pres. Papers*, p. 183). Silence, exile and cunning[23] cannot undercut modern civilization's obsession with control; Mailer concludes woefully that "nihilism might be the only answer to totalitarianism."[24] Melville could only sense that what Mailer calls "a shit storm" was coming (*Cannibals*, p. 41). For Mailer there can be little doubt which way civilization is heading. "That continuing revolution of reason which the Renaissance had begun"[25] is now cresting; a fearsome totalitarianism whose nature it is to "render populations apathetic" and act as "a deodorant to nature" (*Armies*, p. 136) is in control. The "shit storm," Mailer feels, is here. Only because matters are so grave can Mailer conceive of a concordance between man's creative and destructive impulses. Melville lived in an age of anxiety and, like Arnold, wandered ". . . between two worlds, one dead. The other powerless to be born."[26] The twentieth century, of course, has been called the age of anxiety, but Hitler, Stalin and the Rev. Jim Jones, among others, have given evil a face. Mailer, clinging desperately to his intuitions of transcendence, has imagined a sort of Napoleonic God, a great flawed general, simultaneously noble and corrupt but endowed with a heroic conception of destiny, to meet that face.

These Manichaean oppositions have led some of Mailer's critics to conclude that war is Mailer's primary metaphor for experience and his literal subject since *The Naked and the Dead* (1948).[27] Richard Poirier's 1972 study of Mailer in the Viking Modern Masters series[28] makes this assertion. But Poirier's view does not go deep enough. Mailer's Emersonian belief[29] in a universe which is not "A Fact" but "a changing reality whose laws are remade at each instant by everything living, but most particularly man" (*Advertisements*, p. 327), a belief stated in "The White Negro," has not changed since that time. Poirier says Mailer is obsessed by war. This view, in my judgment, is too sweeping. Mailer is interested in RELATION, an idea larger than war and one which subsumes it under its rubric.

Poirier points to Mailer's comment in a 1966 self-interview, "The Political Economy of Time," that "Form in general . . . is the record of a war" (*Cannibals*, p. 370). He holds that this statement is the key to Mailer's aesthetics and also the major thematic chord in his work. But in another self-interview, a piece which Mailer says is "indispensable to understanding *The Political Economy of Time*" (*Cannibals*, p. 261), Mailer qualifies considerably the bellicosity Poirier sees as the linchpin of his work. Poirier mentions this piece, which is called "The Metaphysics of the Belly," but does not note its attempt to extend the ambit of organicism to include "death, perversion, promiscuity, and the fear of hell" (*Cannibals*, p. 283), nor Mailer's assertion that these extreme states are necessary to balance others, because "life seems to come out of the meeting of opposites" (*Cannibals*, p. 281). Consequently, "Beauty, as the Greeks kept nagging, was harmony. Well, it has other qualities as well I hope, danger, ecstasy, promise, the transcendence of terror—all the emotions which give life to us in the West—but harmony, I fear, is what beauty is first. It means that separate parts function in a lively set of rhythms with one another. No organ is too fast or too slow vis-à-vis another organ. The pleasant relation inspires proportions in the outer forms which are healthy, harmonious, and beautiful" (*Cannibals*, p. 265). War for Mailer is only one of a series of relationships which include "the block of marble worked by the sculptor, the audience and the play, a mood and its occasion, the good rider and his good horse, the blocking back and the line-backer, the skier on the snow, the style of sex, a sail into the wind" (*Cannibals*, p. 281).

War is not sought for its own sake but only when it offers focus. Mailer was an early and severe critic of the Vietnam War not only because it bombed civilians and destroyed a complex peasant culture but because it "had no line of battle or discernible climax (an advanced notion which supposes that wars may be in part good because they are sometimes the only way to define critical conditions rather than blur them")" (*Armies*, p. 208).

Because Mailer accepts the romantic notion that man is "roughly more good than evil" (*Advertisements*, p. 336), he can assume that if one follows what he calls the "rebellious imperatives of the self" (*Advertisements*, p. 313) a better world will result. So throughout his writings he hammers on the same exhortation: "Grow or else pay more for remaining the same."[30] For Mailer the choice is no longer between good and evil but between stagnation and growth; man's problem is not his inability to choose good but his inability to choose at all. Mailer's belief in an existential God, a belief which is both paradox and first premise, allows him to maintain his belief in the possibility of human progress without rejecting theism.

But Mailer cannot be sure which way the tide of battle in the cosmos or the nation is flowing. "The schizophrenia of the land" he says, has been "growing more Faustian and more Oriental each season with ABM [anti-ballistic missile] and million-footed folk-rock festivals at the poles, yes, all the incomprehensible contradictions of America might yet come to focus on the possibility that races were at war in America like forces from the cosmos" (*Fire*, pp. 279–80). Mailer is unsure who is winning and why. Was the Lord or the Devil behind the rise of science in the Renaissance and the flight to the moon? If the Renaissance was the time when reason disrupted man's communion with nature, it was also the time of Shakespeare, Marlowe and Donne. So Mailer defines his world with paradoxes and describes himself as a "Left Conservative" (*Armies*, pp. 143, 208), a man whose philosophy is a "private mixture of Marxism, conservatism, nihilism, and large parts of existentialism" (*Armies*, p. 35). He is a former drug addict who feels drugs are the Devil's tool yet is willing to prescribe them for stymied scientists, a non-smoker who once went through three packs a day, a former heavy drinker who says one of the most defeating things he can think of is losing control of himself via alcoholism. He believes in work and has written more than twenty-five books yet continues to get involved in a variety of extraliterary media activities.[31] A firm believer in monogamy, he has been married six times and has nine children. The paradoxes are endless but behind them all is the fact that Mailer, like the American Romantics, sees reality as a mesh of relations.

Like Melville's Ishmael, who had "doubts of all things earthly, and intuitions of some things heavenly,"[32] Mailer believes "we live out our lives wandering among mysteries," our only guide being "the instinctive logic our inner voice tells us is true to the relations *between* mysteries." We cannot trust the individual fact, he continues, because it "is invariably a compression of nuances which alienate the reality." Not the fact, but "the root from which the fact may have evolved" is what should preoccupy us (*Pres. Papers*, pp. 269–70). And the "root" for Mailer, as it was for Emerson, Whitman and Melville, is a processive universe where human possibilities expand and contract with the movement of history.

Melville believed that man could shape his own destiny but was troubled by the problem of evil. To accept the benign determinism of Emerson's cosmos would mean rejecting the possibility of a cosmic principle of evil. Melville could not do this, but he does not seem to have accepted, like Mailer, the possibility that this principle could prevail. Melville's only consolation lay in the continuing search for the bare truth which might reveal the moral balance of the universe—if one existed. His only certainty was that man's destiny is provisional.

Mailer's cosmology is a bulwark against the void Melville stared into, a species of theological brinkmanship which affirms transcendental perception without lapsing into cosmic optimism. Like Melville Mailer believes that man's future is unwritten; like Sartre he rejects as ignoble "the notion of the all-powerful God who takes care of us" (*Advertisements*, p. 351). But Mailer does not believe that man is alone or history is irrelevant or unfathomable or that life ends in death.[33] In his argument for the meaning of sex in *The Prisoner of Sex* (1971), he says, "Yet try to decide there is design in the universe, that humans embody a particular Intent, assume just once there is some kind of destiny intended—at the least!—*intended* for us, and therefore human beings are not absurd, not totally absurd, assume some Idea (or at least some clash of Idea versus ideas) is in operation—and then sex cannot comfortably prove absurd" (p. 136).

In a naturalistic novel, in Norris's *McTeague* or Dreiser's *Sister Carrie*, the characters reflect the surest view of the universe their creators can muster. But if one believes in a universe where the lines of battle between light and darkness are confused and the outcome unknown, if one believes in a flawed, purposeful (but terribly overextended) God, then the need is for a hero of similar proportions. Even as Mailer was writing about "that doubtful day when I sit down to write about my life" (*Advertisements*, p. 99), he had begun to do so. After attempting to separate his artistic and personal worlds in his early novels,[34] Mailer realized that this course clashed with his cosmology. And so, beginning with *Advertisements for Myself* in 1959, Mailer began to incorporate more and more of his personal beliefs and experience in his work. From 1968 to 1975 he published eight nonfiction narratives with himself as narrator-hero.[35] Mailer's vision of an imperfect, striving God whose struggle to fulfill his destiny was intertwined with human history prompted him to conceive a new role for himself: the writer-hero, also imperfect and striving, who sought to cut through the bedeviled communications of the modern world "with the only broadsword God ever gave you, a glimpse of something like Almighty prose."[36] For Mailer, man's ability to advance or hinder God's destiny is incontestable.

In 1856 Hawthorne noted in his journal how Melville would "reason of Providence and futurity, and of everything that lies beyond human ken," but finally could "neither believe, nor be comfortable in his unbelief; and he is too honest and courageous not to try to do one or the other." Norman Mailer has wandered through these same metaphysical deserts searching for the "definite belief" which Hawthorne said Melville could not find.[37] But Mailer's conviction of God's "Intent," his "fondness for order,"[38] coupled with his uncertainty about its fulfillment, has kept him from lapsing into the "annihilation" that Melville spoke of to Hawthorne, and led him to propose a ditheistic cosmology large enough to accommodate the obliquely opposed principles of human freedom and progress, divine providence and limitation, and cosmic evil.

Notes

1. Norman Mailer, *Of A Fire on the Moon* (1970; rpt. New York: New American Library, 1971), p. 409. Quotations from Mailer's work are taken from paperback reprints wherever possible. In most cases, quotations will be identified parenthetically in my text after the first full citation. When two dates are given, the first is the date of original publication in book form.

2. Mailer, *The Deer Park* (1955; rpt. New York, Berkley, 1967). The eschatological fantasies of Marion Faye, the dark genius of *The Deer Park*, demonstrate the range of Mailer's own speculations during the early and middle fifties. See pp. 280–81.

3. Robert Solotaroff is the major exception. In *Down Mailer's Way* (Urbana, Illinois: University of Illinois Press, 1974), he devotes his third chapter to Mailer's existential cosmology, relating it carefully to European existentialism. He does not relate Mailer to the Ameri-

can Romantics, however, as I attempt to do here. Stanley T. Gutman, in *Mankind in Barbary: The Individual and Society in the Novels of Norman Mailer* (Hanover, New Hampshire: University Press of New England, 1975), gives a clear exposition of Mailer's cosmological beliefs (pp. 76–80, 110–16), and notes that Mailer "is firmly rooted in the Emersonian tradition" (p. 79), but does not mention Melville. Jonathan Middlebrook makes reference to Mailer's affinities with the American Romantics (and with a great number of other writers, European and American) in his study, *Mailer and the Times of his Time* (San Francisco: Bay Books, 1976), but the only important attempt to link Mailer with the writers of the American Renaissance is Michael Cowan's "The Americanness of Norman Mailer," *Norman Mailer: A Collection of Critical Essays*, ed. Leo Braudy (Englewood Cliffs, New Jersey: Prentice-Hall, 1972), pp. 143–57. Cowan's thoughtful article focuses on Mailer's ties to Melville and Henry Adams. He does not discuss Mailer's cosmology, however. See also Laura Adams' *Existential Battles: The Growth of Norman Mailer* (Athens, Ohio: Ohio University Press, 1976), pp. 22–24, 119.

4. Mailer, letter to Mike Lennon, October 7, 1974.

5. Mailer, *The Presidential Papers* (1963; rpt. New York: Berkley, 1970), pp. 139.

6. Mailer, *Advertisements for Myself* (1959; rpt. New York: Berkley, 1966), pp. 315, 356, 292.

7. Jean-Paul Sartre, *Nausea* (1938; rpt. New York: New Directions, 1964), p. 112. The narrator of Mailer's "Truth and Being; Nothing and Time: A Broken Fragment from a Long Novel" speaks for Mailer when he says that Sartre "had a dialectical mind good as a machine for cybernetics, immense in its way, he could peel a nuance like an onion, but he had no sense of evil, the anguish of God, and the possible existence of Satan" (*Pres. Papers*, p. 273).

8. Mailer, *St. George and the Godfather* (New York: New American Library, 1972), p. 29. Published only in paperback edition.

9. Mailer, "*Playboy* Interview: Norman Mailer," Interviewer, Paul Carroll (January, 1968), 74. Subsequent quotations from this interview will be identified parenthetically in my text.

10. Marius Bewley explains that "in Zoroastrianism, with which Melville, to some extent at least, was familiar, the world is divided between a good and an evil principle, and they are twin brothers. In the end the good will triumph but their conflict is for the length of time." *The Eccentric Design: Form in the Classic American Novel* (New York: Columbia University Press, 1959), p. 199.

11. Mailer discusses his cosmology and related subjects in numerous passages in his books and in interviews. Besides those cited in this article, his most important comments can be found in the following: *Deer Park* (pp. 280–81); *Advertisements* (pp. 302, 472–93); *Fire* (pp. 75, 128, 189, 411–12); "Norman Mailer: The Final Round," Interviewer: Richard Stratton. *Rolling Stone* (January 16, 1975), 54, 56–57; "Existential Aesthetics: An Interview with Norman Mailer," Interviewer: Laura Adams, *Partisan Review*, 42 (Fall, 1975), 197–207; and "Norman Mailer on Love, Sex, God, and the Devil," Interviewer: Cathleen Medwick, *Vogue* (December, 1980), 269. Major portions of the interviews with Stern, Stratton, Adams and Medwick are collected in Mailer's *Pontifications: Interviews*, ed. Michael Lennon (Boston, Little, Brown and Company, 1982). In the same volume, see also interview with Lennon, "Literary Ambitions."

12. Mailer, *Why Are We in Vietnam?* (1967; rpt. New York: Berkley, 1968), p. 151.

13. Herman Melville, *Moby-Dick*, ed. Harrison Hayford and Hershel Parker (New York: Norton, 1967), p. 144.

14. Richard D. Finholt, "'Otherwise How Explain?' Norman Mailer's New Cosmology," *MFS* (Special Issue: Norman Mailer), 17 (Autumn, 1971), 375–86.

15. Mailer, quoted in "PPA Press Conference," *Publisher's Weekly*, 187 (March 22, 1965), 44.

16. Sam Slovoda, the hero of "The Man Who Studied Yoga," is the type and symbol of

alienated and anxious modern man. In his "fear of new people and novel situations" (*Advertisements*, p. 146), he is exactly opposite the hipster-hero of Mailer's 1957 essay, "The White Negro."

17. *Moby-Dick*, p. 468.

18. According to Mailer, *The Saint and the Psychopath* is a collection of previously published pieces which was sold to Dell Publishing Co. but never released. The quotation comes from *Existential Errands* (1972; rpt. New York: New American Library, 1973), p. 190, where Mailer has published the preface.

19. Melville, *White-Jacket* (Evanston, Illinois: Northwestern University Press, 1970), p. 321.

20. Mailer, *An American Dream* (1965; rpt. New York: Dell, 1966), p. 185.

21. Mailer, letter to Mike Lennon, January 20, 1972. After reading this passage Mailer underscored the word "may" in the last sentence, and noted "this is the core of difficulty in trusting the authority of the senses."

22. "The White Negro" was first published in *Dissent* (Summer, 1957), 276–93. It was reprinted as a paperback by City Lights Books (San Francisco, 1957) and then included in *Advertisements* in 1959.

23. In *Cannibals and Christians* (1966; rpt. New York: Dell, 1967), Mailer says he cannot submit to this "prescription" of Joyce's because he is "too gregarious" (p. 5). Mailer could never accept the kind of isolation Salinger and Pynchon have imposed upon themselves.

24. Mailer, *The Armies of the Night* (1968; rpt. New York: New American Library, 1968), p. 199.

25. Mailer, *The Prisoner of Sex* (1971; rpt. New York: New American Library, 1971), p. 44.

26. Matthew Arnold, "Stanzas from the Grande Chartreuse," *Arnold, Poetical Works*, ed. C.B. Tinker and H.F. Lowry (London: Oxford University Press, 1950), p. 302.

27. Mailer, *The Naked and the Dead* (1948; rpt. New York: New American Library, 1951).

28. Richard Poirier, *Norman Mailer* (New York: Viking, 1972). Jean Radford also follows this line in *Norman Mailer: A Critical Study* (New York: Harper & Row, 1975).

29. Gutman anticipates me on the similarity between Mailer's and Emerson's universes. He says, "In his acceptance of change as a universal principle, and in his ethical injunction to men to continually change and explore ever deeper into themselves and the universe, Mailer is in complete agreement with Emerson" (*Mankind in Barbary*, p. 79).

30. This line, which might be called the pith of Mailer's ethics, first appeared in *Deer Park*, p. 294. It is repeated twice in *Advertisements*, first in "The White Negro" (p. 323), and then in "Advertisements for Myself on the Way Out" (p. 476), the excerpt from Mailer's "long novel" which closes that collecction. Mailer reprints the statement from *The Deer Park* in "The Big Bite," *Esquire* (November, 1962), 134, and then reprints the column in *Pres. Papers*, p. 104. In these last two instances he adds, "I think the line is true. I think its application is more ferocious in America than anywhere I know." Finally, Sergius O'Shaugnessy speaks the line in *The Deer Park: A Play* (New York: Dell, 1967), p. 189.

31. For a discussion of Mailer's opinions of and relations with the media, see Mailer's "Of a Small and Modest Malignancy, Wicked and Bristling with Dots," *Esquire* (November, 1977), 125–48; Robert Lucid, "Norman Mailer: The Artist as Fantasy Figure," *The Massachusetts Review*, 15 (Autumn, 1974), 581–95; and my article, "Mailer's Sarcophagus: The Artist, the Media and the 'Wad,' " *MFS*, 23 (Summer, 1977), 179–87.

32. *Moby-Dick*, p. 314.

33. Mailer rejects what might be called the *sine qua non* of existentialism in positing an afterlife. "The reluctance of modern European existentialism to take on the logical continu-

ation of the existential vision (that there is a life after death which can be as existential as life itself) has brought French and German existentialism to a halt on this uninhabitable terrain of the absurd" (*Pres. Papers*, p. 213). Other references to an afterlife are: *Pres. Papers*, pp. 138, 214 and 246–47; *Errands*, pp. 190, 287–88. Mailer's *The Deer Park: A Play* is set in Hell, a Hell to which people are not necessarily permanently confined. See also Laura Adams' interview with Mailer ("Existential Aesthetics," 206–07). Mailer's continuing interest in life after death is most recently manifested in his novel *Ancient Evenings* (Boston: Little, Brown and Company, 1983), which begins and ends in the afterlife.

34. For a discussion of why Mailer felt obliged to separate his personal and artistic worlds, and how he later reconciled them, see my article, "Mailer's Radical Bridge," *Journal of Narrative Technique*, 7 (Fall, 1977), 170–88. See also chapters 3 and 4 of Jennifer Bailey's *Norman Mailer: Quick-Change Artist* (New York: Barnes & Noble, 1979).

35. The eight books are: *Armies* (1968); *Miami and the Siege of Chicago* (1968; rpt. New York: New American Library, 1968); *Fire* (1970); *Prisoner* (1971); *St. George* (1972); *Marilyn: A Novel Biography* (1973; rpt. New York: Warner, 1975); *The Faith of Graffiti* (New York: Praeger, 1974); *The Fight* (1975; rpt. New York: Bantam, 1976). It should be noted that Mailer becomes less and less interested in himself as a protagonist as this series progresses.

36. Mailer, Introduction to *Deaths For the Ladies (and other disasters)* (1962; rpt. New York: New American Library, 1971), n.p.

37. Nathaniel Hawthorne, *The English Notebooks*, entry for November 20, 1856, reprinted in *The Portable Hawthorne*, ed. Malcolm Cowley (1948; rpt. New York: Viking, 1969), p. 651.

38. Mailer makes this statement in a *Paris Review* interview and prefaces it by disavowing any "love of disruption for the sake of disruption." The interview, which took place on July 6, 1963, is reprinted in *Writers at Work: The Paris Review Interviews* (3rd series), ed. George Plimpton (New York: Viking, 1968), p. 277.

The Quest for Empowering Roots: Mailer and the American Literary Tradition

Michael Cowan*

Few students of Norman Mailer's entire literary career would argue with his friend Jean Malaquais's assessment that "Norman is very much an American writer."[1] From his earliest ambition "to write huge collective novels about American life"[2] to his more recent attention, as he put it, to "matters that are very American: Marilyn Monroe, Muhammed Ali, Henry Miller, Gary Gilmore,"[3] Mailer has searched for powerful symbols of the complexities, contradictions, transcendent possibilities, and final mystery of his nation. And it is a critical commonplace that he has elaborately dramatized himself as a "half-heroic and three-quarters comic" embodiment of

*This essay has been revised and expanded by the author especially for this volume. It appeared originally under the title "The Americanness of Norman Mailer" in *Norman Mailer: A Collection of Critical Essays*, ed. Leo Braudy (Englewood Cliffs, N.J.: Prentice-Hall, 1972), 143–57.

both the contradictions and the possibilities.[4] As a central example of the narcissist he finds embedded in the psyche of most Americans, engaged by a ceaseless and passionate inner dialogue between parts of himself, Mailer has constantly gravitated towards Americans who can most vividly reveal to him who he is.[5] There is clearly self-reference in his assertion that Marlon Brando "is our greatest actor, our noblest actor, and he is also our national lout. Could it be otherwise in America?"[6] It should not surprise us that all his major American heroes, his "representative Americans" (in the Emersonian sense) from John F. Kennedy and Ernest Hemingway to Miller, Monroe, Ali, and Gilmore, are artists. They have offered him not merely examples of living but models of style. Whatever his on-again, off-again hopes for social and psychological revolution in America, Mailer has more typically looked to artistic style—specifically, a romantic style—to wrestle the contradictions of American action and feeling into creative symbiosis. Thus in *The Fight* (1975), after outlining the complex social and metaphysical stakes he finds symbolized by the 1974 Ali-Foreman fight, which he terms a battle between styles,[7] he can argue that "it was as if contradictions fell away with a victory for Ali. That would be a triumph for everything which did not fit into the computer: for audacity, inventiveness, even art. . . . It would certainly come off as a triumph for the powers of regeneration in an artist. What could be of more importance to Norman?" (162). Ali's regeneration becomes counterpart to Mailer's attempt, still reeling from the inconclusive battle recorded in *The Prisoner of Sex* (1971),[8] and finding himself imprisoned in boring "mediocre habits" of thought and expression,[9] to regenerate his own artistic powers by capturing Ali's fighting style in his own book. If Ali can make a comeback, so can Mailer "the literary champ."[10]

Mailer's cry in *Cannibals and Christians* (1966) for American writers who will "clarify a nation's vision of itself" is thus not merely a social but, at base, a religious and aesthetic appeal.[11] Americans' most deeply hopeful dreams, as he argued in his account of the 1967 March on the Pentagon, *The Armies of the Night* (1968), rest on a faith that their nation is "the land where a new kind of man was born from the idea that God was present in every man not only as compassion but as power, and so the country belonged to the people; for the will of the people—if the locks of their life could be given the art to turn—was the will of God."[12] Like Ralph Waldo Emerson and Walt Whitman, Mailer has argued that the key to democratic dreams is a religious dream—a citizenry's often-unconscious vision of its individual and collective bonds with transcendent power—and that it takes an artist to turn that key, to liberate his fellow Americans from their deadening dread of their own freedom and power. Like the graffiti artists whose dangerous art he so admires,[13] Mailer wants to use the blank wall of his contemporary technological society as a canvas on which to paint a colorful communal jungle of psychological, aesthetic, and religious possibility. But he also likes to see his own name in large letters on that wall. If poets, in

Emerson's term, are "liberating gods," Mailer has always wanted to be in the pantheon.

As *Ancient Evenings* (1983) intricately demonstrates, however, the pantheon itself can be a boxing arena where heavyweights slug it out.[14] In a 1980 interview Mailer could argue that Muhammad Ali and Hemingway "come out of that same American urgency to be the only planet in existence. To be the sun. It goes right back to Egypt. A thousand gods but only one sun."[15] Mailer's own literary aspirations have oscillated between wanting to be a "sun" and acknowledging himself as a "son," the bearer of a literary tradition both burdensome and liberating. As a self-consciously American writer, his ambivalence toward his literary forefathers has been two-fold. For he has had to confront not only the use of a non-American but an American tradition. At times he seems to have found himself an exemplar of Emerson's advice to cease listening to the European muses. In 1981 he can suggest that "Americans have a saving instinct—we're not that near to European high culture. . . . In America one can still have the illusion that one is doing something brand new. One can still feel like a pioneer." But he can also acknowledge the price of that "illusion"—its contribution to a destructive national shallowness and arrogance. As he notes, "we didn't start with much culture and we never achieved a truly rich American marrow. We're now in terrible trouble because we're getting to the point where we are destroying our culture at a much greater rate than we are creating it."[16] It may be partly this worry that has prompted him in the last decade to begin exploring ways in which non-American roots—the African sensibility charted in *The Faith of Graffiti* (1974) and *The Fight* and the Egyptian ethos of *Ancient Evenings*—can renew American imaginative life. (There are clearly implicit references to his own literary practice in his recent comment that "Ancient Egyptian is a wonderful language, a very dialectical language. . . . It's a tremendously sensuous language, rather existential. You feel that the ancient Egyptians had already articulated one highly complex and wonderful and rather magical civilization, and yet they were still close to the primitive. Every word in the language is a revelation."[17] This same ambivalence about the exhilaration and the terrible price of rootlessness has affected the ways in which Mailer has responded to his own native literary tradition.

On the other hand, he has been curiously reluctant to acknowledge explicitly his bonds with most of nineteenth-century American literature—perhaps in obedience of Emerson's dictum that "each age . . . must write its own books." At the same time, the buried voices of this indigenous art speak constantly in his own work. For all its contemporary sources, the young Mailer's cry in *Advertisements for Myself* (1959) for a continuous "revolution in the consciousness of our time" also has roots in the school of Emerson.[18] His more recent explorations of karma and reincarnation ride comfortably with Emerson's celebration in "The Poet" of the "cunning Proteus" that he sees as the essence of nature and art.[19] (In this respect, as in many others, *Ancient Evenings* may be a more "American" book than appears at first glance.) Mailer's metaphysics of sex are not unrelated to Whitman's, and even Mailer's scatological preoccupations have at least theoretical justification in Emerson's view that the Poet should "embrace words and images excluded from polite conversation. What would be base, or even obscene, to the obscene, becomes illustrious, spoken in a new connexion of thought."[20]

Not only various Mailer themes but several of his central techniques also find precedents in the strategies of the American Renaissance. The first person singular of *Advertisements for Myself* has a great-grandfather in *Song of Myself*. Mailer clearly knows that the "barbaric yawp" he celebrates in Henry Miller's work and often displays himself has roots in one of Miller's own heroes, Whitman.[21] And we can usefully think of Mailer's own dialectical practice in terms of Emerson's injunction against "foolish consistency" and Whitman's willingness to "contradict myself" in order to "contain multitudes." Certainly his penchant for advancing his own dialectic by means of polar oppositions seems descended from the American Scholar's call to "see every trifle bristling with the polarity that ranges it instantly on an eternal law." Mailer's Manichean "eternal law" may not be Emerson's, but the quest for dignifying metaphysical drama lies behind both. In Mailer's work, as in *Walden* and *Leaves of Grass*, lies an implicit response to Emerson's call in "The Poet" for an American "genius . . . with tyrannous eye, which knew the value of our incomparable materials, and saw, in the barbarism and materialism of the times, another carnival of the same gods whose picture he so much admires in Homer." Even Gary Gilmore knows some Emerson.[22]

This said, we should not deny that, to a modern Manichean existentialist, the Emersonian tradition has refused to acknowledge sufficiently the active evil that Mailer believes essential to heroic drama; it has insufficient taste, in practice, for the earthiness and bloodiness of life (Thoreau's momentary—and unrealized—impulse to devour a woodchuck notwithstanding); it has muted the terrors of ambiguity that haunt the modern soul, and it has therefore not earned its claims to a grand synthesis of the complexities of experience. It is no surprise, therefore, that the one mid-nineteenth-century American writer with whom Mailer has been willing to explicitly affirm some kinship is Herman Melville. The acknowledgement has on occasion been tinged by a playfulness not free from a certain bite. In *The Fight*, the roar of a lion makes him think of Hemingway. Then he remembers a confrontation with a "frolicsome whale" while sailing in the Provincetown harbor. Mailer recalls that "he felt singularly cool. What a perfect way to go. His place in American literature would be forever secure. They would seat him at Melville's feet. Melville and Mailer, ah, the consanguinity of the M's and L's—how critics would love Mailer's now discovered preoccupations (see Croft on the Mountain in *The Naked and the Dead*) with Ahab's Moby Dick" (91–92). If the passage jabs lightly at critics' influence-hunting proclivities, it at the same time points to what, as with Hemingway, was both a resource and a rivalry. One senses Mailer's muted admission that he would dearly love to have beaten the nineteenth-century American master at his own game.[23]

No doubt part of Melville's appeal to Mailer has lain in the mutual immensity of their literary aims. In *Advertisements for Myself*, he proclaims his own ambition "to write a novel which Dostoyevsky and Marx; Joyce and Freud; Stendhal, Tolstoy, Proust and Spengler; Faulkner, and even old moldering Hemingway might come to read, for it would carry what they had to tell another part of the way" (477); and, echoing Ishmael, he speaks of this novel as "a descendant of *Moby-Dick* which will call for such time, strength, cash and patience that I do not know if I have it all to give, and so will . . . avoid the dream"(156). Mailer's proclamation prompted F. W. Dupee to argue that "the attraction of *Moby-Dick* to Mailer . . . seems to consist largely in its bulk, profundity, and prestige. It is to him . . . an image of literary power rather than a work to be admired, learned from perhaps, and then returned to its place of honor."[24] In fact, however, Mailer's response to *Moby-Dick* has been more intricate and versatile than Dupee suggests. Another reason for his attraction is implied in his discussion in *Cannibals and Christians* of the backgrounds of modern American literature: ". . . Tolstoy and Dostoyevsky divided the central terrain of the modern novel between them. Tolstoy's concern . . . was with men-in-the-world, and indeed the panorama of his book carries to us an image of a huge landscape peopled with figures who changed that landscape, whereas the bulk of Dostoevsky's work could take place in ten closed rooms: it is not society but a series of individuals we remember, each illuminated by the terror of exploring the mystery of themselves . . . one can point to *Moby-Dick* as a perfect example of a novel in the second category—a book whose action depends upon the voyage of Ahab into his obsession . . . " (128). Mailer's writing has raised a siege of both sides of this terrain, with many a guerilla raid across boundaries. And Melville has been one commanding scout along that frontier. A century before Mailer, he had explored the terrors as well as the exhilaration that flowed from Americans' proclamation of themselves as "new men," seemingly cut free of the past and launched on a perilous voyage to "remake" themselves. Melville, among others, has helped Mailer explore the contemporary dimensions of this intensely ambiguous quest.

One of Mailer's responses to the Melvillean voyage of adventure is perhaps reflected in the harbor view and nautical decor of his Brooklyn Heights duplex apartment, with its ropes and rigging leading to the upper floors. Another representative response is his proposal in *Cannibals and Christians* to build cloud-reaching cities whose buildings "could begin to look a little less like armored tanks and more like clipper ships," and whose airborne residents could "feel the dignity of sailors on a four-master at sea . . . returned to that mixture of awe and elation, of dignity and self-respect and a hint of dread, that sense of zest which a man must have known working his way out along a yardarm in a stiff breeze at sea" (237). It is just these sorts of complex feelings that Stephen Rojack experiences as he walks around the parapet of Barney Kelly's penthouse apartment: "as used up as a sailor who has been tied for hours in the rigging of a four-master beating through a storm."[25] Perhaps there is even a hint of Melville in Mailer's assertion, during his 1969 campaign for mayor of New York City, that voters for him and Jimmy Breslin "are voting for an embarkation upon an unknown journey, which may end with the city of New York being cut loose from the mainland of America and being shipped out to sea."[26]

Mailer's engagement with Melville begins early in his career. We are told in *The Naked and the Dead* (1948) that Robert Hearn's senior essay, for which he "has been given a magna" at Harvard, is entitled *A Study of the Cosmic Urge in Herman Melville*.[27] The world that Hearn attempts unsuccessfully to come to terms with on Anopopei (perhaps this is why Mailer gives him a magna rather than a summa) is a wild landscape dominated by the mania of a commander and the presence of an unconquerable leviathan. "The biggest influence on *Naked*," Mailer remarked, perhaps somewhat flippantly, in 1951, "was *Moby-Dick*. . . . I was sure everyone would know. I had Ahab in it, and I suppose the mountain was Moby Dick."[28] It is unwise to press too solemnly for precise parallels between the two novels. Hearn, for example, may resemble Ishmael in his intellectual background, his speculative habits, and the ennui that drives him onto the uncharted sea of war, but in his confrontation with Cummings and Croft he comes closer to expressing what Melville calls the "unaided virtue" of Starbuck. Cummings and Croft share the role of Ahab. And the heterogeneous backgrounds and values of Croft's patrol make it a paler version of the *Pequod's* crew. Like Melville's whalers, each soldier of the patrol finds himself on a mission that comes to involve not only a primal struggle with social authority and a non-human wilderness but a nightmarish war with the ambiguities and divisions of his own inner nature.

The central symbol of these ambiguities and dangers is Mount Anaka itself, which, like Moby Dick, casts its awesome presence over the entire novel, inspiring men to conquest but also confronting them with naked ambiguities about themselves and their world. Anaka is unreachable not only physically but intellectually; like Moby Dick or the doubloon that Ahab nails to the *Pequod's* mast, the mountain is always viewed partially. And as in Melville's novel, the varying and even conflicting meanings that individual characters read into Anaka tell as much about themselves as about the mountain. To Gallagher, for example, "the mountain seemed wise and powerful, and terrifying in its size. Gallagher stared at it in absorption, caught by a sense of beauty he could not express. The idea, the vision he always held of something finer and neater and more beautiful than the moil in which he lived trembled now, pitched almost to a climax of words . . . but it passed and he was left with a troubled joy, an echo of rapture" (447). Roth fears the mountain—it seems to him "so open, so high"—and prefers even the suffocating jungle "to these naked ridges, these gaunt alien vaults of stone and sky. . . . The jungle was filled with all kinds of dangers but they did not seem so severe now . . . But here, one misstep and it would be death. It was better to live in a cellar than to walk a tightrope" (638). Hearn finds that the mountain "roused his awe and then his fear. It was too immense, too powerful. He suffered a faint sharp thrill as he watched the mist eddy about the peak. He imagined the ocean actually driving against a rockbound coast, and despite himself strained his ears as though he could hear the sound of such a titanic struggle" (497). To Croft too "the mountain looked like a rocky coast and the murky sky seemed to be an ocean shattering its foam upon the shore." But Croft finds Anaka more compelling than does Hearn: "The mountain and the cloud and the sky were purer, more intense, in their gelid silent struggle than any ocean and any shore he had ever seen. The rocks gather themselves in the darkness, huddled together against the fury of the water. The contest seemed an infinite distance away, and he felt a thrill of anticipation at the thought that by the following night they might be on the peak. Again, he felt a crude ecstasy. He could not have given the reason, but the mountain tormented him, beckoned him, held an answer to something he wanted. It was so pure, so austere" (496–97).

Whereas Hearn is more impressed with the dangers and ambiguities suggested in his mind by Anaka—"It was the kind of shore upon which huge ships would founder, smash apart, and sink in a few minutes" (498)—Croft is more compelled by the intensity and purity of its challenge to his own powers: "He led the platoon up the mountain without hesitation. . . . Despite all the exertion of the preceding days, he was restless and impatient now, driven forward by a demanding tension in himself. . . . He was continually eager to press on to the next rise, anxious to see what was beyond. The sheer mass of the mountain inflamed him" (635). And his failure to conquer Anaka is important not for what it tells him about his physical limitations but for what it has revealed to him about his inner nature: "Deep inside himself, Croft was relieved that he had not been able to climb the mountain . . . [and] was rested by the unadmitted knowledge that he had found a limit to his hunger" (701).

As *The Naked and the Dead* suggests, Mailer at the very outset of his career was mining *Moby-Dick* not only for major analogues to the adventure that he has constantly stressed as an essential component of America's psychic and social health but, equally important, for a major symbol of the ambiguities and dangers that attend such excursions. Significantly, when Mailer took on the mantle of "Historian" in the late sixties, he found Melville's book also a useful reference point for determining how far his fellow citizens had departed from their "organic" heritage. Observing the 1964 Republican convention (in an article reprinted in *Cannibals and Christians*), he is reminded of the degeneration that security-minded Americans have allowed to take place in the cultural tradition of which Melville was a part: "The American mind had gone from Hawthorne and Emerson to the Frug, the Bounce, and Walking the Dog, from *The Flowering of New England* to the cerebrality of professional football in which a quarterback must have not only heart, courage, strength and grace but a mind like an I.B.M. computer. It marks the turn we have taken from the Renaissance. There too was the ideal of a hero with heart, courage, strength, and grace, but he was expected to possess the mind of a passionate artist. Now the best heroes were—in the sense of the Renaissance—mindless . . . " (28–29).

This "mindlessness" to which the American imagination has degenerated shows itself in the degeneration of America's major symbols of power. By the time Moby Dick has reached the rudderless world of D. J. in *Why Are We in Vietnam?* (1967), it has become merely the occasion for sophomoric wordplay: "Herman Melville go hump Moby and wash his Dick."[29] Whereas the American Renaissance's major symbol of power, Moby Dick, fused profound ambiguity with dignifying epic drama, contemporary America's major symbols of power, such as the Pentagon, have become not only faceless but utterly without dramatic personality, have become, in fact, "anonymous" signs of the failure of the adventurous symbolizing imagination in American public life. As Mailer treats it in *The Armies of the Night*, the Pentagon becomes almost a travesty on Melville's mighty leviathan:

> . . . it is doubtful if there was ever another building in the world so huge in ground plan and so without variation. . . . The Pentagon, architecturally, was as undifferentiated as a jellyfish or a cluster of barnacles. One could chip away at any part of the interior without locating a nervous center. . . . High church of the corporation, the Pentagon spoke exclusively of mass man and his civilization; every aspect of the building was anonymous, monotonous, massive, interchangeable. . . . For . . . [the Mobilization Committee's] revolutionary explorers, the strangeness of their situation must have been comparable to a reconnaissance of the moon. . . . it was impossible to locate the symbolic loins of the building—paradigm of the modern world indeed, they could explore every inch of their foe and know nothing about him . . . (252–53).

It may seem somewhat ludicrous to compare the Pentagon to the great whale's "pasteboard mask" through which Ahab wants obsessively to strike or to see in its facelessness the ultimate unknowability that Ishmael describes in "The Tail": "Dissect him how I may, then, I but go skin deep; I know him not, and never will. But if I know not even the tail of this whale, how understand his head? much more, how comprehend his face, when face he has none?" But Mailer feels the same incongruity. The easiest way into the Pentagon, he reminds us, is through its shopping center and cafeteria, and he finds "something absurd" in this possibility. "To attack here was to lose some of one's symbolic momentum—a consideration which might be comic or unpleasant in a shooting war, but in a symbolic war was not necessarily comic at all" (254). The decline in the power of the epic symbol is thus not only a reflection of a degeneration of national value but a terrifying reminder of how difficult it is for a contemporary American writer to create an image that again will move his countrymen to heroic action. Mailer is reminded again of this challenge in 1969 when he visits, in preparation for *Of a Fire on the Moon* (1970), the Vehicle Assembly Building at Cape Kennedy where Apollo 11 is being built. His first tentative attempt at surrounding the vehicle in epic hyperbole is challenged by the official language in which the vehicle is encased: "VAB—it could be the name of a drink or a deodorant, or it could be suds for the washer. But it was a name for this warehouse of the gods. . . . Nothing fit anything any longer. The art of communication had become the mechanical function, and the machine was the work of art. What a fall for the ego of the artist. What a climb to capture the language again!"[30]

But this imaginatively degenerated world is all that Mailer has. Loving America too much to leave it, he must dig for redemptive metaphors in his native soil. He is thus obviously pleased that, in contrast to the lack of real drama that a super-plastic Miami offers him in his account of the 1968 conventions, *Miami and the Siege of Chicago* (1968), bloody, stockyard-smelling Chicago "gave America its last chance at straight-out drama" and thus provides potential "salvation of the schizophrenic soul."[31] Watching the overwhelming battle at the Chicago Hilton between the protesters and the police, he searches for a mighty image appropriate to the dramatic occasion and finds one in *Moby-Dick*: ". . . it was as if the war had finally begun, and this was therefore a great and solemn moment, as if indeed even the gods of history had come together from each side to choose the very front of the Hilton Hotel before the television cameras of the world and the eyes of the campaign workers and the delegates' wives, yes, there before the eyes of half the principals at the convention was this drama played, as if the military spine of a great liberal party had finally separated itself from the skin, as if, no metaphor large enough to suffice, the Democratic Party had here broken in two before the eyes of a nation like Melville's whale charging right out of the sea" (172).

What is interesting about this passage is not merely that Mailer is searching for an epic symbol with which to give weight yet another time to the dialectic of American life, but that he has self-consciously chosen to do so by means of a traditional symbol transformed for his own purposes. Melville's Leviathan, as Mailer treats him, is no longer merely a natural force against which the American must wage his epic and perhaps tragic frontier wars. It has become a symbol of the split at the center of the American's sense of identity. Moby Dick is not merely a frontier threat, but a humanized resource from the past that an embattled contemporary writer can use in his continuing struggle to redeem the present.

Mailer, of course, has not treated the American past with the fullness of intricacy of Nathaniel Hawthorne, William Faulkner, or even his rival Gore Vidal. Rather, he has distilled that past down to what he considers its symbolic essence—in that sense, in fact, he does approach Hawthorne. Central to that essence, as he sees it, is a dream of revolutionary adventure on behalf of an apocalyptic quest for identity, both personal and collective. The two central images of the American tradition are a large individual (perhaps a madman, perhaps a saint, perhaps both) in vast space and an epic battle in that same landscape. It is the latter image in particular that gives resonance to the 1967 March on the Pentagon, as described in *Armies*: "As Lowell and Mailer reached the ridge and took a turn to the right to come down from Washington Monument toward the length of the long reflecting pool which led between two long groves of trees near the banks to the steps of Lincoln Memorial, out from that direction came the clear bitter-sweet excitation of a military trumpet resounding in the near distance, one peal which seemed to go all the way back through a galaxy of bugles to the cries of the Civil War and the first trumpet note to blow the attack. The ghosts of old battles were wheeling like clouds over Washington today" (105).

It is not that Mailer sentimentalizes this symbolic past. His battleground is strewn with corpses, of cowards as well as of heroes, of demons as well as of saints. In 1967 he argued that modern Western civilization has "never paid for the crimes of the past; now we're trying to bury them. That's one reason the technological society advances at such a great rate: it frees people from having to look back into the horrors of the past."[32] Like Hawthorne, Mailer believes that corpses not given full rites (and rights) will rise to haunt a present that has tried to forget them. Thus he could suggest in 1977 that "dread was the ongoing uneasiness of those whose roots were cut . . . dread was the communal American experience."[33] If American rootlessness, viewed benignly, could be seen as a welcome liberation from a dark past, it could also, viewed through a more brooding lens, be understood as a dispossession. In *Marilyn* (1973), musing on the "void in one's sense of identity" that makes Marilyn Monroe, like most Americans, a "spiritual orphan," Mailer notes that, "With the exception of the Indians, we are a nation of rejects . . . transplanted by the measure of every immigration of the last three hundred and fifty years."[34] Mailer notes in *Marilyn* that if American arrogance is "the pride of the weed that knows it is the true flower of the garden" (29), American dread is the deeper knowledge that one in fact has been uprooted from that garden, has suffered a fall. The Marilyn that Mailer creates in *Of Women and Their Elegance* (1980) reflects this anxious quest for nourishing roots in the face of constant displacement: "Once I stay overnight in a place, my personality gets into everything. Moving out is as bad as pulling out. I grow roots like I've gone crazy. I might as well be a weed or some undistinguished flower."[35]

Increasingly in his writing, particularly since the mid-sixties, Mailer has been willing to venture the notion that the quest of a weed for its roots may in fact have as much existentially heroic possibility as the quest for the unknown future—may, in fact, be part of the same journey. If to be modern—or American—is to be rootless, Mailer suggests in *Existential Errands* (1972) that "we can never locate our roots without a voyage of discovery" (336). Like many classic American voyages, Melville takes the *Pequod* not only toward a vision of a national future but into a realm of ancient realities and mysteries. So does Mailer in *The Fight* and *Ancient Evenings*. Like Henry Adams, he has increasingly staked out points in a pre-American past to help him read the Sphinx in America's future.

While in Washington to participate in the March on the Pentagon, Mailer stays at the Hay-Adams hotel and, in the course of pondering his emerging mission as self-proclaimed "Historian" finds himself wondering "if the Adams in the name of his hotel bore any relation to Henry" (66). In a 1981 interview, he was to acknowledge the hinted connection: "Henry Adams . . . obviously had a vast influence on me but I never knew he did until I started to write *The Armies of the Night*."[36] As various critics have noted, it is in this book that Mailer first dons the third-person narrative guise used by his fellow Harvard alumnus in *The Education*, and for much the same reason. Alan Trachtenberg remarks that "the implausible assault upon the Pentagon . . . becomes the perfect vehicle to bring Mailer's own inner experience into focus, and Mailer himself, 'a comic hero,' a 'figure of monumental disproportions,' becomes the perfect figure through which 'to recapture the precise feel of the ambiguity of the event and its monumental disproportions.' Much like Henry Adams in his *Education*, Mailer here discovers an aptness between his own postures in the world and the crazy configurations of the world itself."[37]

Like Adams, Mailer has increasingly treated his work as the rather ironic story of an education whose value as preparation for succeeding in or least understanding a rapidly changing modern world is at best ambiguous. Whereas Adams claims to be an eighteenth-century child trying to prepare in the nineteenth century for a twentieth-century civilization, Mailer seems a nineteenth-century romantic (with a trace of the puritan) trying to straddle the twentieth century in order to seize a twenty-first century that has arrived before its time. Like Adams, Mailer sees history as an accelerating movement from unity to multiplicity. What could be more Adams-like than Mailer's statement in *Of a Fire on the Moon* that: "It was the first century in history which presented to sane and sober minds the fair chance that the century might not reach the end of its span. It was a world half convinced of the future death of our species yet half aroused by the apocalyptic notion that an exceptional future still lay before us. So it was a century which moved with the most magnificent display of power into directions it could not comprehend. The itch was to accelerate—the metaphysical direction unknown" (48). Like *The Education*, much of Mailer's most engaging work can be seen as an embattled poet's ambivalent search for a metaphorical structure that will at least bring the illusion of order to the multiplying force fields of modern experience.

One of the most crucial force fields for both writers is sexual. In a 1981 interview with Barbara Solomon, Mailer argues that, to the best of his recollection, he has "never read much Adams," but he does state that "I know for certain that I read one long chapter of *The Education of Henry Adams* in my freshman reader at Harvard."[38] He undoubtedly is referring to Adams's often-anthologized chapter, "The Virgin and the Dynamo." Mailer's controversial arguments in *The Prisoner of Sex* and *Marilyn*, two key products of his "third-person" phase from the late sixties to mid-seventies, are presided over in part by the spirit of Adams's own meditations on the historical, psychological, and metaphysical relationship of sexuality and technology. Like Adams, Mailer assumes, in *Prisoner*, the role of "acolyte" in search of enlightenment about the mysteries of women's power, and his conclusion that women's reproductive capacity is the very essence of their power echoes Adams's argument that the Virgin "was goddess because of her force; she was the animated dynamo; she was reproduction—the greatest and most mysterious of all energies; all she needed was to be fecund."[39] Like Adams's Madonna, Mailer's Marilyn Monroe, at her highest artistic moments on the screen, embodies the reunification of Venus and Virgin, sexuality and purity, and mysteriously transcends the modern electronic medium in which her image lives. In *Marilyn* he calls her "sweet angel of sex" and "every man's love affair with America" (15); she represents to Mailer the victory of art over technology, of faith over history. And her tragic and mysterious death, like those that fill *The Education*, confronts her metaphorical lover Mailer not only with the fragility of modern faith and art but with the painful knowledge that the only important beauty is that which reflects "the record of a war."[40]

For all his romantic attraction to the mysterious power of female fecundity and artistry, however, Mailer has seemed most comfortable applying Adams to a male-dominated world, such as that of the astronauts in *Of a Fire on the Moon*. Mailer's meditation on the meaning of Apollo 11 is framed usefully by Adams's comments in the last chapter of *The Education*. Approaching New York in 1905 by boat, Adams finds the view of the technologically wondrous city "more striking than ever—wonderful—unlike anything man had ever seen—and like nothing he ever much cared to see. The outline of the city became frantic in its effort to explain something that defied meaning. Power seemed to have outgrown its servitude and to have asserted its freedom. The cylinder had exploded, and thrown great masses of stone and steam against the sky. The city had the air and movement of hysteria, and the citizens were crying in every accent of anger and alarm, that the new forces must at any cost be brought under control. . . . He was beyond measure curious to see whether the conflict of forces would produce the new man, since no other energies seemed left on earth to breed. The new man could be only a child born of contact between the new and the old energies" (500).

It is in much the same spirit of distaste and guarded respect that Mailer observes the "bomb" that he believes Apollo 11 to be. And out of much the same curiosity that leads Adams to formulate "A Dynamic Theory of History," Mailer begins to formulate "a psychology of astronauts" to help explain the "new men" who must guide the bomb's powers.

As preparation for this task, Mailer rather wryly takes on the kind of role that Adams finds for himself in the latter part of *The Education*—that of a senior American statesman and philosopher whom the world has by-passed and who therefore must make a virtue out of being an important if detached observer of the rapidly changing scene. If Adams felt little in common with the twentieth century, he still saw himself as an audience for it. Mailer describes himself in similar terms: "He has learned to live with questions. Of course, as always, he has little to do with the immediate spirit of time. . . . he has never had less sense of possessing the age. He feels in fact little more than a decent spirit, somewhat shunted to the side. It is the best possible position for detective work" (4). This role of "somewhat disembodied spirit" has an important artistic virtue for Mailer: "He might be in superb shape to study the flight of Apollo 11 to the moon. For he was detached this season from the imperial demands of his ego. . . . he felt like a spirit of some just-consumed essence of the past" (6).

A philosophical but playful spirit from the past, Mailer probes the meaning of American technology at the Manned Spacecraft Center at Cape Kennedy in much the way that Adams probes the implications of the dy-namo at the Chicago, Paris, and St. Louis Expositions. Viewing the dy-namo as "a symbol of infinity," Adams treats it as the most appropriate symbol of the age's moral values: "Before the end, one began to pray to it. . . . Among the thousand symbols of ultimate energy, the dynamo was not so human as some, but it was the most expressive" (380). Similarly, Mailer describes the Vehicle Assembly Building as "the antechamber of a new Creation":

> . . . he came to recognize that whatever was in store, a Leviathan was most certainly ready to ascend the heavens—whether for good or ill he might never know—but he was standing at least in the first cathedral of the age of technology, and he might as well recognize that the world would change, that the world *had* changed, even as he had thought to be pushing and shoving on it with *his* mighty ego. And it had changed in ways he did not recognize . . . The change was mightier than he had counted on. The full brawn of the rocket came over him in this cavernous womb of an intensity, this giant cathedral of a machine designed to put together another machine which would voyage through space. Yes, this emergence of a ship to travel the ether was no event he could measure by any philosophy he had been able to put together in his brain (55).

Facing the force of the dynamo and its problematic relationship to the force of the Virgin, Adams argues that he can search for a means of measurement only by becoming "a pilgrim of power." Mailer adopts the same strategy: "He would be, perforce, an acolyte to technology" (56).

As a reluctant acolyte, Mailer forces himself to treat the Apollo 11 not merely as a dynamo but as the moral equivalent to the Virgin of Mont St. Michel and Chartres. Describing the spotlighted rocket on the night before the launch, he wryly suggests that "she looked like a shrine with the lights upon her. In the distance she glowed for all the world like some white stone Madonna in the mountains, welcoming footsore travelers at dusk" (59). He sees white Protestant America, long deprived of a Madonna, as hopefully investing the rocket with all the powers of comfort and cure for their alienation: "All over the South . . . they would be praying for America tonight—thoughts of America served to replace the tender sense of the Virgin in the Protestant hearts" (61).

American technology, then, has attempted to harness the forces of nature which Melville had symbolized by Moby Dick, and Mailer is willing as detached observer to leave ambiguous the question of whether the launching of Apollo 11 shows man taming nature or nature's revenge on man—further, whether the rocket is a "Sainted Leviathan"—Moby Dick canonized by the American dream—or "a Medusa's head" whose only powers are those of death (84). The rocket launch is thus the latest and one of the most dramatic of America's frontier encounters with the wilderness, and Mailer, as grimacing "acolyte to technology," identifies himself with all Americans who feel compelled to continually search for their identity by means of such ambiguous confrontations: "A tiny part of him was like a penitent who had prayed in the wilderness for sixteen days, and was now expecting a sign. Would the sign reveal much or little?" (98).

The response to Mailer's question is appropriately less an answer than an image. As the rocket rises, the worlds of the Dynamo, the Virgin, and Moby Dick—of technology, imagination, and nature—merge into a new, powerful, but intensely ambiguous symbol of the American dream. The launch is immensely "more dramatic" than he has anticipated:

> For the flames were enormous. No one could be prepared for that . . . Two mighty torches of flame like the wings of a yellow bird of fire flew over a field, covered a field with brilliant yellow bloomings of flame, and in the midst of it, white as a ghost, white as the white of Melville's Moby Dick, white as the shrine of the Madonna in half the churches of the world, this slim angelic mysterious ship of stages rose without sound out of its incarnation of flame and began to ascend slowly into the sky, slow as Melville's Leviathan might swim, slowly as we might swim upward in a dream looking for the air. And still no sound.
>
> Then it came . . . an apocalyptic fury of sound equal to some conception of the sound of your death in the roar of a drowning hour, a nightmare of sound, and he heard himself saying, 'Oh, my God! oh, my God! oh, my God! oh, my God! oh, my God! oh, my God!' . . . and [had] a poor moment of vertigo at the thought that man now had something with which to speak to God . . . (99–100).

If the flight of Apollo 11 has renewed once again a feeling for the cosmic implications of the American enterprise, it has also again pointed to the overwhelming nightmares that the enterprise inevitably carries with it, and Mailer can even suggest that the God who directs this modern *Pequod* may be a colossal Ahab gone monomaniacal: "The Power guiding us . . . was looking to the day when all of mankind would yet be part of one machine . . . an instrument of divine endeavor put together by a Father to whom one might no longer be able to pray to since the ardors of His embattled voyage could have driven Him mad" (151–52). But the terror of such a possibility seems ultimately less important to Mailer than the sheer drama it creates. For the feeling of high drama reassures him that he is once again in an epic arena where the divided halves of the American psyche can meet in potentially creative combat: "It was somehow superior to see the astronauts and the flight of Apollo 11 as the instrument of . . . celestial or satanic endeavors, than as a species of sublimation for . . . aggressive and intolerably inhuman desires. . . . Aquarius preferred the . . . assumption that we were the indispensable instruments of a monumental vision with whom we had begun a trip" (152).

This "assumption" is one that Mailer has found it increasingly difficult to embody in his American-based writing of the past decade or so. It has seemed harder and harder for him to find experiential equivalents in the post-Watergate era for his Manichean epic vision of American possibilities, or to use symbolic resources like Moby Dick and Madonna to vivify these possibilities. For all his efforts to penetrate the bland facades of the 1972 presidential conventions in *St. George and the Godfather* (1972), and to suggest the fires of apocalyptic civil religion that he believes burn underneath, he is finally forced to admit that "he never found the major confrontation for which he looked."[41] If the battle still rages, it has gone underground. It rarely breaches the increasingly monotonous surface of American life. Such breaches are themselves increasingly encapsulated by the technology of modern life, as Marilyn Monroe's and Marlon Brando's are—except in rare moments—imprisoned in film. Nonetheless, Mailer has continued his search for those moments of vision, and he has continued, if in increasingly muted ways, to bring the force of a native literary tradition to bear on those moments. In the Bantu philosophy in which he frames *The Fight*, for example, it is possible to find an Adamsesque musing on "the old idea that man was a force in a field of forces" (38–43). The heavyweight championship is "a magnetic field" (125), and Ali and Foreman are like "magnetic poles," enacting a high ritual of "attraction and repulsion" (177–78). In fact, we might take a risk, in light of Mailer's explicit reference to Melville early in the book (92), and consider the ritual he recounts, for all its allusions to Hemingway and Conrad, as a new voyage of the *Pequod*, with American black men in both of the commanding roles: an Ahabian Ali—"America's Greatest Ego," Mailer had called him in *Existential Errands* whose "essential message to America all these years" was that he "is

simply not comprehensible, for he could be a demon or a saint. Or both!"
(4)—and a Foreman, described in *The Fight* as a "prodigy of strength" like
a lion and a bull (97, 195, 202), who takes on attributes of the Leviathan.
Perhaps the title of Chapter 14, "The Man in the Rigging," refers not only
to Ali on the ring's ropes but to a Black Ahab confronting his highest challenge, one that requires him to regain something vital—a title—he has lost,
just as Melville's captain searches to revenge his lost limb. Like *Moby-
Dick*, the contest is a legend-making confrontation: "the rarest war of all—
a collision between different embodiments of divine inspiration" (47). And
if this analogy is at all plausible, we might find Mailer himself fair game for
the part of Ishmael, an observer who "had climbed the mast into a squall
of magical forces" (123) and who, in trying to observe the fight "with two
eyes instead of one" (122), takes on the dialectical vision that Ishmael associates with the sperm whale's separated eyes.

Mailer's disappearance as an overt actor from his major works of the
past decade, in fact, can be compared usefully to the disappearance of Melville's first-person narrators in most of his writing after *Moby-Dick*. And his
themes, too, take on some of the resonances of the later Melville. In his
grandest achievement of the seventies, *The Executioner's Song*, he moves
along with Melville's Pierre and Bartleby literally into a prison, from which
the metaphorical dead-walled prison of society itself may be more clearly
contemplated. And in its sustained meditation on the nature of social justice, and on the problematic relationship between secular and religious visions of crime and punishment and of life and death, Mailer's "novel"
places itself in the company of *Billy Budd*.[42] If the story of Billy shows that
an adamic innocent can be a murderer, Mailer suggests that a cold-blooded
murderer can also be, in ways both American and universal, an innocent.
Both tales seem more engaged by the consequences rather than by the
causes of individuals' acts of murder. They focus on the assumptions that
underlie society's own execution apparatus and on the questions of faith
and courage that confront all humans as they approach their inevitable
death. The mysteries of Budd and Gilmore are communal resources. If sailors treat a chip of the spar on which Billy was hung "as if it were a piece
of the cross," Gilmore's donation of all parts of his body for transplants, his
ritual dismemberment, makes him the host of strange kind of communion
ceremony.

And it is the narrators of both tales who quietly but firmly preside over
those rituals. As the narrator-authored "folk" ballads—"Billy in the Dar-
bies" and the "old prison rhyme"—that end both works imply, it is finally
the artist who preserves the hero, who keeps the dead alive, who becomes,
as in Emerson and Whitman, the principle of reincarnation. In *The Fight*,
Mailer nominally effaces his famous ego, taking on simply the name "Norman" as a means of "acquiring an anonymous voice" in the service of his
narrative. This voice takes him on a kind of Virgilian journey into Bantu
philosophy, which sees humans as "in a field of all the forces of the living

and the dead" (38). On this journey, he learns that "Nommo" in Bantu means "the Word" (40). Can we resist the possible play on "Nommo" and "Norman"? If the individual ego goes underground, the written art remains to assert its power as a part of the "field of forces." It enters the dozens of voices of *The Executioner's Song*—a complexly orchestrated and "executed" chant—and glides through the constantly shifting and blending voices of *Ancient Evenings*. It affirms not merely the inevitability of finite death, a topic from which Americans have often fled, but the possibility of a continuing life through the power of the word. Mailer has constantly tried, over a long literary career, to use language to suggest that power. On the final pages of *Of a Fire on the Moon*, looking at a fragment of dead moon rock brought back from the lunar wilderness and now separated from him by a sterile technological casing, he still finds the rock giving off to his imagination, like a blade of Whitman's grass, the smell of new life: ". . . he liked the moon rock, and thought—his vanity finally unquenchable—that she liked him. . . . there was something young about her, tender as the smell of the cleanest hay, it was like the subtle lift of love which comes up from the cradle of the newborn. . . . and so he had his sign, sentimental beyond measure, his poor dull senses had something they could trust . . . " (472).

Ancient Evenings begins with a similar Whitmanesque meditation—"Is one human? Or merely alive? Like a blade of grass equal to all existence in the moment it is torn? Yes. If pain is fundament, then a blade of grass can know all there is" (3). And the ecstatic assertion of the novel's concluding voice that "I must enter into the power of the word" (709) is simply one of Mailer's latest attempts to evoke the power of art to celebrate an ongoing process that requires the collaboration of man and god. For all its attention to violence, pain and death, the novel (significantly, part of a longer uncompleted epic) is yet the latest in Mailer's series of hymns to openness and renewal, the most recent of his irrepressible attempts to both placate and move beyond the American literary gods from whose roots, among others, he springs.

Notes

1. Jean Malaquais, quoted by Hilary Mills in *Mailer: A Biography* (New York: Empire Books, 1982), 95. Indirectly but considerably helpful in thinking about Mailer's place in American literary tradition is Sacvan Bercovitch, *The American Jeremiad* (Madison: Univ. of Wisconsin Press, 1978), 176–210 and passim.

2. Norman Mailer, *Pontifications*, ed. Michael Lennon (Boston: Little, Brown, 1982), 147. This paperback collection of interviews (1958–81) appeared first with Mailer's non-fiction of the seventies as *Pieces and Pontifications* (Boston: Little, Brown, 1982). Because each of the hardback volume's halves begin with page 1 in order to accommodate their publication later that year as separate paperbacks, I refer here and elsewhere to these paperback editions.

3. *Pontifications*, 189.

4. *Pontifications*, 153.

5. Henry Miller, for example. See Mailer's discussion of Miller and narcissism in *Genius and Lust: A Journey Through the Major Writings of Henry Miller* (New York: Grove, 1976), 173–94.

6. *Pieces*, 128.

7. Mailer, *The Fight* (Boston: Little, Brown, 1975), 200.

8. Mailer, *The Prisoner of Sex* (Boston: Little, Brown, 1971).

9. *The Fight*, 31.

10. *The Fight*, 35.

11. Mailer, *Cannibals and Christians* (New York: Dial, 1966), 98.

12. Mailer, *The Armies of the Night: History as a Novel, The Novel as History* (New York: New American Library, 1968), 316.

13. Mailer wrote about these urban artists in his nonfiction essay, *The Faith of Graffiti* (New York: Praeger, 1974).

14. Mailer, *Ancient Evenings* (Boston: Little, Brown, 1983).

15. *Pontifications*, 161–62.

16. *Pontifications*, 185.

17. *Pontifications*, 189. John T. Irwin's *An American Hieroglyphics: The Symbol of the Egyptian Hieroglyphics in the American Renaissance* (New Haven: Yale Univ. Press, 1980) offers suggestions that might usefully be applied to Mailer, particularly his examination of the American Romantics's meditation on the sources of language and identity.

18. Mailer, *Advertisements for Myself* (New York: Rinehart, 1959), 17.

19. See Michael Cowan, "The Loving Proteus: Metamorphosis in Emerson's Poetry," in *Characteristics of Emerson, Transcendental Poet*, ed. Carl F. Strauch (Hartford: Transcendental Books, 1974), 11–12. Representative of the critics who have glanced, generally quite briefly, at Mailer's possible ties to Emersonian romanticism are Stanley T. Gutman, *Mankind in Barbary: The Individual and Society in the Novels of Norman Mailer* (Hanover, New Hampshire: Univ. Press of New England, 1975), 78–80; see also Benjamin T. Spencer, "Mr. Mailer's American Dreams," in *Prospects: An Annual of American Culture Studies*, vol. 2, ed. Jack Salzman (New York: Burt Franklin, 1976), 144–45. Most discussions have focused on ties of theme rather than of literary technique.

20. We might also note Whitman's meditations on man as a compost heap and Thoreau's assertion, in the climactic thawing railroad-cut episode in *Walden*, that there is a "somewhat excrementious" character to Nature's operations.

21. Mailer links Miller with Whitman in *Prisoner*, 118.

22. Mailer, *The Executioner's Song* (Boston: Little, Brown, 1979), 390.

23. J. Michael Lennon, in "Mailer's Cosmology," *Modern Language Studies* 12 (Summer 1982):18–29, offers a detailed and persuasive comparison of the central dimensions of Mailer's metaphysics to Melville's and other American Romantics. Of various critics' briefer comparisons of Mailer and Melville, some of the more useful passing comments can be found in what remains the most stimulating general study of Mailer's work, Richard Poirier's *Norman Mailer* (New York: Viking, 1972), especially 135–36. Surprisingly, given Mailer's relentless explorations of the psychology and metaphysics of dread, obsession, and murderous and suicidal impulses, few attempts have been made to link him with that dark master of the "imp of the perverse," Edgar Allan Poe.

24. F. W. Dupee, "The American Norman Mailer," *Commentary* 29 (February 1960):129.

25. Mailer, *An American Dream* (New York: Dial, 1965), 258.

26. Mailer, *Existential Errands* (Boston: Little, Brown, 1972), 351.

27. Mailer, *The Naked and the Dead* (New York: Rinehart, 1948), 345.

28. Mailer, quoted by Harvey Breit, *The Writer Observed* (New York: World, 1956), 200.

29. Mailer, *Why Are We in Vietnam?* (New York: Putnam's, 1967), 26.

30. Mailer, *Of a Fire on the Moon* (Boston: Little, Brown, 1970), 55–56.

31. Mailer, *Miami and the Siege of Chicago* (New York: World, 1968), 90.

32. *Pontifications*, 40.

33. *Pieces*, 32.

34. Mailer, *Marilyn: A Biography* (New York: Grosset & Dunlop, 1973), 27.

35. Mailer, *Of Women and Their Elegance* (New York: Simon and Schuster, 1980), 27.

36. *Pontifications*, 149.

37. Alan Trachtenberg, "On the Steps of the Pentagon," *Nation* (27 May 1968), 701. The most extensive analysis of the Adams-Mailer connection, which appeared after the 1972 version of this article, is Gordon O. Taylor, "Of Adams and Aquarius," *American Literature* 46 (March 1974):68–82.

38. *Pontifications*, 186.

39. Henry Adams, *The Education of Henry Adams*, ed. Ernest Samuels (1918; rpt. Boston: Houghton Mifflin, 1973), 384.

40. *Cannibals and Christians*, 370.

41. Mailer, *St. George and the Godfather* (New York: New American Library, 1972), 221.

42. Mailer's familiarity with *Billy Budd* is clearly reflected in the playful comparison of two Harvard classmates to Budd and Claggart (*Pieces*, 2–3), and in his 1968 suggestion that "an ambitious high school dramatics teacher might have picked" David Eisenhower "to play Billy Budd" (*Miami*, 30).

Prolegomenon to a Biography of Mailer
                                              Robert F. Lucid*

"Every time I get into the newspapers I injure myself professionally," Mailer remarked in 1980, and much of this portion of the biography will confirm, or at least test out this proposition.[1] Mailer was claiming that whenever aspects of his personal life became public, the result undermined his relationship with the reading and book-buying public, and in the seventies he was quite possibly correct. It had not always been so: in the sixties, one could argue, his newspaper notoriety enhanced his professional appeal, even though his private life was immensely more unconventional then than it became in the seventies. The truth seems to be that the public recollection of the earlier Mailer was what kept getting into the newspapers in the later decade, and it scarcely mattered that Mailer's current private life was

*This essay, which covers the period from 1970 to 1983 has been excerpted by the author from a long piece discussing his authorized biography of Mailer. The biography is scheduled to be completed in 1987.

comparatively unremarkable. His tolerance for alcohol remained good and he liked to drink at a party, but he drank moderately otherwise and he went to far fewer parties than before. He had been quick, in the earlier days, to fight when he felt challenged, but now he tended to forgo such confrontations and boxed mostly with gloves, for exercise. His love life, after the final break in 1975 with Carol Stevens, became notably monogamous, as he formed a relationship which led (after much legal storminess) to marriage in 1980 with Barbara Norris, a tall strikingly beautiful model, actress, and painter who worked under the name of Norris Church. From an earlier marriage she brought to the household her small son Matthew, and together she and Mailer produced his eighth child, John Buffalo. Through the earlier two decades Mailer had always surrounded himself with male friends who served if not as an entourage at least as a close personal circle. But as the seventies moved forward this phenomenon began noticeably to fade and Mailer, while still entirely clubable and pleased to stay in touch with friends, moved socially in a less structured way than he had before. What is remarkable is that while all of this was true, and while he was addressing himself to his fiscal burden in very much the way a furniture mover, short of helpers, addresses a grand piano, he was represented in the media quite differently. It was as if a totally wrongheaded press agent had set out to confirm that though our times may have changed one thing remained constant: we still had with us the same Norman Mailer. It was not an identity likely to win him new friends, and to a considerable extent he played the part of the wrongheaded press agent himself. In 1971 he strangely boxed with José Torres on a television talk show;[2] later that year he quarreled with Gore Vidal on the *Dick Cavett Show*;[3] in 1974 he published a poem in the *New Republic* which ended with the line, "All hail fucking;"[4] in 1977 he publicly punched Vidal at a Boston cocktail party;[5] and, in what may well have been his most controversial act of the decade, he published *Marilyn*, his biography of Marilyn Monroe.[6] Somehow, the idea of an apparently unregenerate Mailer going back in time and addressing the life and death of the most celebrated movie actress of the 1956–62 period drove many people, among them many reviewers, nearly crazy with anger. The *need* of the seventies audience to let Marilyn Monroe "rest in peace," undisturbed by the diggings of an iconoclast like Mailer, showed itself in very vigorous ways. The book itself, after all, was a decently respectful tribute to a colleague, and its questioning of the coroner's verdict of death by suicide certainly was an inspired piece of guesswork. So the corrosively hostile reception of the book, and indeed the hostility at the simple announcement of the book's coming publication, forces one to conclude that it was not really the book that caused the anger.[7] It had to be Mailer, Mailer himself, and the cause of the anger was almost surely to be discovered in the new historical circumstances both author and audience were experiencing. Mailer had exhorted that audience since at least 1956 to face up to the twin realities of self and history.[8] In doing so, in hammering away at the certainty of pre-apocalyptic anticipation, he had absolutely identified himself with this frame of reference, and he was identified with it still. No matter that it was actually absent from the pages of *Marilyn*, where the once-dominant theme of inextricability between interior self and exterior history had been replaced by a far more static analytic structure. It remained true that Mailer seemed to his audience to be woefully unsynchronized with the reality of his time, and for this he quite clearly was not to be forgiven. The fact that a small army of others had become unsynchronized as well, that in reality the whole culture, caught flatfooted, had been imaginatively immobilized by the change of decades, served to create no common bond. Mailer had said that the most and said it most forcefully; he was therefore culpable.

All this tended, as he put it, to injure him professionally. In the professional arena he spent the decade on two parallel lines of endeavor. The first began in 1971 and received formal acknowledgement in 1974, when Mailer signed a million-dollar contract with Little, Brown to write a multivolume novel. He worked on the first volume, *Ancient Evenings*, throughout the seventies and until its publication in 1983.[9] The second, and the most apparent, line of activity was a series of volumes, published in the seventies, all of which clearly had been written as a part of a process of reassessment and reunderstanding (not to speak of the process of earning a living). *St. George and the Godfather* (1972),[10] his fourth and last account of the national political conventions, was followed a year later by *Marilyn*. In 1974 he published *The Faith of Graffiti*,[11] an essay on New York's ghetto artists accompanied by photographs of their work. He broke off from his work on *Evenings* again in 1975 to produce his third-world account of the Muhammad Ali championship fight in Zaïre, *The Fight*,[12] and in 1976 for his anthology (including his extended commentary) of the work of Henry Miller, *Genius and Lust*.[13] He also collected his convention narratives into a volume, *Some Honorable Men: Political Conventions, 1960–1972*, published in 1976;[14] and in 1978 published a facsimile of the typescript of his 1943 novel about an insane asylum, *A Transit to Narcissus*.[15] In *The Fight* he showed genuine, even very exciting power, and it was striking to see how the old countdown vocabulary, now so inappropriate to the American scene, fit beautifully into the context of the third world. But it was plain that his major commitment of imagination was not to be discovered here, and that the most important portion of the real fruits of his efforts in the seventies would appear in the fiction.

So the seventies will be handled in the biography as a rite of passage, for Mailer as an artist and for the individual at large in the American culture as well. The passage from the pre-apocalyptic vision of the sixties through a clearly post-apocalyptic state of consciousness at the start of the eighties was, in a sense, the business of the period, as in very large part it was the business of Mailer's work. It can hardly be mere coincidence that at decade's end the two tracks of Mailer's imaginative endeavors converged into an imaginative work of tremendous power, power altogether comparable in its magnitude to that generated by *The Armies of the Night* (1968),[16] but as different from that apocalyptic testament as a lonely moon is different from a bursting sunrise. The new book was *The Executioner's Song* (1979),[17] and from a biographical point of view the most immediately relevant thing that it did was get Mailer out of debt.

Coping with this debt, organizing his life so as to keep it from growing worse while still keeping up with his vast array of financial obligations, had been the actual story of his life during most of these years. It was a story not without interest, to be sure: his discovery that his system of keeping accounts was not satisfactory to the IRS cost him many thousands of practically unpayable dollars; the reorganization of his cash flow by Norris Church and a new accountant accomplished real wonders in savings; his total abstinence from alcohol for an extended period provided him with a hitherto unsuspected method of much-needed weight control. But there was a distinct absence of glamour in all this, and as this section of the biography is brought to a close it will be on a note of diminished intensity in terms of the life story. Strategically, this should set the stage for the next and final section of the book, where we will encounter a new vitality—different from the frantic urgency of the early years, but a clear turning around of what some had begun to see as an irreversible personal decline.

Part Four of the book will show us a Mailer we had not seen before producing a body of work we had not anticipated before, and the design will be to infer from these two phenomena the emergence of a cultural or historical period, previously inexplicable to us, which we can only now begin to understand. Soon after the publication of *The Executioner's Song*, Mailer left for England to perform his cameo role in Milos Forman's 1982 film version of E. L. Doctorow's novel *Ragtime*,[18] and while he was there he went to Germany to promote his book and to cooperate with Jeffrey Van Davis and J. Michael Lennon in the shooting of a documentary devoted to the story of his life. The *Ragtime* episode introduces a kind of retrospective or nostalgic glamour into his life, and the Davis film, *Norman Mailer: The Sanction to Write* (which turns out to be a good and successful film) provides the opportunity for a retrospective with regard to the whole life story.[19] The intention here in the biography will be to produce a kind of portrait of the artist as survivor of the cataclysm: not the mushroom cloud explosion he had spent so many years anticipating, but the actual slow sinking into an imaginative bog that in the 1970s really was experienced by almost all the rest of his artistic generation. The concrete proof of his survival, indeed of his prevailing, will be shown to be *The Executioner's Song*, and the focus of the discussion of that book will be upon the figure of the outlaw. In his re-creation of Gilmore he separates himself off, declining the gambit of simple self-identification or even self-characterization in the narrative, and this tells us something about how he has pulled back from the idea of the omnipotence of the individual presence, imaginatively speaking.

But more important than this distinction is the change in the concept of what an outlaw *is*, and how one comes to be created. In the fifties, Mailer rang a big bell in the cultural imagination when he struck that imagination with the figure of the artist-outlaw. By combining the presentation of this figure with the argument that the artist was really only the writ-large representative of the audience-individual in the culture, he gave his audience the opportunity to share the experience of rebellion. What the rebellion was directed against, in this first incarnation, was the suffocating smother of parental authority. The first outlaw was getting rid of the threat of being embraced into permanent immobility by a social and institutional establishment that was fundamentally parental. The figure was resonant not only because Mailer delineated it brilliantly, but because, apparently, it seemed to his audience to be true. But in 1979 a much different audience, in a profoundly different historical situation, was presented by Mailer with a very different kind of outlaw, and this one rang the bell again. Gary Gilmore, so far from exploding against parental smother, was the ultimate orphan, murderously rampant in the face of parental desertion. Mailer presents him not clinically, but through the voices and consciousnesses of all the non-violent, non-murderous people around him, and the biography will argue that in doing so Mailer entangles the imagination of his audience in its own historically orphaned situation. When Mailer went one stage further, and brought forth Gilmore's living, presumably redeemable counterpart, Jack Henry Abbott, he set the stage for a much wilder and apparently terrifying entanglement. Abbott was a prisoner at the Marion federal penitentiary in 1978 when be began corresponding with Mailer about prison life. Mailer praised his literary abilities to prison officials and, when Abbott was paroled, gave him a job and helped arrange for the publication of his prison letters, *In the Belly of the Beast*, to which Mailer contributed the preface.[20]

The drama created by the appearance of Abbott's book, of Abbott himself, and then of the killing of Richard Adan by Abbott in July of 1981 (while on parole in New York City), will be given full treatment in the next portion of the book. Even the most furious indictments of Mailer's role in this drama reveal, the argument will assert, that Mailer had been terribly on target with this new outlaw conception. Gone were the lofty dismissals of, say, James Atlas in the *New York Times Magazine* profile published just before the appearance of *The Executioner's Song*.[21] The attacks on Mailer now were directed at an imaginer too intolerably powerful to be countenanced in our threatening time. If we measure a man by the paradoxically respectful fury of the attacks his enemies deliver, we must conclude from the Abbott episode that Mailer has more than returned to the position of major cultural imaginer. This section of the biography will address a different Mailer, living a different life, creating a different body of work in the context of a deeply different time, but what remains the same is the magnitude of his presence. Indeed one could argue that the Mailer figure is more deeply with us than ever, having proved with this last long comeback that he is, in the historical sense, evidently indestructable.

There is danger in the use of such vocabulary as "major cultural imaginer" in connection with Mailer, however, because it calls to mind visions of an artistic pantheon, an Olympus populated by imaginations so much more powerful than those of normal people as to suggest a race of gods. Such a view of artists and their art is quite common, after all, and in its context Mailer must be seen not as a divine but as an essentially Promethean figure; no god himself, he steals their fire, infuriating the devout by the profane uses to which he often puts it. Thus he follows *The Executioner's Song*, for which even the most mandarin critics were prepared to welcome him into the Pantheon, with *Of Women and Their Elegance* (1980), a narrative as told by Marilyn Monroe, a book in some places very nearly as recklessly bad as the consensus of furious reviewers has held the whole thing to be.[22] Why does he *do* such things? The question echoes and re-echoes like some tremendous refrain, not just at this comparatively late point in his life but all through it—certainly since the great personal attempt at emancipation after *The Deer Park* was published in 1955.[23] Directed not only at certain pieces of writing but at all kinds of things—the marriages, the episodes, the recklessness, all the rest of it—the question might perhaps occupy us for a space as we drive in conclusion towards a consideration of what may be, by all presently ascertainable judgements, his most powerful imaginative accomplishment to date. If *Ancient Evenings* marks Mailer's artistic outer limit (at this writing), what is the specific relationship between that achievement and the life that led up to it?

Let us be quite clear about what we mean. Critics differ about what the things are in Mailer's life that he should not do or should not have done, but rare is the Mailer watcher who will fail to identify *some* area of enormous error, some symptom of inner inadequacy but for which the artist might have done himself full justice. Some see the error in what they call his lesser work, the things indeed like *Of Women and Their Elegance*, or the *Esquire* columns of 1962–64,[24] or the periodic attempts at poetry,[25] or the many, many other pieces said to have been written only for the money. (The profit motive supplies a knee-jerk metaphor; in the early seventies I heard a prominent Stalinist critic at a Wesleyan University conference denounce Mailer's action in having followed up the best-selling *The Naked and the Dead* with the commercially hopeless *Barbary Shore* as a classic example of "selling out.")[26] Others identify Mailer's mistake as megalomania; an inability inside his work to get off the subject himself, and an even more serious inability to in any case *stay* inside his work, avoiding that media spotlight which it seems has always been the nemesis of the true artist. (James Joyce's "Silence, exile and cunning," is the standard medicine prescribed for this condition, and Mailer once jokingly described himself as "too gregarious" to stomach it.)[27] Still others, citing the penknife stabbing of his second wife Adele in 1960, the fascination with combat, with violent actions and with psychopathic personalities, identify Mailer simply as a dangerously unstable personality (*Time* magazine noted that New Yorkers were saying that Mailer should be indicted as an accessory in the Jack Abbott murder prosecution.)[28] Less relentless critics, conceding Mailer's basic emotional stability, nevertheless identify him as almost hopelessly immature, salving a sexual insecurity by piling up wives, children, girlfriends, outlandish escapades—like running for the office of mayor of New York in a campaign that cost an incredible amount of money and generated more publicity than the plague—and in effect not being a serious person. (In fact, McGeorge Bundy, according to an eyewitness, during the most intense American military effort in Vietnam, accused Mailer at a party of not being a serious person. Mailer invited him outside.) It is this kind of criticism, whose range is only suggested here, that gives such resonance to the question: Why does he do such things?

A way of answering, of course, would be to enter the assorted arenas: argue about whether Mailer's potboilers are really potboilers; whether he is really wasting his substance in self-advertisement; whether media exposure is actually bad for the artist's creative energy; debate the question of how destructively he relates to violence; make the case that Bundy, at bottom, is both more violent and more immature than Mailer could ever be. Some such discourse is appropriate and will indeed occur in the course of the narrative overall, but the point here is a different one. Whether his extra-artistic activities, whatever they may be, are sensible or nonsensical, Mailer certainly knows that he is engaging in them and has in fact provided us with an important explanation for why he does what he does. He once shaped the answer in response to a question by Steven Marcus in a *Paris Review* interview. He said that he did the things that he did outside his fiction writing so that he could "keep in shape" as a novelist, but "in a peculiar way." To illustrate, he told a story about the fighter Harry Greb, who had his own highly unconventional training methods:

> Harry Greb, for example, was a fighter who used to keep in shape. He was completely a fighter, the way one might wish to be completely a writer. He always did the things which were necessary to him as a fighter. Now, some of these things were extremely irrational, that is, extremely irrational from a prize-fight manager's point of view. That is, before he had a fight he would go to a brothel, and he would have two prostitutes, not one, taking the two of them into the same bed. And this apparently left him feeling like a wild animal. Don't ask me why. Perhaps he picked the two meanest whores in the joint and so absorbed into his system all the small, nasty, concentrated evils which had accumulated from carloads of men.[29]

One notes the lines: "He was completely a fighter, the way one might wish to be completely a writer. He always did the things that were necessary to him. . . ." In the final analysis, the thesis of this life story of Norman Mailer is that his life has been lived out of his wish to be completely a writer, and that he always did, or at least tried to do, the things that were necessary to him as a writer. One does not mean that he planned it all, clear and calculating—though a very considerable amount of clear calculation certainly did go on—but that he came, just about in the middle of the journey, to see that this was, beneath it all, what he was really doing. Identifying the things that were necessary to him as a writer—finding his two whores, to use the blunt terms of the Greb parable—was clearly a hit-and-miss process, more than once nearly costing him the whole game, but he proceeded with a kind of plan. The plan was to find the things necessary to allow himself to be wholly a writer through the operation of his unconscious—through the use of what he called his navigator. As early as 1958, in trying to explain the radical, destructive life-styles of the figure of the Hipster, he explained himself as writer still better. "The unconscious, you see, has an enormous teleological sense," he said, "it moves toward a goal . . . it has a real sense of what is happening to one's being at each given moment—you see— . . . the messages of one's experience are continually saying, 'Things are getting better,' or 'Things are getting worse.' For me. For that one. For my future, for my past."[30]

Navigation, of course, is the means by which we get where we want to go, and if we accept the proposition that where Norman Mailer wants to go is that place where he can be "completely a writer," then we understand, to some useful degree, the course that his navigator has plotted. The Harry Greb parable implies that literary commentators, critics, kibbitzers of various persuasions, are like prizefighter managers: they think they know what will keep the fighter in shape, what kind of life he should lead and what kind to avoid. Clearly, Mailer's life challenges this set of assumptions, and in its risk-taking, consequence-accepting, and in many ways punishing struggle adds up to a kind of practical argument for playing close to the line. Certainly it adds up to the argument that such a life can produce not simply the major effort but perhaps even the extraordinarily major achievement which is *Ancient Evenings*, the very conception of which argues for the soundness of the navigator principle. In 1972, after all, Mailer's conscious mind didn't have a historical clue. Consciously, he still *thought* in apocalyptic historical terms, in which individual personality stood at the center of impending historical climax. Yet at the same time he was following his navigator toward a novel that he himself found bewildering: a novel set so far back in time as to be out of history altogether; a narrative in which climax was perceived as inconsequential; a fictional world where separate, individual identity and even individual consciousness was brushed aside as the most transparent kind of illusion. *Ancient Evenings* may make it in the long critical haul or it may fall short, but the radical character of its design, the scope of its ambition, and the still more ambitious scope and radical plan of the trilogy it leads off, must give the world pause. Such a spectacle must, indeed, lead us relentlessly back to contemplate the life that made its production possible.

For one thing, it is a life that vigorously goes on. Mailer's robust state of health, indeed, is a fact that is more annoying than any other to a certain kind of Mailer critic. All those years of all those vices, and after he turns sixty his greatest physical affliction is that once in a while he gets a mild case of the gout. In his association with others in his personal life—men, women, and children—with the reading and watching audience, with his work and with himself, the present Mailer is a man of whom, as a recent reviewer has remarked, the fiery young Mailer of 1955 would not be ashamed.[31] This is saying a good deal, considering the angry impatience of that young man, and the vaulting ambition that drove him forward into his life. It is perhaps not too much to say now that Norman Mailer, young and old, will for some considerable time to come occupy a special place within the collective imagination of his culture. Figures that the cultural imagination fix upon, in its need for nourishment and a kind of energizing iconography, can come and go very quickly. At the start there are the mere celebrities, the presences that satisfy certain short-term needs—and Mailer has certainly been a celebrity. A celebrity hero is one who lasts a little longer than usual, who comes to seem more necessary than the short-term figure—and Mailer has certainly been a celebrity hero. A legend, one supposes, is what emerges when a celebrity hero starts to accumulate a real lore: written stories, images with some claim to relative permanence, books even. If all this lasts long enough a legendary hero is born. Certainly Norman Mailer, feet of clay, warts and all, is a legend now, and a hero of his own legend. There is, of course, a final stage beyond this. It is the stage at which apotheosis takes place, and a legend becomes permanent in the cultural imagination. We call such a thing a myth, and when the thing comes to that it becomes inseparable from us, like one's childhood, or like the culture's past. Mailer is no myth, to be sure. A figure becomes a myth, if ever, only after death: indeed that act of apotheosis is probably a rebuttal to death, a denying of it. But the living Norman Mailer's life story, like his work, belongs to his living audience as much, now, as it belongs to him, and as the shape of his time becomes clear and comprehensible to the historians who follow us it may well turn out that he will seem in some mythical way to have gone beyond his own legend at last. He may seem finally to have embodied our time.

Notes

1. Norman Mailer, "Prisoner of Success: An Interview with Paul Attanasio," in *Pontifications*, ed. Michael Lennon (Boston: Little, Brown, 1982), 134. Conducted in 1980, this interview originally appeared in the *Boston Phoenix* (24 February 1981), 2–3, 11.

2. José Torres, former light-heavyweight boxing champion, has been a close friend of Mailer's for about 20 years. Mailer wrote the preface to Torres's book, *Sting Like a Bee: The Muhammad Ali Story* (New York: Abelard-Schuman, 1971).

3. Mailer's account of his quarrel with Vidal was included in his essay on television, "Of a Small and Modest Malignancy, Wicked and Bristling with Dots," *Esquire* 88 (November 1977):125–48. The essay was reprinted in book form in 1980 (Northridge, California: Lord John Press), and was included in *Pieces*, Mailer's essays written in the seventies (Boston: Little, Brown, 1982).

4. Mailer, "Gladiators: For Hemingway," *New Republic* (30 November 1974), 22.

5. For an account of this incident see Nancy Collins, " 'The Fight,' Starring Mailer and Vidal," *Boston Globe* (28 October 1977), 24–25; and Hilary Mills, *Mailer: A Biography* (New York: Empire Books, 1982), 418–19.

6. Mailer, *Marilyn: A Biography* (New York: Grosset & Dunlop, 1973).

7. The many hostile reviews are typified by that of Jean Stafford, "Norman Mailer should be bull-whipped for what he did to Marilyn Monroe," *Vogue* 162 (September 1973):288–89, 342, 344. For a summary of the controversy surrounding the book, see "Much Ado about Mailer's 'Marilyn,' " *Publisher's Weekly* (30 July 1973), 45.

8. Mailer's exhortations appeared regularly in his column for the *Village Voice*, titled "Quickly," which appeared weekly from 11 January through 2 May 1956.

9. Mailer, *Ancient Evenings* (Boston: Little, Brown, 1983).

10. Mailer, *St. George and the Godfather* (New York: New American Library, 1972).

11. Mailer, *The Faith of Graffiti* (New York: Praeger, 1974).

12. Mailer, *The Fight* (Boston: Little, Brown, 1975).

13. Mailer, *Genius and Lust: A Journey Through the Major Writings of Henry Miller* (New York: Grove Press, 1976).

14. Mailer, *Some Honorable Men: Political Conventions, 1960–1972* (Boston: Little, Brown, 1976).

15. Mailer, *A Transit to Narcissus* (New York: Howard Fertig, 1978).

16. Mailer, *The Armies of the Night: History as a Novel, The Novel as History* (New York: New American Library, 1968).

17. Mailer, *The Executioner's Song* (Boston: Little, Brown, 1979).

18. E. L. Doctorow, *Ragtime* (New York: Random House, 1974).

19. Jeffrey Van Davis, producer, director; Michael Lennon, interviewer, consultant, *Norman Mailer: The Sanction to Write* (1982). Distributed by Picture Start, 204 W. John St., Champaign, Illinois 61820.

20. Jack Henry Abbott, *In the Belly of the Beast: Letters from Prison* (New York: Random House, 1981).

21. James Atlas, "Life With Mailer," *New York Times Magazine* (9 September 1979), 53–55, 86, 88, 90, 92, 94, 96, 98, 102, 104, 107.

22. Mailer, *Of Women and Their Elegance* (New York: Simon and Schuster, 1980).

23. Mailer, *The Deer Park* (New York: Putnam's, 1955).

24. Mailer's *Esquire* column, "The Big Bite," appeared from November 1962 to December 1963. All but the final column were reprinted in subsequent Mailer collections: *The Presidential Papers* (New York: Putnam's, 1963); *Cannibals and Christians* (New York: Dial, 1966); *The Idol and the Octopus* (New York: Dell, 1968); and *Existential Errands* (Boston: Little, Brown, 1972).

25. Most of Mailer's poetry is collected in *Deaths for the Ladies (And Other Disasters)* (New York: Putnam's, 1962).

26. Mailer, *The Naked and the Dead* (New York: Rinehart, 1948); *Barbary Shore* (New York: Rinehart, 1951).

27. *Cannibals and Christians*, 5.

28. Lance Morrow, "The Poetic License to Kill," *Time* (1 February 1982), 82.

29. Mailer, quoted in a 6 July 1963 interview with Steven Marcus, *Writers at Work: The Paris Review Interviews* (3rd series), ed. George Plimpton (New York: Viking, 1967), 274. Abridged versions of the interview are reprinted in *Cannibals and Christians*, 209–21, and *Pontifications*, 17–27.

30. Mailer, *Advertisements for Myself* (New York: Rinehart, 1959), 386.

31. I cannot locate this insightful comment, but believe it appeared in a review of *The Executioner's Song*.

INDEX

185